Efficiency Measurement in Health and Health Care

This book provides a concise synthesis of leading edge research in the theory and practise of efficiency measurement in health and health care. Whilst much of the literature in this area is confusing and impregnable, Hollingsworth and Peacock show the logical links between the economic theory underlying efficiency, the methods used in analysis and practical application of measurement techniques including Data Envelopment Analysis and Stochastic Frontier Analysis.

The book outlines which methods are most suitable in which setting, how to specify valid models, and how to undertake a study and effectively disseminate results. The current state-of-the-art is assessed in terms of methods and published applications, and practical applications of advanced methods, including analysis of economies of scale and scope, variable weightings, specification testing and estimation of the efficient production of health are undertaken. Finally, the way forward in efficiency measurement in health is outlined, mapping out an agenda for future research and policy development.

This book will be of interest to students, academics and practitioners alike, particularly those engaged with health economics and efficiency measurement in health care.

Bruce Hollingsworth is Associate Professor at the Centre for Health Economics at Monash University, Melbourne.

Stuart J. Peacock is Senior Scientist and Director of the Centre for Health Economics in Cancer at the British Columbia Cancer Agency and the University of British Columbia, Vancouver.

Routledge International Studies in Health Economics
Edited by Charles Normand
London School of Hygiene and Tropical Medicine, UK
and
Richard M. Scheffler
School of Public Health, University of California, Berkeley, USA

1. **Individual Decisions for Health**
   Edited by Björn Lindgren

2. **State Health Insurance Market Reform**
   Toward inclusive and sustainable health insurance markets
   Edited by Alan C. Monheit and Joel C. Cantor

3. **Evidence Based Medicine**
   In whose interests?
   Edited by Ivar Sønbø Kristiansen and Gavin Mooney

4. **Copayments and the Demand for Prescription Drugs**
   Domenico Esposito

5. **Health, Economic Development and Household Poverty**
   From understanding to action
   Edited by Sara Bennett, Lucy Gilson and Anne Mills

6. **Efficiency Measurement in Health and Health Care**
   Bruce Hollingsworth and Stuart J. Peacock

Efficiency Measurement in Health and Health Care

Bruce Hollingsworth and
Stuart J. Peacock

Routledge
Taylor & Francis Group
LONDON AND NEW YORK

First published 2008 by Routledge
2 Park Square, Milton Park, Abingdon, Oxon OX14 4RN

Simultaneously published in the USA and Canada
by Routledge
270 Madison Avenue, New York, NY 10016

Routledge is an imprint of the Taylor & Francis Group, an informa business

Typeset in Times New Roman by Keyword Group Ltd
Printed and bound in Great Britain by MPG Books Ltd, Bodmin

British Library Cataloguing in Publication Data
A catalogue record for this book is available from the British Library

Library of Congress Cataloging-in-Publication Data
Hollingsworth, Bruce.
Efficiency measurement in health and health care / Bruce Hollingsworth and Stuart J. Peacock.
p. ; cm. — (Routledge international studies in health economics ; 6)
Includes bibliographical references and index.

1. Medical care—Cost effectiveness—Measurement. 2. Health facilities—Cost effectiveness—Measurement. 3. Health facilities—Labor productivity—Measurement. 4. Organizational effectiveness—Measurement. I. Peacock, Stuart. II. Title. III. Series.

[DNLM: 1. Economics, Medical. 2. Data Interpretation, Statistical. 3. Efficiency, Organizational—economics. 4. Health Resources—economics. 5. Health Services—economics. 6. Models, Economic. W 74.1 H741e 2008]

RA410.5.H59 2008
362.1068—dc22
2007034241

ISBN 10: 0–415–27137–1 (hbk)
ISBN 10: 0–203–48656–0 (ebk)

ISBN 13: 978–0–415–27137–0 (hbk)
ISBN 13: 978–0–203–48656–6 (ebk)

Contents

Figures

Tables

Foreword

What ratio of doctors to nurses should a busy emergency room staff? Should a managed care organization (MCO) expand by hiring generalists or specialists? Would a county health facility do more good if it had more psychiatrists and fewer psychologists? How many hospitals in a province should be licensed to perform heart surgery? Should a country spend more on preventive care and less on treatment, and if so, for which preventive services? Do countries with market-based health-care systems perform better than those that rely more on regulation?

Although, as pointed out by Bruce Hollingsworth and Stuart Peacock in this fine book, economists (sometimes slip up occasionally) imply that there are right and wrong answers to questions such as these, there are not. So called 'normative' questions – those asking what *ought* to be, can only be answered by using values and opinions. In some sense, this is a shame, because questions like those listed above are the most intriguing ones. Few are interested, say, in the input–output relationship between the number of pharmacists and the quantity of pills dispensed – which is a 'positive' or factual sort of question.

This is not to say that we can't make decent progress in grappling with the above list of questions. In fact, decision makers can benefit enormously from studies of economic efficiency. To use the second question as an example, a good efficiency study can tell the MCO manager how a given amount of resources spent on generalists versus specialists will affect the number of patients served and what services were received. An even better study might compare health outcomes for the two alternatives per unit of spending. This leads us far closer to answering the question, and thus the information would be welcomed by most decision makers. Other factors, of course, would still come into play; for example, patient preferences, community desires and medical regulations, to name a few.

To illustrate, throughout the world there is much debate about whether costly new medical technologies improve health outcomes. In the United States, the debate is particularly intense. Fisher and colleagues (2003), for example, find no relationship between medical spending and a variety of outcomes. In one set of studies examining the elderly, they found that individuals in high-spending regions of the country receive 60 per cent more care for myocardial infarctions, hip fractures and colourectal cancer, but fare no better. The higher spending stems from 'more frequent physician visits, especially in the inpatient setting, more frequent tests and minor (but not major) procedures, and increased use of specialists and hospitals' (p. 273). In contrast, Cutler and McClellan (2001) find that increased medical technology and spending for a variety of conditions, including heart-attack care, low birth weight infants, depression, and cataracts, far outweigh its costs. For heart attacks, over a 15-year period, spending rose by 4.2 per cent per year, but the increase in quality-adjusted life years was such that they estimate a benefit to cost ratio of seven to one, such that 'the net benefit of technology changes is so large that it dwarfs all of the uncertainties of the analysis' (p. 18).

Who is right?

That's where this book comes in. It provides a much-needed 'soup to nuts' treatment on the critical economic concept of efficiency. It begins with the necessary theory, defines measures of efficiency in health and health care, illustrates how efficiency studies are done – including a very useful review of available software – reviews and re-analyses previous work, and posits where the field should go. In reading it, I was surprised by (a) how many studies have been done, especially using data envelopment analysis, but conversely by (b) how little we still know to help us address the critical normative sorts of questions listed earlier. The material about the state-of-the-art on alternative techniques, along with the authors' nuanced discussion of the pluses and minuses of each, is especially valuable.

Hollingsworth and Peacock explore this contradiction, in part, by employing the adage, 'have software – will analyse'. They make a compelling case that most of the research appears to be supply driven – because academics need to publish – rather than demand driven (an unfortunate but not altogether shocking possibility). In particular, they posit that *the* two most important potential demanders have hardly entered the picture: the units being analysed (e.g. hospitals) and policy makers. This alone should give us pause for thought.

Essentially, what the authors are calling for is for something that is quite appropriately in vogue now in other realms of health services research, namely translational research. In this case, studies that can be used by the private decision makers (the units being analysed) and public decision makers (those in the public policy world) who have to grapple with the efficiency issue. A good portion of the book is devoted to detecting and trying to understand particular outlier cases. By trying to get inside this 'black box', one can learn much about what characteristics of an organization lead to enhanced efficiency. But in this respect the field of efficiency analysis is still in its infancy.

It is not entirely obvious as to *why* there is a large disconnect between the supply and demand for research on efficiency in health and health care. The actual reasons, I think, relate to some assertions the authors make in the last chapter:

> … efficiency analyses may not provide organizations with the requisite information to make decisions and take action. Efficiency analyses tend to focus on the organization as the unit of analysis, but this may provide them with little insight about where and how actual technical improvements could be made.

> Most analyses appear to be targeted at academic users, and are little utilized by either policy makers or organizations. To be more useful, the analytical techniques need further development. There needs to be greater confidence that the results are reliable. This means greater attention to model construction (as well as underlying theory), especially better understanding of the nature of production of health care and of production constraints. Also, analysis needs to be more specific. Instead of merely quantifying the extent of inefficiency, analyses need to identify the nature and form of inefficiency; and therefore, what can be done about it. These challenges are not straightforward and academic researchers need to work more closely with policy makers and organizations in order to meet them.

One area in which practice still lags theory is in incorporating true outcomes as part of efficiency analyses. As pointed out repeatedly in the book, efficiency is hardly just about costs; benefits are half of any benefit-to-cost ratio. Much lip service is paid to this but more needs to be done. Take an example from the United States. For many years, MCOs have established networks of preferred providers. Patients who seek care from such providers usually get a discount. These networks are supposedly chosen on the basis of 'performance', but too often, performance is mainly what is cheap for the insurance company – that is, providers with whom they receive the biggest discounts. We are still waiting for the time when performance in terms of medical outcomes is the make-or-break as to whether a provider will be deemed as 'preferred'.

Although one could claim that this is due to the state-of-the-art in quality measurement not being far enough along, I think another reason is more important. In health care, where consumers often have difficultly in obtaining and comprehending information about quality, organizations have an economic incentive to go for the cheap rather than the efficient. I thus behoove researchers to lead the charge as to what constitutes proper analyses of efficiency. That, I think, ultimately is the aim of this book.

Thomas Rice
UCLA School of Public Health

Acknowledgements

Dr Bruce Hollingsworth is a Victorian Health Promotion Foundation Fellow and Associate Professor at the Centre for Health Economics (CHE), Monash University, Melbourne. Dr Stuart Peacock is a Michael Smith Foundation for Health Research Scholar and Director of the Centre for Health Economics in Cancer at the British Columbia Cancer Agency and the University of British Columbia, and is also an Honourary Senior Research Fellow, CHE at the Monash University. He acknowledges previous funding by the National Health and Medical Research Council. The book builds upon work originally published in our PhD dissertations. We are especially grateful to Dave Parkin, Phil Dawson, and Pete Smith for introducing us to, and teaching us about, efficiency measurement, and for supervising our early work in this area. We would also like to thank Bonnie McCoy, Amanda Geddes and Lynette McGowan for their help with preparing the manuscript.

We have drawn upon several papers published and presented over the years by the authors, both solely and jointly with others. We thank the following publishers for their permissions: John Wiley, The Royal Society of Medicine Press, Springer and Blackwell and the RAND corporation, for use of material from the following papers:

DaVanzo, J. and Gertler, P. (1990) 'Household Production of Health: A Microeconomic Perspective on Health Transitions', RAND Note no. N–3014–RC, RAND Corporation.

Hollingsworth, B. (2004) 'Non Parametric Efficiency Measurement', *Economic Journal*, **114**: 307–311.

Hollingsworth, B. (2003) 'Non-Parametric and Parametric Applications Measuring Efficiency in Health Care', *Health Care Management Science*, **6**(4): 203–218.

Hollingsworth, B. and Parkin, D. (2003) 'Efficiency and Productivity Change in the English National Health Service: Can Data Envelopment Analysis Provide a Robust and Useful Measure?', *Journal of Health Services Research and Policy*, **8**: 230–236.

Hollingsworth, B. and Street, A. (2006) 'The Market for Efficiency Analysis of Health Care Organisations', *Health Economics*, **15**(10): 1055–1059.

Hollingsworth, B. and Wildman, J. (2003) 'The Efficiency of Health Production: Re-estimating the WHO Panel Data using Parametric and Nonparametric Approaches to Provide Additional Information', *Health Economics*, **12**(6): 493–504.

We are grateful to Dave Parkin, Andy Street and John Wildman for agreeing to the inclusion and adaptation of the above work. An example given in Chapter 6 is drawn from an original paper jointly authored by Bruce Hollingsworth, Nancy Devlin and Dave Parkin. We are grateful to Nancy and Dave for agreeing to its inclusion here. They also (with agreement for BH) published the example separately as part of Chapter 8 in Advances in Health Economics (Eds. A. Scott, A. Maynard and R. Elliot, 2003). Thanks to Wiley for permission to use this.

Finally, special thanks go to Tom Rice for writing the foreword. We are grateful for his patience, and to have a foreword written by an economist of Tom's calibre adds incalculable value to the text.

1 Introduction

There has long been a perception that health services could be operating more efficiently. Concern over efficiency arises because health service resources are scarce, and given those scarce resources, health services cannot meet all the demands and needs of the population they serve. Some of those demands and needs will therefore go unmet, irrespective of how, when, where and to whom health services are provided. Inefficiency in the provision of health services will then result in greater levels of unmet need in the community and poorer levels of population health.

The commonly held view that health services could be operating more efficiently has been debated at the government level in the vast majority of countries. This debate has provided the impetus for radical health system reforms in many developed and developing countries in the last 20 years. Reform has occurred at different levels, for example at the state/local level in the USA and at the national level in the UK, and has taken many diverse forms, for example managed competition in the Netherlands and integrated care in New Zealand. However, despite the pervasive concern over efficiency and its role in driving health system reform, until relatively recently there have been few attempts to measure efficiency in health services, at least in terms recognizable to an economist.

Efficiency is a term widely used in economics, commonly referring to the best use of resources in production. From the 1950s onwards, following the seminal work of Farrell, economists have typically distinguished between two types of efficiency: technical efficiency and allocative efficiency (Farrell 1957). Technical efficiency refers to the maximization of outputs for a given level and mix of inputs, or conversely the minimization of input use for a given output level. Technically efficient behaviour can be mapped by plotting the different combinations of inputs that maximize outputs, which economists term the production frontier. Thus if an organization, such as a hospital, is technically efficient it is operating on its production frontier. Allocative efficiency refers to the maximization of outputs for a given level of input cost, or conversely the minimization of cost for a given output level. Allocative efficiency can be mapped by plotting the different combinations of inputs that minimize cost, which is termed the 'cost frontier'. Similarly, allocative efficiency implies a hospital is operating on its cost frontier. When combined, technical and allocative efficiency comprise the 'overall' efficiency of an organization.

To measure the efficiency of an organization we therefore need knowledge of the production and/or cost frontier. In practice the frontier is made up of those organizations which are the most efficient in the sample of organizations under analysis. That is, the frontier consists of those organizations which produce a given level of output from the least inputs (or least cost), or produce the maximum output given a certain level of inputs (or cost). The level of inefficiency of organizations not lying on the frontier is estimated relative to these efficient organizations. Furthermore, efficiency changes from one period to the next – 'technological or productivity change' – can also be measured.

There are two main alternative empirical approaches to estimating frontiers: data envelopment analysis (DEA) and stochastic frontiers. These approaches have two fundamental differences. Stochastic frontiers, based on econometric regression techniques, are parametric and therefore require specification of a particular functional form. DEA, based on linear programming techniques, is non-parametric and does not require specification of the functional form. DEA is also non-stochastic, assuming that the distance an organization lies from the efficient frontier is due entirely to inefficient behaviour. Conversely, stochastic frontiers assume that the distance an organization lies from the frontier will be due a combination of random measurement error and inefficient behaviour. To date the application of stochastic frontiers to the analysis of health services has been somewhat limited. By contrast, DEA has been used extensively, with hundreds of published applications. This is perhaps because one advantage of DEA is that it is the only method available which easily allows the estimation of multiple input–multiple output models. Econometric methods usually require some degree of aggregation of the dependent variable.

This text defines efficiency clearly and its relationship to health and health care. There is confusion in this area at present. For example, *The Handbook of Health Economics* (Culyer and Newhouse 2000) is criticized by Rutten *et al.* (2001) for failing to address production and cost functions, and as an exercise the reader may wish to try and find a definition of efficiency in these volumes.

In what follows, we logically lead the reader through this potential maze, going on to a practical 'how to do' section, with a review of the software available to actually apply these methods. Following this exposition of theory and methods we give an up-to-date literature review of applications of efficiency measurement in health care, drawing out important methodological and policy implications of work undertaken so far. Following on from this and in part based on lessons learnt in the text we report new examples of practical applications of advances in this area. This is work which has been, and is being, undertaken by the authors, in collaboration with others. This includes a comparison of the different methods of analysis, with consequent policy implications; analysis of economies of scale and scope; modelling and consequences of restricting the weighting given to different variables; model specification; the efficiency of the production of health, as well as health care; and analysis in differing health-care settings.

Finally, we look to the future, based on our knowledge of what has been undertaken, what is currently being undertaken, and what needs to be done to advance this critical area in health economics. In summary, our text is a synthesis of theory, practice and leading edge research, separating the wood from the trees. It should appeal to a wide audience, including academics, practitioners and students, who find this area confusing and impregnable at present. This is especially important given the increasing references to the importance of efficiency in health services throughout the developed and developing world, from the level of the individual patient and the efficient production of health, through to the efficiency of entire countries and their health-care systems.

This chapter provides an introduction and description of the significance of the book, following the theme outlined above. It outlines the rationale for examining efficiency in the health sector, drawing on the established principles of economics and health economics. The chapter concludes with an outline of the book, and what each chapter seeks to achieve.

Why measure efficiency in the health sector?

Reinhardt (1998) castigates distinguished economists for misuse of the word 'efficiency' in the health-care environment. He singles out Nobel laureates Milton Friedman and Gary Becker as being 'cavalier' in using the term efficiency in normative statements regarding health policy. Reinhardt goes on to state that advocating one system above another, for example a market system as opposed to a system characterized by government intervention, based on efficiency as defined by certain economists is not based on what he calls 'economic science' and that comparing systems with different social goals makes no sense. This does not mean efficiency should not be measured, but that the term itself should not be 'misused'.

In this book we draw on Reinhardt's vision of economic science and attempt to avoid making normative statements as to what efficiency should be. We define efficiency in the strictest economic sense and go on to look at quantitative means of measurement in the context of well-specified models, founded on economic principles. Suffice to say the term 'efficiency' is frequently used inappropriately, and if economists as guardians of the term cannot use it appropriately, its misuse by others is inevitable. In particular, efficiency does not just mean operating at the lowest cost or achieving the best outcomes possible, regardless of costs. Both sides of the equation need to be examined together. As economics students learn at an early stage, production depends on the inputs to and outputs from the process. Looking at one side of the equation in isolation is ultimately meaningless for the efficiency analyst. Unfortunately this basic lesson is often forgotten, although it has been revived in some health economics texts recently (Folland *et al.* 2001; Rice 2002). Rice (2002) also points out the potential confusion in the view that 'markets are efficient and governments are inefficient'. He argues that this view is wrong as it is based on 'a misunderstanding of economic theory as it applies to health'. The economic assumptions for a market system to operate efficiently are not met in the health sector, which is why there is government intervention in all countries in this sector. This book does not seek to advocate one health system over another. We seek to clarify what efficiency is in economics terms, and how it is applied to the production of health care and health itself. It does not review each available system in terms of whether markets or their alternatives are 'best', or even critique these systems (others such as Rice (2002) have undertaken this comprehensively). We should also state at the outset that we are not writing a book about efficiency and equity in health systems, although of course we acknowledge that these considerations run hand in hand. There is a vast literature on this already (for example, see Chapters 9, 10, 34 and 35 of *The Handbook of Health Economics* (Culyer and Newhouse 2000)).

Our intention is to focus on the theory of and measurement of efficiency in health, which has received far less attention in health economics texts. We have produced a framework for how economists who ply their trade in the health sector can consider and measure efficiency based on economic theory. No more, no less.

Outline of the book

Health and efficiency

The concepts and definitions of efficiency adopted in health economics have often been confused, and have received relatively little attention in the literature. Chapter 2 introduces the reader to key concepts and definitions in studying efficiency in the health sector. Efficiency is often defined in a range of ways, and this has implications for both analysis and policy makers. We discuss the range of definitions of efficiency in health economics and the implications of this. The chapter offers a structured presentation of concepts and the theory of production from the economics and health economics perspective. Using the economic theory of production, we introduce readers to key concepts, including technical efficiency, cost minimization, allocative efficiency, and production and cost functions, drawing an important distinction between the production of *health* and the production of *health care*. Finally, we discuss relevant output measures and health economic efficiency concepts.

Efficiency measurement techniques

In Chapter 3, we discuss the theory and measurement of efficiency. The theoretical foundations are based on the work of Farrell (1957) and include the theory of production and cost frontiers and their relationship to production and cost functions, leading on to the measurement of technical and allocative efficiency using radial measures. We then describe three alternative approaches to measuring efficiency in the health sector: ordinary least squares (OLS) regression analysis, data envelopment analysis (DEA), and stochastic frontier analysis (SFA).

OLS draws on Feldstein's seminal work on efficiency in the health sector (Feldstein 1967), which uses classical linear regression to estimate a cost/production functions for a sample of health-care providers. Residuals from these models can be used to tell us which providers are above or below average efficiency levels, as measured by the OLS average, and by how much. Criticisms of this approach include that OLS does not identify truly efficient behaviour as efficiency estimates are not related to a production frontier, but are based on average performance.

DEA creates a production frontier for a sample of providers using linear programming. It identifies efficient providers, which make up the frontier, and provides estimates of efficiency of all other providers relative to that frontier. The key features of DEA are described, including: non-parametric and non-stochastic estimation of the frontier; multiple inputs and outputs; and, input minimization versus output maximization variants of DEA models. Malmquist indices are then described, which are a means of measuring productivity over time using DEA. The index can be decomposed to show if changes are due to technology change (movements in the frontier from one year to the next), changes in efficiency (how far a provider moves from the frontier in each time period), and changes in scale of operation.

SFA estimates the production/cost frontier for a sample of providers using regression based techniques. The frontier is estimated by decomposing the error term into two parts – a one-sided error term that measures inefficiency and a more usual normally distributed error term that captures random influences. Key features of SFA are described, including: parametric and stochastic estimation of the frontier; choice of functional form; choice of distribution for the inefficiency term; testing of model assumptions; the treatment of casemix; estimation of economies of scale and scope; estimation of marginal costs; and, interpretation of rankings of efficiency. The chapter ends with a comparison of DEA and SFA as alternatives for frontier estimation.

Measuring efficiency in health services

Chapter 4 develops a framework for the practical modelling and measurement of efficiency in health services. Several issues are considered, from model specification to feeding back of results to those who may actually find them to be useful.

We structure this chapter around a number of questions: What is to be measured? Why? And for whom? In most cases the answer to the first question is relatively straightforward. We could be looking at the technical efficiency of a sample of hospitals, for example. The second and third questions are sometimes more difficult. Initially, we are usually concerned with increasing the amount of health care that can be delivered given certain resources, but increasingly factors such as quality of care are introduced, making analysis complex. Careful consideration of a range of other factors is important, for example in examining efficiency in the hospital sector how do we account for teaching and research, and the impact of this on health care? For whom we are measuring efficiency is also of interest. Studies can range from an academic exercise to advance a particular technique, to a study commissioned by health authorities to develop a practical measure for health service managers? Or, is the study to develop a 'high level' measure to be used to promote health system level efficiency?

To undertake an efficiency measurement study several practical steps need to be taken once the study perspective has been established. These include data collection, model specification, sensitivity analysis and reporting of results. So far 'rules of thumb' have often been used to guide choices for each of these steps. We examine this trend, and look more closely at validation techniques. The translation of empirical findings into policy tools is another area that has received little attention in the literature. We show how you can feed-back study findings to decision makers and demonstrate some critical factors in translating results from efficiency measurement studies into practical policy instruments.

Importantly analysts need to choose an appropriate software package for data analysis. We review the current software available to undertake efficiency measurement analysis, ranging from complex to easy to operate, each with advantages and disadvantages.

Applications of efficiency measurement in health services

Next, Chapter 5 undertakes a comprehensive review of applications of efficiency measurement in health care. Papers are reviewed from the perspective of determining methods and data used, models specified, sensitivity analysis used, and validity and robustness of techniques. Results are summarized in a form of meta-analysis and some implications drawn.

This review contextualizes the lack of direction in this area, perhaps due in part to the lack of information available to researchers on what has been undertaken so far. It is important for a researcher in the field to examine the directions taken by their peers, in order to place ones own work in context. It is hypothesized that much work undertaken and published in this area is of the nature of 'have software – will analyse', perhaps setting a dangerous precedent, in terms of research that has a weak underlying basis in economic theory. This may mean 'efficiency' results being produced that potentially lead to policy changes based upon invalid models and unreliable information.

Drawing out the consequences of the literature helps us to set in place robust foundations and guidelines for a research agenda in this area. We also make the references we find in the review available in the form of a database, published as an appendix which summarizes comprehensively all our findings – a useful resource in itself.

Advanced applications and recent developments

Based on our in depth knowledge of current practice in this area, and our own research in progress, Chapter 6 covers some of the areas that are currently in deficit in research terms. For example, comparison of different methods of analysis, and potential policy implications. We compare SFA and DEA methods in terms of cost and production frontiers, testing robustness and properties of the efficiency measures generated. We critically explore the appropriateness of techniques under alternative study assumptions, settings and perspectives, and, importantly, over time.

We then examine the impact on efficiency of the size of health care 'provider units', and the scope of different services offered – is it more efficient to specialize, or diversify and jointly produce a selection of outputs?

Within efficiency modelling different variables may be perceived as more important than others, for example within a hospital it may be that teaching is seen as more important than providing a minor injury service. We explore whether the means of restricting the weights given to variables within the analysis, so that differing levels of importance are attached to different variable, are valid, and whether results can be used to inform policy choices.

Efficiency measurement to date has, in the main, estimated the production of health care. Health care is just one input into the production of health itself. We look at the efficiency of the production of health using data on oral health and health care in order to establish what the impact of the production of health care is on the production of health. Finally, we extend the application of efficiency measurement, introducing quality adjusted health care outcome variables.

Future directions in theory and practice

Chapter 7 summarizes progress in efficiency measurement in health and health care, and sets a tentative research agenda for the future.

It is asked why efficiency measurement has gained in popularity, despite criticisms of the efficiency measurement tools available? Is it because of the relative ease with which researchers can now employ frontier methods? Is it also attributable to the potential uses of efficiency measurement in decision making?

How might techniques be used most effectively? For target setting for health service providers, for example determining input/output mix? For monitoring or benchmarking performance, for example filtering of complex information and identifying outlying providers? For evaluation of performance, for example estimating inefficiency from managerial practice? And, for determining efficient reimbursement rates? The extent to which efficiency measurement techniques have been successfully used for these purposes is discussed, and suggestions are made as to how it can be used more widely in the future, especially the potential for efficiency measurement to inform reimbursement policy.

We conclude, as active researchers in this area, that there are positive ways forward. Over the course of this book we map some of these critical pathways in the most effective and user friendly manner possible, without ever losing sight of the economic theory which we believe must underpin them.

2 Health and efficiency concepts

Introduction

Health professionals and policymakers are placing increasing emphasis on efficiency in the health sector. Efficiency considerations have been central to health system reforms in many countries, including the US, the UK, the Netherlands and Australia. However, discussion of efficiency in the literature is sometimes unclear, with several different definitions of efficiency in the health sector appearing in different contexts. The task for the analyst is to precisely define the production process of interest, the relevant output for that process and the efficiency question to be addressed.

In this chapter we introduce the reader to key concepts and definitions in studying efficiency in the health sector. Inspection of the economics and health economics literature suggests that efficiency is defined in a range of ways, with different implications for both methods of analysis and decision making. Our departure is the economic theory of production, which is used to introduce readers to the key concepts of technical efficiency, cost minimization, allocative efficiency and production and cost functions. In order to properly consider efficiency we then draw a distinction between the production of health and the production of health care. We conclude with a discussion of relevant output measures and efficiency concepts in health economics.

The economic theory of production

The foundation of the economic theory of production is simple: production involves the use of goods and services of various types to generate output. These goods and services are inputs which are transformed into output in a production process.

Economists distinguish between three types of inputs (termed the factors of production): land, labour and capital. Land represents inputs from natural resources, labour the inputs from human endeavour, and capital the machines, plants and buildings that make production possible. The treatment of capital in production theory is sometimes controversial, as capital assets which are used to generate output have themselves been produced. Some forms of capital will emerge as part of the final output (e.g. the headlights in a car) which are sometimes referred to as circulating capital or intermediate outputs. However, some forms of capital will never emerge as a consumable output (e.g. the car assembly building) which are referred to as fixed capital. The task for the analyst is to carefully define the final output of interest and the different types of inputs used in its production.

Production processes may have many different economic, social and political dimensions. For example, production may be organized within a privately owned profit-making firm or it may take place within a non-profit government entity. As we will discuss later, production processes in health care may be organized in many different ways. However, first we need to introduce some theoretical building blocks. Our starting point is to consider a model of production where there is only one output.

Production and efficiency in the single-output model

The production function

In any production process it is important to know how much output can be produced from different combinations of inputs. The production function defines the possibilities. It does so by mathematically specifying the range of technically possible combinations of inputs in the production process and resulting output. As we will discuss throughout the book, the production function is the central concept in the economic theory of production.

The single-output model considers a single homogenous output, y. The technical relationship between inputs and output is represented by the production function:

$$y = f(x_1,\ldots,x_n) \tag{2.1}$$

where $(x_1,\ldots,x_n)$ are the n factor inputs in the production process, and $f(\cdot)$ is the technology that producers face. The production function shows the maximum possible level of production which can be achieved, given the state of technology, for different levels and types of inputs. Technology is assumed to be fixed, known and available to all producers. Equation 2.1 therefore describes a purely technical relationship, summarizing the technical constraints on producers and the production process.

Figure 2.1 shows the production function graphically. For simplicity, the horizontal axis shows different amounts of all inputs on the same axis. All points on, or to the right of, the production function (PF) are technically possible. For example, output y^0 can be produced using the different combinations of inputs shown by A and B, where B uses more inputs than A. All points to the left of PF are not technically possible: given the current state of technology it is not feasible to produce y with fewer resources than combination A.

Technical efficiency

The production function allows us to say something about the efficiency of different production processes. For the given state of technology, the production

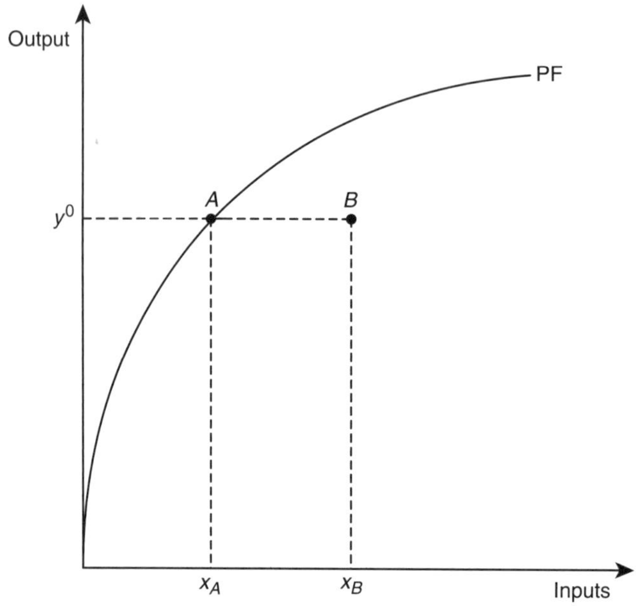

Figure 2.1 The production function.

function maps the technically efficient combinations of physical quantities (as opposed to costs) of inputs: those combinations of inputs which use the least resources to produce a given level of physical quantities (again, as opposed to costs) of output. Points to the right of PF represent inefficient production processes, as the same level of output could have been produced using fewer resources. Alternatively, technical efficiency may be defined as maximizing output for a given level of inputs.

As well as understanding the relationship between different combinations of inputs and output, a producer may want to know about the relationship between a single input and output. For example, a hospital may want to know how many more hernia operations could be performed by employing more surgeons. Economists describe this relationship in terms of the marginal contribution of an input to output. Marginal means one extra, and in this context refers to the extra output that would be produced if one extra unit of a specific input was added (with all other inputs held constant). In this simple example, the marginal contribution of surgeons may be expressed as the additional hernia operations performed per extra surgeon, with all other inputs – such as anaesthetists, nurses and operating rooms – held constant.

The marginal contribution of the *i*th input to output is called the marginal product of input *i*. This is given by the partial derivative of output with respect to input *i*:

$$\mathrm{MP}_i = \delta y \,/\, \delta x_i \tag{2.2}$$

where MP_i is the marginal product of input x_i. Because the marginal product shows the rate at which output changes in response to changes in x_i, it also provides a measure of the returns to an input in the production process.

A useful way of visualizing the production function is by constructing 'isoquants' ('iso' stands for equal and 'quant' for quantity). An isoquant shows all the combinations of inputs which would produce a given level of output in a technically efficient manner. The isoquant for output y^0 is given by:

$$y^0 = f(x_1, \ldots, x_n) \tag{2.3}$$

Figure 2.2 shows the isoquants (I^0 and I^1) for output levels y^0 and y^1 when there are two factor inputs x_1 and x_2. For simplicity we will call x_1 labour and x_2 capital. Any combination of labour and capital on the curve I^0 is capable of producing y^0. Combination *A* uses more labour and less capital than *B* (*A* is more labour intensive than *B*), whereas *B* is more capital intensive than *A*. To increase output beyond y^0 more labour and/or capital is needed.

Isoquants do not cross and are generally assumed to be convex to the origin. Convexity means that the returns to an input diminish as greater and greater amounts of that input is used in production. For example, the number of hernia operations performed by the first surgeon employed by the hospital may be greater than the number performed by the tenth surgeon. Why might we expect this? There are only so many hernias that a hospital will need to surgically repair each year (assuming incidence and prevalence of hernias are finite) so additional

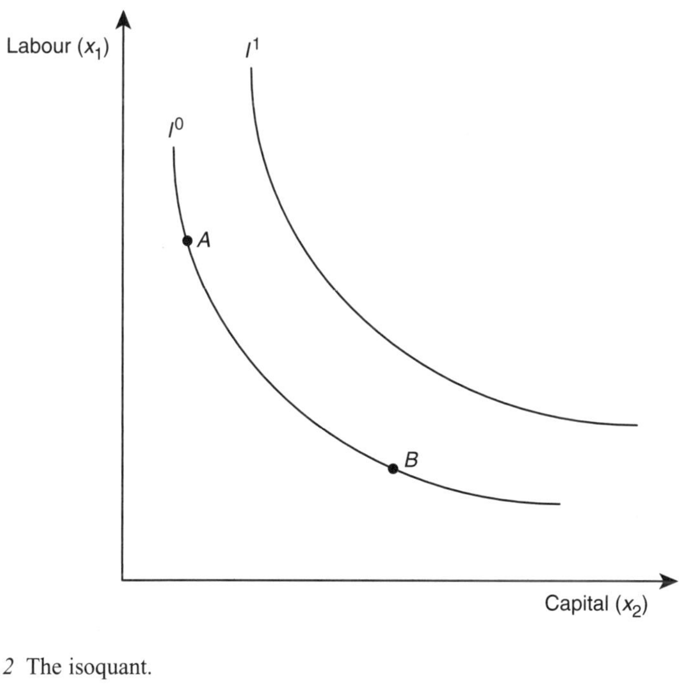

Figure 2.2 The isoquant.

surgeons may have fewer patients needing treatment and therefore perform fewer operations. The slope of an isoquant shows the marginal rate of technical substitution between inputs. This is the rate at which inputs may be substituted for each other whilst maintaining the same level of technically efficient production. In the two-input case the slope of the isoquant is given by the ratio of the marginal products for each input:

$$\mathrm{MRTS}_{21} = \mathrm{MP}_1 \,/\, \mathrm{MP}_2 \tag{2.4}$$

where MRTS_{21} is the marginal rate of technical substitution of input 2 for input 1 (the rate at which x_2 must be substituted for x_1 to remain on that isoquant).

Economies of scale

Changes in the relative proportions of inputs lead to movements along an isoquant, but changes in the scale of production lead to movements between isoquants. Changes in scale, or returns to scale, may be achieved by varying all inputs used in the production process in the same proportion. If an equiproportionate increase in inputs yields the same proportionate increase in output then the production process exhibits constant returns to scale (e.g. a 10 per cent increase in all inputs leads to a 10 per cent increase in output). If an equiproportionate increase in all inputs yields a greater than proportionate rise in output then increasing returns to scale are present, and conversely if the rise in output is less than proportionate then decreasing returns to scale are present. Production functions may exhibit constant, increasing and decreasing returns to scale over different ranges of outputs. A convenient measure of returns to scale is given by the elasticity of scale:

$$\varepsilon = (\mathrm{d}y/y) \,/\, (\mathrm{d}x/x) \tag{2.5}$$

where ε is the elasticity of scale, $\mathrm{d}y/y$ is the proportionate change in output resulting from the change in inputs, and $\mathrm{d}x/x$ is the proportionate change in all inputs (which is assumed to be the same for each input). If $\varepsilon = 1$ constant returns to scale are present, $\varepsilon > 1$ indicates increasing returns and $\varepsilon < 1$ decreasing returns. Alternatively the elasticity of scale can be defined for the general case of n inputs in terms of marginal products where:

$$\varepsilon = \sum_{i=1}^{n} \mathrm{MP}_i (x_i \,/\, y) \tag{2.6}$$

Cost minimization and allocative efficiency

The production function is central to the economic theory of production because it provides some of the information needed to calculate the costs of output.

Without it we would not know the amounts of resources required to produce different levels of output. Adding market prices for factor inputs allows the calculation of costs based on the production function. This allows producers to determine whether or not they should engage in production activities, by allowing them to compare their costs with the market prices for output. Combining factor prices with the production function yields the cost function.

A producer's cost function shows the minimum-cost combination of inputs required to produce a given level of output. If input prices, w, are given (producers cannot influence the price of inputs) then a cost function can be derived giving the least-cost combinations of inputs required for all different levels of output. In the two-input case, the levels of inputs which minimize cost for a given level of output can be found where the isoquant (for that output level) is tangential with an isocost line (see Figure 2.3). An isocost line is a line representing all combinations of inputs which can be purchased for a fixed amount of money. For two inputs the isocost line is given by:

$$C = w_1x_1 + w_2x_2 \tag{2.7}$$

where w_1 and w_2 are the prices of inputs 1 and 2 respectively. The slope of the isocost line is then the ratio of the factor prices, and must be equal to the slope of the isoquant for the tangency condition to hold, such that costs of production are minimized when:

$$(w_1/w_2) = (\text{MP}_1/\text{MP}_2) \tag{2.8}$$

Alternatively this condition can be written as:

$$(w_1/\text{MP}_1) = (w_2/\text{MP}_2) = \text{MC} \tag{2.9}$$

If, and only if, this condition holds, the costs of production are minimized. The cost minimization condition given by Equation (2.9) states that the cost of increasing output by one unit when adding more of input 1 must be equal to the corresponding cost for input 2. That is, the marginal cost (MC) of producing one extra unit of output must be the same irrespective of which additional inputs are used.

In Figure 2.3 the parallel lines are isocost lines. An increase in total costs shifts an isocost line further from the origin, so that cost represented by the isocost line C^3 is greater than C^2, and C^2 is greater than C^1. A change in the relative prices of factor inputs changes the slope of an isoquant. Assuming a producer chooses a desired output level y^0 and wishes to minimize costs, the producer must first choose a combination of inputs which lie on the appropriate isoquant I^0. The problem then is to choose from all the points on I^0, the point which crosses or touches the isocost line closest to the origin. Isocost line C^1 is irrelevant as I^0 does not cross or touch it. It is possible to produce with the combination of inputs represented by point A, with cost C^3. However, it is also possible to

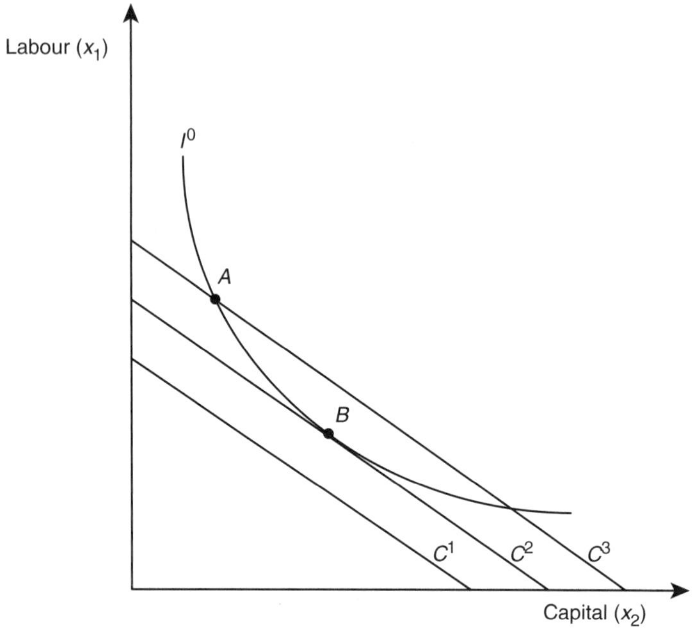

Figure 2.3 Isoquants, isocosts and cost minimization.

produce at point *B*, with a lower cost of C^2. In fact, it is easy to see that *B* is the point at which costs are minimized, because every isocost line representing a lower cost than C^2 (closer to the origin) does not have a point which touches or crosses I^0.

In the economic theory of production, when cost minimization occurs allocative efficiency is achieved. Allocative efficiency involves selecting combinations of inputs (e.g. mixes of labour and capital) which produce a given amount of output at minimum cost (given market prices for inputs). Allocative efficiency implies technical efficiency, but the reverse does not hold.

Production and efficiency in the multi-output model

Technical efficiency

The model described above can easily be extended to include more than one output. In the multi-output production function each output is assumed to be homogeneous in its own characteristics, but different to other outputs. The production function is written:

$$y = f(x_1, \ldots, x_n) \tag{2.10}$$

where y now represents a vector of $(y_1,...,y_m)$ outputs, $(x_1,...,x_n)$ are the n factor inputs, and $f(\bullet)$ is technology which is taken as given. For simplicity, we consider a two-output, two-input model below, where the production function is given by:

$$y = f(x_1, x_2) \tag{2.11}$$

where y is a vector of two outputs y_1 and y_2. Production in the two output case can be conveniently represented by a production possibilities frontier (PPF) for a given level of inputs, as shown in Figure 2.4. Note, the axes for this diagram represent output levels for y_1 and y_2. The PPF maps the technically efficient combinations of outputs for a given level of inputs. For example, a producer may vary the combinations of y_1 and y_2 represented by A or B and be technically efficient. If outputs are completely variable (there are no limits on how the producer can change the mix of y_1 and y_2) the producer can choose any combination of outputs on the PPF. Combinations of outputs inside the PPF are technically feasible but inefficient because production could be expanded for at least one output for the given resources available. Combinations outside the PPF are not possible due to constraints imposed by technology. As we will show later, the PPF is a key concept in the practical measurement of efficiency.

The marginal product of the ith input is given by

$$MP_i = \delta y / \delta x_i \tag{2.12}$$

where MP_i is now the contribution of input i to total output of both y_1 and y_2. If the production y_1 and y_2 can be separated into two separate and discrete processes, then the marginal contribution of each input to each output can be found. In this case the product specific marginal products are given by:

$$MP_i^1 = \delta y_1 / \delta x_i \tag{2.13}$$

$$MP_i^2 = \delta y_2 / \delta x_i \tag{2.14}$$

where MP_i^1 is the marginal product of input i in the production of y_1, and MP_i^2 is the marginal product of input i in the production of y_2. The marginal rate of technical substitution for the two inputs, x_1 and x_2, is given by:

$$MRTS_{21} = MP_1 / MP_2 \tag{2.15}$$

which is the MRTS for the total production of both outputs. Again, if the production of each output can be considered as a separate process, then an MRTS can be calculated for the two inputs for the production y_1 and y_2 separately using the ratio of the product specific marginal products shown in 2.13 and 2.14.

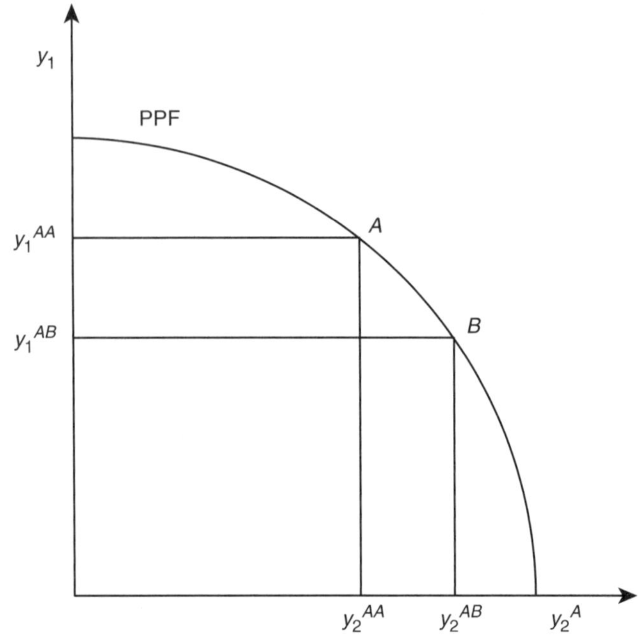

Figure 2.4 The production possibilities frontier.

Cost minimization and allocative efficiency

Allocative efficiency in the multi-output model occurs when the costs of production for all outputs are minimized. This is achieved when factor inputs are employed in proportions which minimize production costs given market prices for those inputs. The multi-output cost function is derived from the allocatively efficient production of outputs, and maps the cost minimizing levels of output for given input prices.

The multi-output cost function is derived using duality theory. Rearranging the general production function in Equation (2.10) into its implicit form, the m output and n input multi-output production function can be written:

$$g(y, x_1,..., x_n) = 0 \qquad (2.16)$$

The implicit form of the production function shows the maximum levels of outputs for a given level of resources. The production function can now be written in terms of a maximization problem where outputs are maximized subject to technological constraints, and non-negativity constraints on the inputs. The cost minimization problem which is solved to find the multi-output cost function is the dual of this production function maximization problem. The cost minimization problem requires that the factor input prices, $w_1,\ldots,w_n$, are fixed and exogenously determined. The cost minimization problem may then be written:

$$\min_{x_1,\ldots,x_n} \sum w_i x_i$$

subject to $y = g(y^0, x_1,\ldots, x_n)$

$$x_i \geq 0 \qquad i = 1,\ldots,n \tag{2.17}$$

where the objective function represents total cost, the first constraint is the production function where y^0 is the specified output level for the vector y, and the second constraint represents the non-negativity constraint on inputs. This formulation of the problem can be written as the Lagrangian function:

$$L = \sum w_i x_i + \lambda g(y^0, x_1, \ldots, x_n) \tag{2.18}$$

The first order conditions on inputs for the minimization of L are:

$$\frac{\partial L}{\partial x_i} = w_i + \lambda g_i = 0 \qquad i = 1, \ldots, n \tag{2.19}$$

and by dividing the ith condition by the jth condition we can obtain:

$$\frac{w_i}{w_j} = \frac{g_i}{g_j} \tag{2.20}$$

so cost minimization must satisfy the constraint that the ratio of input prices must equal the MRTS for those inputs. The term λ in the multi-output problem has the interpretation of a measure of the rate at which minimized cost is reduced as the production function constraint is relaxed.

Solution of the cost minimization problem for input levels yields the conditional input demands, x_i^*, which represent the amounts of inputs that minimize cost for given factor prices and output levels. The conditional input demand for the ith input is given by:

$$x_i^* = x_i\, (y, w_i,\ldots,w_n,) \tag{2.21}$$

The optimal values for inputs can then be used to construct the cost function which relates minimized production cost to input prices and outputs:

$$C = w_i x_i^* = c\, (y, w_i,\ldots,w_n,) \tag{2.22}$$

The multi-output cost function then maps the allocatively efficient sets of outputs for given factor prices. As in the single product model, allocative efficiency implies technical efficiency, but technical efficiency does not imply allocative efficiency.

The cost function for the two output and two input model can then be written:

$$C = w_1x_1^* + w_2x_2^* = c\ (y,\ w_1,w_2,) \tag{2.23}$$

Economies of scale

Economies of scale in the multi-output model are more complex than in the single-output model. In the single-output model above, economies of scale are defined according to the proportionate response of outputs to equiproportionate changes in inputs. However, in the multi-output model different outputs can be changed in different proportions when there is an equiproportionate change in inputs.

Using the multi-output cost function shown in Equation (2.10), a measure of scale economies across the entire set of $(y_1,\ldots,y_m)$ outputs can be developed. First the concept of ray average cost is required, which is a measure of how total cost varies with equiproportionate changes in output levels (holding all other variables constant). Ray average cost is given by:

$$\text{RAC} = [C(\text{y})]\ /\ t \tag{2.24}$$

where RAC is ray average cost, C(y) is the cost function for the vector of outputs y, and t is the equiproportionate change in all outputs in the vector y. Hence RAC is the ratio of total cost to the proportionate change in output level. From this a measure of economies of scale for the general case of m outputs can be written:

$$S_m = \frac{C(\text{y})}{\sum_{i=1}^{m} y_i C_i(\text{y})} \tag{2.25}$$

where

$$C_i(\text{y}) = \partial(C(\text{y})\ /\ \partial(y_i)) \tag{2.26}$$

S_m is the ratio of the ray average cost to the marginal cost of the composite output y. The properties of the measure S_m are the same as for the elasticity of scale in the single-output model, where $S_m = 1$ constant returns to scale are present, $S_m > 1$ implies increasing returns, and $S_m < 1$ implies decreasing returns to scale.

Individual outputs may also exhibit product specific scale economies. A measure of product specific returns to scale can be developed using the notion of the incremental cost of a product, y_i, which refers to the addition to total cost from the production of that output. The measure is given by:

$$S_i = \frac{IC_i(y)}{y_i C_i(y)} \tag{2.27}$$

where

$$IC_i = C(y) - C(y_{m-i}) \tag{2.28}$$

where IC_i is the incremental cost of output i, and $C_i(y)$ is the marginal cost of output i. IC_i is the total incremental cost of output i, which is the cost of producing the vector of outputs y less the cost of production if output i was no longer produced and all other outputs were held constant (including any product-specific fixed costs). The measure S_i takes a value greater than one if product-specific scale economies are present, and equal to one, and less than one if constant and decreasing product-specific economies of scale are respectively present.

Economies of scope

The multi-output model raises the possibility that the production process(es) for different outputs are inter-related. This is known as joint production. Joint products are produced in such a way that a change in the amount of one output necessarily involves a change in the amount of another output. For example, a farmer raising extra chickens will also increase egg production. In this situation a producer will incur joint costs in producing chickens and eggs, and the allocation of costs to the different outputs may become arbitrary. Joint production also raises the possibility of economies of scope. These are factors which make it cheaper to produce a range of related outputs than to produce each output on its own.

Joint production and economies of scope arise from two sources. The first is the presence of public inputs in production. Once acquired for use in producing one output, public inputs are available costlessly for use in the production of other outputs. An example of this type of input may be coal in coal-fired power stations where the fuel is purchased to produce electricity, but is also available for the production of steam (if steam is also deemed to be a valuable output). However, examples of public inputs are rare. The second source relates to inputs which are shared between products due to indivisibilities in production and which generate common or overhead costs. These inputs are quasi-public inputs: inputs which can be shared between outputs in production without complete congestion. Common costs are costs which are incurred when production of one output cannot be increased without reducing production of at least one other output. Examples of quasi-public inputs are much more common; for example, straw, water and shelter for chickens and eggs.

Economies of scope allow technically efficient production of multiple outputs using fewer resources than would have been used in producing those outputs separately. Non-joint production occurs when each output has a separate production function and there are no economies of scope, such that in the two-output, two-input case:

$$y_1 = f(x_1, x_2) \tag{2.29}$$

$$y_2 = f'(x_1, x_2) \tag{2.30}$$

Conversely under joint production, economies of scope exist and the production of one output varies with the level of production of at least one other output, which can be written as:

$$y_1 = f(y_2, x_1, x_2) \tag{2.31}$$

$$y_2 = f'(y_1, x_1, x_2) \tag{2.32}$$

However, economies of scope are more commonly examined using the multi-output cost function. The cost function in the two-output, two-input case may be written:

$$C = c\,(y_1, y_2, w_1, w_2) \tag{2.33}$$

where w_1 and w_2 are the factor prices of inputs x_1 and x_2 respectively. If economies of scope are not present (production is non-joint) each output will have a separable cost function:

$$C^1 = c\,(y_1, w_1, w_2) \tag{2.34}$$

$$C^2 = c\,(y_2, w_1, w_2) \tag{2.35}$$

such that the marginal cost of producing output i is independent of the level of output j. The presence of economies of scope would imply that the joint production of both outputs would reduce the total costs of production below the sum of the total costs of producing each output separately. In the two-product case:

$$C(y_1, y_2) < C(y_1, 0) + C(0, y_2) \tag{2.36}$$

where the multi-output cost function displays subadditivity, implying one firm or organization can produce a given level of both outputs at a lower cost than two firms specializing in the production of y_1 and y_2 respectively.

A measure of the degree of economies of scope in the two-output case is given by:

$$SC_m = \frac{C(y_1) + C(y_2) - C(y)}{C(y)} \tag{2.37}$$

which measures the relative increase in costs from separating the production of y_1 and y_2.

The production of health and health care

The production of health

Individuals demand health care for its desired impact on their health and well-being (Culyer 1978). They do not (at least in general) derive utility directly from the consumption of health care itself. Hence, the demand for health care is derived from the demand for health. In its simplest form, the production of health improvements from health programmes may then be thought of as a two-stage process. Resources (e.g. labour and capital) are combined to produce health programmes, which are consumed by individuals to produce improvements in their health. Health care may therefore be thought of as an intermediate output in the production of health improvements (other determinants of health include a wide range of socio-economic, environmental, cultural and demographic factors). Concepts of efficiency will vary according to which part(s) of these production processes are to be considered.

Figure 2.5 shows a model of health production. It draws on Grossman's seminal work on the production of health (1972a, 1972b) and is adapted from DaVanzo and Gertler (1990).

Health is considered to be a durable good in the model which individuals can invest or disinvest in over time. At the start of any time period (*t*) the individual has an endowment of health (H). Over the course of that period their health will change (ΔH) so that the endowment of health for the next period is (H + ΔH). Changes in the individual's health may be exogenous (outside of their control), for example declining health due to age or illness; or endogenous (within their control), for example changes in health-related behaviour.

In the short term an individual's health endowment is taken as fixed: it has been determined by their past actions and circumstances. However, in the long term individuals are able to influence health endowments in future periods through choices relating to health inputs (B) (which include health care) and other commodities (X). Investments in health are made through the consumption of health care and other health inputs, such as diet, exercise, education, housing, etc. Similarly, individuals may make disinvestments through their consumption choices, such as smoking, high trans-fat diet, etc. In fact, a number of studies have suggested that health care is a relatively weak determinant of health when compared to other determinants such as nutrition, education and lifestyle

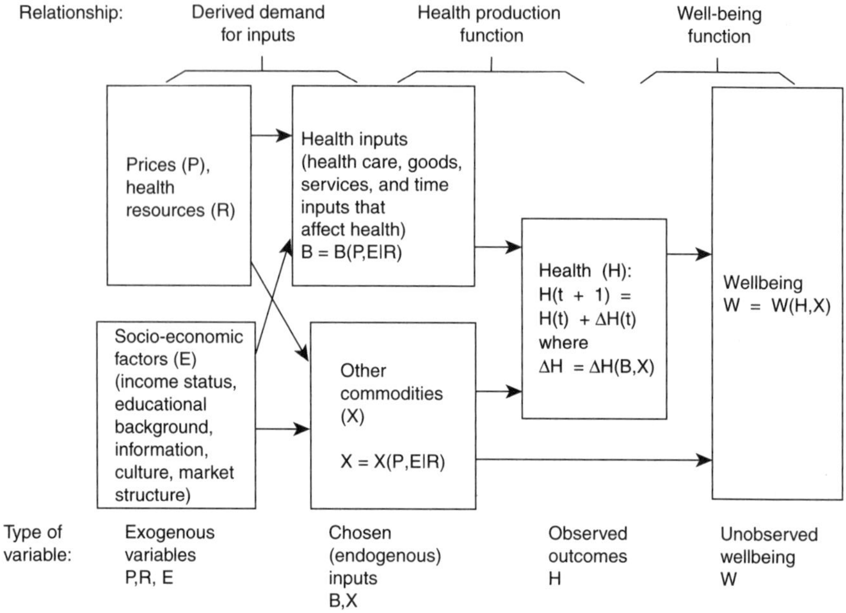

Reproduced from DaVanzo and Gertler (1990) with permission from the RAND corporation.

Figure 2.5 A model of the production of health.

(Auster *et al.* 1969; Newhouse and Friedlander 1980; Hadley 1982; Brook *et al.* 1983; Valdez *et al.* 1985). However, there is some evidence that the contribution of health care to health is increasing over time in developed countries (Hadley 1988). The health production function describes the process by which health inputs are transformed into improvements in health. In this context, efficiency concepts relate to the relationship between health inputs and associated improvements in health.

As noted above the demand for health inputs is derived from demand for health. In the model, the demand for health is, in turn, derived from the individual's desire to maximize their well-being (W). Well-being reflects both choices relating to health inputs and choices relating to the consumption of other commodities (X) which contribute to well-being. Consumption of these other commodities is influenced by prices (P), resource constraints (R) and the impact of socio-economic factors on preferences (E).

The production of health care

In a competitive health-care market, service providers are assumed to pursue the goals of profit maximization and cost minimization. That is, they pursue technical and allocative efficiency goals. Consumers have perfect information about health benefits from consuming health programmes and market prices for programmes provide appropriate price signals, so that individuals maximize their health and well-being subject to resource constraints. However, the health sector is not characterized by many of the features of the competitive market.

On the demand side, asymmetric information exists between health-care providers and consumers. Patients typically have much less information on the relationship between health care and its potential benefits than doctors. Further, even given the necessary information, patients will often lack the training and education required to interpret it correctly. Consumers may also lack detailed knowledge about their own health needs, the availability of health services and treatment options open to them. On the supply side, health service providers rarely operate in competitive market conditions, especially in the hospital sector.

Markets tend to be monopolistic or absent (i.e. the government directly pays for and provides health care), property rights are poorly defined and managers are only loosely accountable to owners, and significant transaction costs lead to imperfections in the pricing system.

Asymmetric information gives rise to the doctor–patient agency relationship, which is the central feature of the health-care market. Individuals' lack of information concerning the timing of their health-care consumption and the effectiveness of treatments means that the patient relies on the provider's assessment of expected outcomes. That is, the doctor acts not only as the provider of services, but also as the patient's agent. The agency relationship is an institutional response to the consumer's lack of information. However, if the agent does not pursue goals that are consistent with maximizing the patient's health and well-being, then the agency relationship becomes another source of market failure. In practice, clinical decisions are based on doctors' estimates of the likely effectiveness of a given treatment where there will always be some uncertainty surrounding the outcome. Doctors have considerable autonomy in how they provide health programmes which has resulted in wide variations in practice styles (Wennberg 1988). The costs of providing a given programme may therefore vary widely, and may be influenced by factors such as training and skill of service providers, local complication rates and differences of opinion between experts.

The market failures that characterize health-care markets indicate that the link between health programmes and improvements in consumers' health is far from straightforward. There are no guarantees that service providers will combine labour and capital efficiently in the production of health care. Providers may be pursuing goals other than efficiency, they may face imperfect (or no) market prices and the benefits of health programmes may be uncertain.

Health outcomes and health-care outputs

Using Figure 2.5 we can define outputs in the production of health and health care in two ways: in terms of improvements in health (health outcomes) or the production of health programmes (intermediate outputs in the production of health). Each has different implications for defining efficiency.

In recent years, a substantial literature has developed on the measurement of health outcomes from the consumption of health care. Health outcomes refer to the impact of a specific health-care intervention on the health status of an individual or group of individuals (Donabeidan 1969). There are a great number of possible ways to measure health outcomes, some examples are: biomedical indicators (e.g. changes in blood pressure); survival measures (e.g. changes in life expectancy); generic quality of life measures in the form of health profiles (e.g. the Nottingham Health Profile and the SF-36 questionnaire); and utility instruments (e.g. the EuroQol or EQ-5D, the SF-6D, and the Health Utilities Index) which are used to combine the quality and quantity of life dimensions of health using the Quality Adjusted Life Year (QALY) or one of its variants. A more detailed discussion of the measurement of health outcomes is given by elsewhere by Drummond *et al.* (2005).

Approaches to defining the outputs of health programmes have focused mainly on the hospital sector, and in particular, on inpatient interventions for specific conditions (Butler 1995). The main task has been to find an appropriate conceptual measure of output for different interventions which may draw on many different resources (e.g. nursing and physician care, laboratory tests, surgery, drugs, etc.). Interventions may also take many different forms, including in terms of their objectives (whether they seek to prevent, diagnose, cure, etc. symptoms and illnesses). Empirical approaches to measuring health-care outputs have included measuring output in terms of episodes of illness in primary, secondary and tertiary sectors, episodes of inpatient care and length of inpatient stay (Scitovsky 1964). However, these measures are still very crude. For example, a one-day inpatient stay in obstetrics for a woman giving birth cannot said to be the same output as a one-day stay for hernia-repair surgery. Interventions and outputs differ substantially between different health conditions. They also differ according to the severity of the condition for each individual patient (referred to as casemix factors). The response has been the development of output measures which reflect both the underlying condition and the severity of that condition for different patients. The most commonly used casemix adjusted measures of health-care output are Diagnosis Related Groups (DRGs). A detailed discussion of the relative merits of the different health care based output measures is provided elsewhere by Butler (1995).

Proponents of the use of health outcomes as the unit of analysis for efficiency argue that these measures reflect the primary objective of providing health care. The appeal of this argument is not in dispute but the approach has difficulties in practical application. In particular, there is no consensus on the most appropriate vehicle to employ in measuring health outcomes. This is evident when one considers the wide range of quality of life measures that are available using different constructs, methodologies and questions. While the health outcomes field is advancing rapidly, these difficulties have led many researchers to use health-care output measures as proxies for health outcomes.

While health-care outputs have the advantage that they are conceptually less troublesome than health outcomes, they also have major shortcomings. First, as with health outcomes, there is no consensus as to what is the best measure of health-care output. Second, while measures such as inpatient episodes and bed days (for instance) have the advantage that they can be aggregated across all forms of hospital inpatient care to provide a single measure of output, these measures do not fully reflect the heterogeneity of outputs produced in health care. They have the danger of treating programmes for schizophrenia and coronary artery bypass grafts as the same commodity. Robust measures of health-care output should attempt to pick up the large variety of different outputs in health care, both in terms of the different types and quality of care available.

A more fundamental issue is that the use of health outcomes as the unit of analysis presents problems in attributing cause to effect. Establishing the link between resources and health outcomes requires simultaneous estimation of the health and health-care production functions. Health care is characterized by complex decision-making processes involving managers and health-care professionals, large and diverse organizations such as hospitals, and inherent uncertainty about expected health outcomes. These factors make the specification of a single mechanistic relationship between inputs and health outcomes impractical (McGuire and Westoby 1983). To avoid some of these problems research has focused on economic evaluation to determine the relative cost-effectiveness of alternative interventions for specific conditions. By using careful clinical trial design, researchers have sought to estimate the links between health-care interventions, an individual's characteristics and health outcomes. However, the number of interventions considered in an economic evaluation is often limited b the costs and expected value of the information from clinical trials. Alternative methods of providing interventions are often overlooked, meaning that potential efficiency gains may be ignored. However, these efficiency gains may be examined through analysis of the health-care production function.

Efficiency, health and health care

As we outlined earlier in the chapter, economists typically distinguish between two types of efficiency in production processes: technical and allocative efficiency. The meaning and importance of technical and allocative efficiency may change depending on whether the production of health or health care is being examined.

There are two possible approaches to defining efficiency in relation to the production of health: to define efficiency in terms of the whole production process which converts factor inputs into health outcomes; or to define efficiency in terms of the production of health outcomes from treatments. Under the first approach technical efficiency relates to the combinations of inputs which minimize resource use for a given level of health status improvement, or maximizing health gain for a given level of inputs. Allocative efficiency relates to that combination of inputs which minimize the cost of producing a given level of health gain. Allocative efficiency implies that the marginal cost per extra unit of health status improvement must be equal across all inputs.

Under the second approach, treatments are used as the inputs in the production of health outcomes, rather than factor inputs. Technical efficiency relates to the combinations of treatments which minimize resource use for a given level of production of health gain, or which maximize health gain for a given level and mix of treatments. Allocative efficiency relates to that combination of treatments which minimize the cost of producing a given level of health gain for given treatment prices. Treatments are considered to be a 'black box': the efficiency with which health care is produced is not examined, just the efficiency with which health outcomes are produced from treatments. Allocative efficiency now implies that the marginal cost per extra unit of health outcome must be equal across all treatments. This is, perhaps, the most familiar definition of allocative efficiency in health economics: allocative efficiency implies that the ratio of marginal cost to marginal benefits (marginal health outcomes) should be equal across treatments.

Technical efficiency in the production of health care occurs if inputs are combined to produce a given level of health care at minimum resource use, or when health-care output is maximized for a given set of inputs. Allocative efficiency in the production of health care occurs when an input combination minimizes the cost of producing a given level of health care, for given input prices. This occurs when the ratio of the price of inputs to their marginal products is equal across all inputs; that is, the marginal cost of producing an extra unit of health-care output from each input is the same.

This leaves the possibility of six different options for defining efficiency in the production of health and health care which are summarized in Table 2.1. It is perhaps not surprising then that the health economics literature is rather inconsistent in its definitions of efficiency and their implications for policy (Birch and Gafni 1992). Applied research has focused mainly on three of the above concepts

Table 2.1 Efficiency, health and health care.

Inputs	*Outputs*	*Technical efficiency*	*Allocative efficiency*
Factor inputs	Treatments	Minimum physical quantities of resources for given level of treatments	MC of producing an extra unit of treatment equal across factor inputs
Factor inputs	Health outcomes	Minimum resources for given level of health outcomes	MC of producing an extra unit of health status improvement equal across factor inputs
Health programmes	Health outcomes	Minimum treatments for given level of health outcomes	MC of producing an extra unit of health status improvement across treatments

(either explicitly or implicitly): technical and allocative efficiency in the production of health care and allocative efficiency in the production of health outcomes from health-care interventions.

Allocative efficiency in the production of health outcomes has, however, represented by far the largest area of efficiency-based research in health economics. Techniques to assess the production of health outcomes from health-care interventions have included economic evaluations of alternative health interventions (Drummond *et al.* 2005), and priority setting techniques including cost per QALY league tables and programme budgeting and marginal analysis (Mooney *et al.* 1992). These approaches have generally focused on health-care interventions and treatments as the unit of input, attaching cost figures to the resources used in making up those interventions.

Empirical studies of technical and allocative efficiency in the production of health care have focused on analysis of health-care production and cost functions. Increasingly these studies are using the frontier-based approaches of DEA and SFA to analyse efficiency. This literature is reviewed in Chapter 5.

3 Efficiency measurement techniques

Introduction

This chapter discusses the theory of, and alternative techniques for, measuring efficiency. We first describe the theoretical foundations of efficiency measurement. These foundations are based on the pioneering work of Farrell (1957) and include the theory of production and cost frontiers and their relationship to production and cost functions, and the measurement of technical and allocative efficiency using radial measures of distance to the production/cost frontier. We then go on to describe three alternative approaches to measuring efficiency in the health sector: ordinary least squares (OLS) regression analysis, data envelopment analysis (DEA), and stochastic frontier analysis (SFA).

OLS regression methods draw on Feldstein's seminal work on efficiency in the health sector (Feldstein 1967). This approach uses classical linear regression models to estimate a cost or production function for a sample of health-care providers. The residuals from these models may then be used to estimate whether given providers are above or below average efficiency levels, and by how much they are above or below the average. Average efficiency is estimated using the OLS regression line. The criticisms of this approach will then be discussed – primarily that OLS regression does not identify truly efficient behaviour as efficiency estimates are based on average performance and not on the production frontier.

DEA plots the production frontier for a sample of providers using linear programming techniques. It identifies efficient providers – those lying on the frontier – and provides estimates of the technical and allocative efficiency of all other providers relative to those which are efficient. The key features of DEA are described, including: non-parametric and non-stochastic estimation of the frontier, the handling of multiple inputs and outputs, input minimization versus output maximization, formulations of the model, interpretation of weights in the model, dual values identification of the peer group of providers, estimation of economies of scale, interpretation of targets for inefficient units, the treatment of casemix, and the interpretation of efficiency rankings including regression analysis of rankings. The Malmquist index is then described, which is a means of measuring productivity in terms of efficiency changes over time using DEA. The index can be decomposed to show if changes are due to technology changes (movements in the frontier from one year to the next), changes in efficiency (how far a provider moves from the frontier in each time period), and scale changes.

SFA is used to estimate the production/cost frontier for a sample of providers using regression-based techniques. This approach estimates the frontier by decomposing the error term into two parts – a one-sided error term that measures inefficiency and a more usual normally distributed error term that captures random influences. The key features of stochastic frontiers are described, including: parametric and stochastic estimation of the frontier, choice of functional form, choice of distribution for the inefficiency term, testing of model assumptions, the treatment of casemix, estimation of economies of scale and scope, estimation of marginal costs, and interpretation of efficiency rankings.

The chapter concludes with a brief comparison of DEA and SFA as alternative frontier estimation techniques.

Efficiency measurement and Farrell

In Chapter 2 we introduced two key concepts: technical and allocative efficiency. Technically efficient combinations of inputs are those combinations which use the least resources to produce a given level of output (for a given state of technology). Alternatively, technical efficiency may be defined in terms of maximizing output for a given level of input. Allocative efficiency involves selecting combinations of inputs (e.g. mixes of labour and capital) which produce a given amount of output at minimum cost (given market prices for inputs). Farrell's seminal work introduced two further concepts (Farrell 1957): radial measures of efficiency and overall (economic) efficiency.

These concepts are illustrated in Figure 3.1. The figure considers a simple example of producing a single output (y) from labour (x_1) and capital (x_2) inputs, where the parallel lines represent isocost lines and I^0 an isoquant. Assuming a producer chooses a desired output level y^0, the producer must first choose a combination of inputs which lie on I^0 to be technically efficient. Production at the point *C* would be technically inefficient because the producer could produce y^0 using both less labour and capital. Keeping the same mix of inputs, a producer would be technically efficient if they produced at point *A*, which lies on the isoquant. Farrell's measure of technical efficiency is based on the line *OC*, which passes through *A* and *C*. *OC* is often referred to as a radial measure of efficiency as it measures efficiency in terms of distance from the origin. Technical efficiency (TE) at point *C* is given by:

$$\text{TE} = OA/OC \qquad (3.1)$$

where TE must take a value greater than zero and less than or equal to one ($0 < \text{TE} \leq 1$). If TE = 1 the producer is technically efficient and is operating on the isoquant. If TE < 1 the producer is technically efficient. The lower the value of TE, the less technically efficient the producer is.

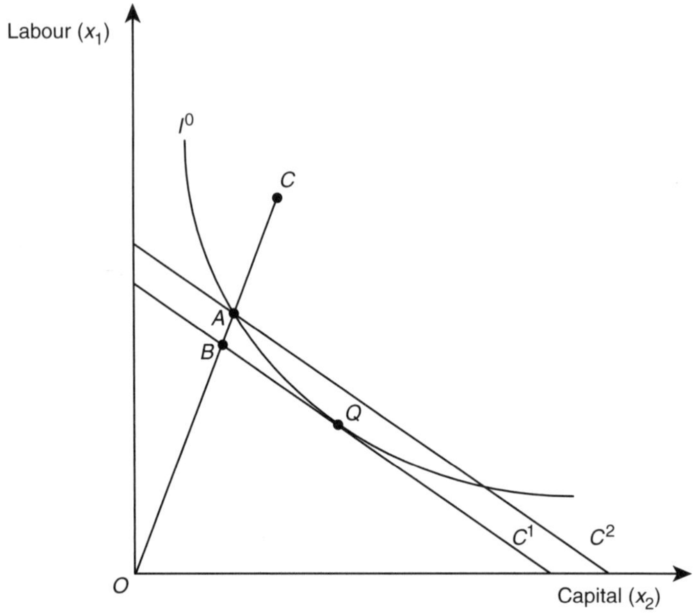

Figure 3.1 Radial efficiency measurement and Farrell.

If we now assume a producer wishes to minimize costs they will choose the combination of inputs at point Q where the isocost line C^1 is tangential to I^0. If the producer chooses an input mix along the line OC and is technically efficient they will produce at point A, as described above, which lies on the isocost line C^2, which implies they are not minimizing costs. For the input mix given by the line OC, the producer would need to produce at the point B to be minimizing costs. This is one of Farrell's key insights: allocative efficiency (AE) can now be measured by:

$$\text{AE} = OB/OA \tag{3.2}$$

where similarly AE must take a value greater than zero and less than or equal to one ($0 < \text{AE} \leq 1$), and where AE is less than 1, this implies that production is not allocatively efficient. AE can therefore be interpreted as a measure of excess costs arising from using inputs in inappropriate proportions.

Farrell's TE and AE terms can be combined to generate a measure of overall (economic) efficiency (OE):

$$\text{OE} = \text{TE} \times \text{AE} = (OA/OC) \times (OB/OA) = OB/OC \tag{3.3}$$

where OE also lies in the range ($0 < \text{OE} \leq 1$). OE can be interpreted as the ratio of the cost of producing one unit of technically efficient output to the cost of producing one unit at point *C* (for given factor prices).

Ordinary least squares (OLS) regression

Early work in the empirical measurement of technical efficiency concentrated on OLS regression approaches to estimating health-care production functions. Feldstein's seminal study employed OLS models to estimate a variety of production functions for acute non-teaching hospitals in the UK National Health Service (Feldstein 1967). He estimated production functions using a variety of functional forms, and then interpreted the residuals from these regressions as a measure of the technical efficiency of each hospital. In the OLS approach, a hospital with a residual of zero is interpreted to be producing at 'average technical efficiency' compared with other hospitals in the data set. A hospital with a negative residual is interpreted to be operating 'below average technical efficiency', and a hospital with a positive residual to be operating 'above average technical efficiency'. More formally, Feldstein's specification is given by:

$$y_i = \beta_i x_i + v_i \tag{3.4}$$

where y_i is a vector of outputs, x_i is a vector of inputs, and v_i is the error term which is assumed to follow the assumptions of the classical linear regression model error term. Since the error term v_i is distributed symmetrically the estimated function cannot be interpreted as a frontier. Instead the OLS model plots the 'average' relationship between inputs (the independent variables) and outputs (the dependent variables) in the hospitals being studied.

This presents two significant problems for the analyst wishing to measure efficiency. First, the OLS residuals only provide a measure of (in)efficiency compared to 'average' production practices. This measure sheds no light on how far each hospital may be from the production frontier; that is, how (in)efficient each hospital is compared to efficient production practices (Barrow and Wagstaff 1989) as the frontier is not estimated. Second, the interpretation of OLS residuals as pure measures of (in)efficiency is questionable, as residuals will also capture noise, those random influences on production which are outside of the hospital's control (Wagstaff 1987), measurement error and unobservable heterogeneity (Jones 2000).

In the late 1970s these criticisms led independent research teams to develop DEA and SFA as alternative approaches to estimating production and cost frontiers, which we now discuss.

Data envelopment analysis

The development of DEA into a practical research tool in the 1970s opened up new methods of examining health-care production (Charnes *et al.* 1978;

Cooper *et al.* 2004). DEA uses observed input and output data from health-care providers to directly plot the production frontier using mathematical programming techniques. The approach is non-stochastic and non-parametric: avoiding problems of specifying a functional form for the frontier. It also allows direct comparisons of efficiency between providers based on their observed production. DEA has proved to be particularly useful for analysing production in the public sector where there is market failure or outputs are not traded using market prices (Ganley and Cubbin 1992).

There are numerous examples of applications of DEA in the health sector, including studies of hospitals (Sherman 1984; Banker *et al.* 1986; Register and Bruning 1987; Sexton *et al.* 1989a; Burgess and Wilson 1993; Ozcan and Luke 1993), the effect of hospital ownership on efficiency (Grosskopf and Valdmanis 1987; Ozcan *et al.* 1992; Valdmanis 1992), maternity care (Boussofiane *et al.* 1991), nursing (Nunamaker 1983), pharmacies (Färe *et al.* 1992), public health programmes (Pina and Torres 1992), and primary health-care services (Huang and McLaughlin 1989). It is by far the most common method for analysing efficiency in health care (see Chapter 5).

DEA uses quantities of inputs consumed, and the corresponding outputs produced, to calculate the relative efficiencies of provider units. The technique is attractive as it is able to incorporate multiple outputs and inputs simultaneously, without having to aggregate either into a less meaningful index. Furthermore, DEA does not require specific knowledge, or restrictive mathematical assumptions, concerning the exact ways in which inputs in the provision of care are transformed into the outputs of the care process.

DEA operates by identifying a group of units against which a single chosen unit can be compared. The comparison group is defined as those units which have produced at least the same level of output, using fewer inputs, than the unit under study. Therefore, the modelling process identifies those units which appear to be operating relatively more efficiently than others, and which group of units should be used in comparison with any particular provider unit chosen for study. However, some important factors in the provision of services may not be adequately captured by the model (for example differences in local hospital policies) but DEA does offer the potential for exploring these factors. By examining the comparison group of units, and the unit under study, DEA can be used to examine the impact of any factors in terms of their effects on service provision levels for given levels of resources. Therefore DEA provides a tool for analysing both input and output relationships, and possible other factors which are important in determining output levels.

The technique produces a measure of a health-care producer's efficiency by the method proposed by Farrell (1957) which is based on the ratio of by how much a particular producer could reduce its inputs and still maintain the same level of output. The measure is independent of output prices and is solely based on technical efficiency issues, which has clear advantages for the use of DEA in the public sector where price information is frequently absent. This measure is constrained to lie between 0 (no output) and 1 (technical efficiency).

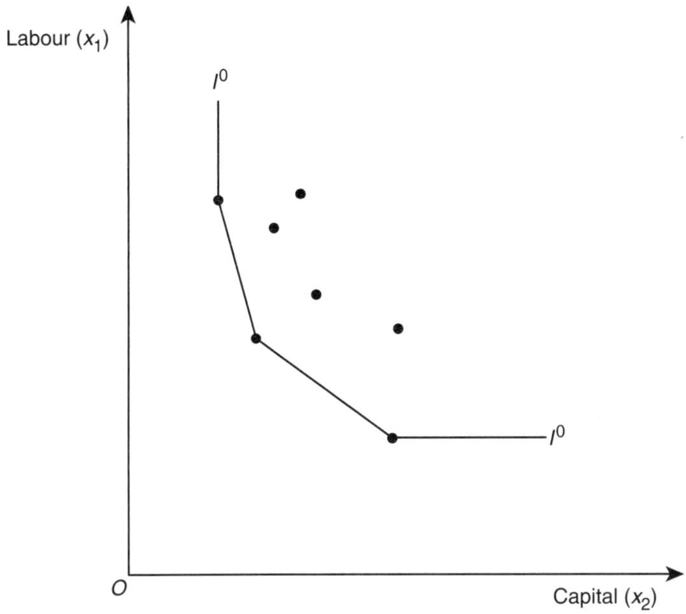

Figure 3.2 The DEA production frontier.

Because the production function is not directly observable, DEA estimates a realized production frontier based on input and output data. The frontier maps the least resource use input combinations from historic data, is assumed to be convex to the origin, and always has a non-negative slope. The DEA frontier is illustrated in Figure 3.2. This figure again considers a simple, single-output, two-input example. The dots represent different producers and the quantities of inputs they used to produce a given level of output. The DEA frontier (I^0I^0) consists of straight lines joining the points that represent the most efficient producers. Inefficient producers lie to the right of the frontier. The complete production frontier is easily inferred for all levels of output, the analysis can be extended to cover both multiple inputs and outputs, and the assumption of constant returns to scale can be easily dropped (see p. 35).

The general mathematical formulation of the DEA model centres on decision-making units (DMUs). DMU is a term widely used in the DEA literature intended to represent any type of producer or service provider being studied. Consider a model of n DMUs, and the general case with m inputs and s outputs. The *jth* DMU can be represented in terms of its input and output vectors:

$$\text{Input vector } \mathrm{x_j} = (x_{ij},\ldots, x_{mj}) \tag{3.5}$$

$$\text{Output vector } \mathrm{y_j} = (y_{ij},\ldots, y_{sj}) \tag{3.6}$$

If we are interested in analysing the efficiency of a given producer (called DMU 0), we must establish the group of other DMUs against which comparison will be undertaken. DEA analyses frontiers by mapping straight lines or planes between different combinations of DMUs. Therefore we are interested in identifying the linear combinations of other DMUs that produce at least as much of all the *s* outputs as DMU 0, the unit under study. A linear combination of such DMUs is referred to as the comparison group. The usual method is to represent a comparison group by a vector of weights:

$$\lambda = (\lambda_i, \ldots, \lambda_n) \tag{3.7}$$

where λ_j is the weight attached to DMU*j*. The first condition which must be met is that the comparison group must produce at least as much output, in all *s* dimensions, as the unit under study, DMU 0. This condition is given by:

$$\sum_{j=1}^{n} y_{rj}\,\lambda_j \geq y_{r0} \qquad r = 1, \ldots, s \tag{3.8}$$

The second condition to be met is that the weighted comparison group must use no more than a fraction of the *m* inputs which DMU 0 uses. This fraction is h_0. The model presented here assumes constant returns to scale for simplicity, and hence h_0 is constant across all inputs. This condition is given by:

$$\sum_{j=1}^{n} x_{ij}\,\lambda_j \leq h_0\, x_{i0} \qquad i = 1, \ldots, m \tag{3.9}$$

The fraction is bounded such that $0 \leq h_0 \leq 1$. The minimized value of h_0 is the measure of (relative) technical efficiency of DMU 0. The efficient comparison group is that which minimizes h_0, and the vector of optimal weights λ gives the weight attached to each DMU in forming the efficient comparison group. The model can be represented by a linear programme which finds the optimal values of h_0 and λ.

$$\text{Minimize } h_0 \tag{3.10}$$

Subject to:

$$\sum_{j=1}^{n} y_{rj}\,\lambda_j \quad \geq y_{r0} \qquad r = 1, \ldots, s \tag{3.11}$$

$$\sum_{j=1}^{n} x_{ij}\lambda_j - x_{i0}h_0 \quad \leq 0 \qquad i = 1, \ldots, m \tag{3.12}$$

$$h_0, \lambda_j \quad \geq 0 \qquad j = 1, \ldots, n \tag{3.13}$$

The assumption of constant returns to scale under DEA can be dropped, with the mathematical transition to a variable returns to scale model relatively straightforward. This formulation of the DEA model is sometimes referred to as the BCC model (Banker *et al.* 1984). A variable returns to scale frontier can be found by adding the additional constraint:

$$\sum_{j=1}^{n} y_{rj}\lambda_j \qquad \geq y_{r0} \qquad r = 1, \ldots, s \tag{3.14}$$

Figure 3.3 illustrates DEA frontiers under constant returns to scale (CRS) and under variable returns to scale (VRS). The section *AB* of the VRS frontier exhibits increasing returns to scale, *BC* exhibits constant returns to scale, and *CD* decreasing returns to scale. For a given DMU, *G*, the distance *EF* measures the effects of economies of scale in production, and *FG* measures 'pure' inefficiency. Clearly, more DMUs will be deemed to be efficient under variable returns to scale, as under an assumption of constant returns to scale any economies of scale are (incorrectly) included in the measure of inefficiency.

DEA (in the formulation presented above) does not account for the influences of casemix on producer efficiency in the production of health care (see Chapter 2). One approach to modelling the effects of casemix is to include the patient characteristics

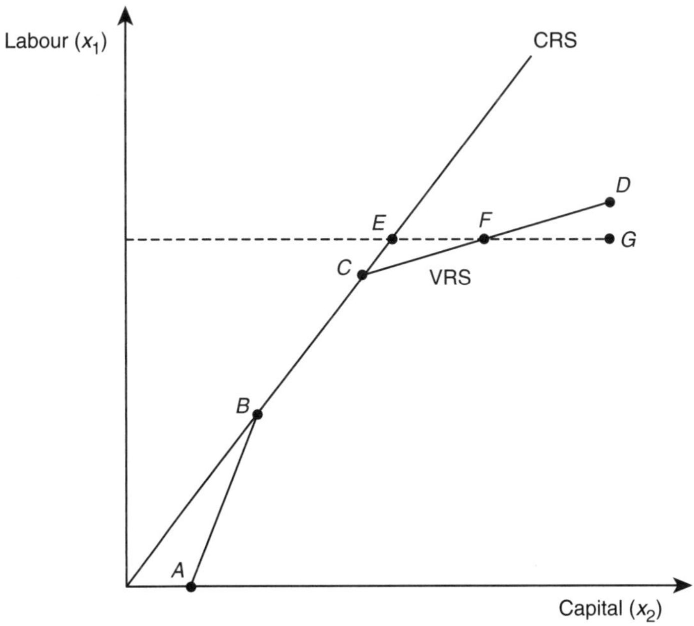

Figure 3.3 Constant and variable returns to scale under DEA.

(for patients at different health-care DMUs) as a type of input in the production frontier. However, this approach may be inconsistent with economic theory, as patients are not inputs which are transformed to make the final product (which in this case is a health-care intervention). Instead, patients consume treatments to (hopefully) produce improvements in their health status. The characteristics of patients will influence the production of health care in order to produce these health status improvements, hence patient characteristics may be better viewed as factors which shape the environment within which the production of health care occurs, rather than inputs in the production process.

DEA models can easily incorporate this approach to patient characteristics (casemix factors) by modelling the effect of casemix on the overall production process. The method typically involves adding a second stage of analysis to the DEA approach. The first stage of the model involves running a DEA model based on physical inputs and treatment-based outputs to yield efficiency scores for DMUs, as shown previously. The second stage then takes these efficiency scores and regresses them against unit-level casemix variables to assess the impact of a patient's socio-demographic and clinical characteristics on the production process and efficiency (Sexton *et al.* 1989a; Chilingerian 1995). Hence, casemix factors are used to explain variations in observed efficiency levels of provider units.

An advantage of this approach is that statistical modelling of variations in the efficiency score allows the most important casemix determinants of (in)efficiency to be chosen on statistical grounds by their significance in the second stage regression. If patient characteristics are included as inputs in the DEA model, the choice of casemix variables is essentially arbitrary. Moreover, if the latter approach was adopted, DEA would show the unit with the lowest value for a given casemix variable to be efficient, and use this value as a reference point for assessing the efficiency of other providers. Clearly, deeming a unit to be efficient in such a case is undesirable.

Since the efficiency score produced by DEA lies within the range of 0 to 1, it does not represent a true continuous variable. This violates assumptions of the classical linear regression model and makes estimates derived from an OLS regression inconsistent (Maddala 1988). The efficiency score distribution is best described by a censored normal distribution (Maddala 1988). A censored distribution is one in which a limiting value(s) exists on the observed variable whereby observations lying beyond the limit are assigned the value of the variable at the limit. In DEA this limit is 1, which is imposed by the linear programmes used in DEA. Thus censoring takes place at 1, whilst efficiency scores below 1 take their 'true value'. More simply the censoring can be summarized by:

$$\text{DEA efficiency score} = \begin{cases} \text{actual score} & \text{if score} < 1 \\ 1 & \text{otherwise} \end{cases} \tag{3.15}$$

An important distinction is drawn in the econometrics literature between truncated and censored distributions. Truncated distributions are those where observations are omitted or missing for either the dependent or independent variables (Greene 1992). The DEA efficiency scores contain a full set of observations, but observed values are limited at 1. Hence it is appropriate to treat the score as having a censored distribution. The DEA score does not exactly fit the theory of censored distributions, however, in that a censored distribution has a hypothetical normally distributed variable underlying it which is not directly observable (Maddala 1988). In terms of providing a robust model with which to analyse the DEA efficiency score it is still most appropriate to treat the score as having a censored distribution, as this is the closest approximation of the DEA score distribution available (Chilingerian 1995). The appropriate regression model to use when the dependent variable has a censored distribution is the Tobit censored model (Greene 1992). The Tobit model estimates a regression line which allows for hypothetical efficiency scores above 1. Therefore the regression model identifies characteristics of patient populations which are strongly associated with a set of 'adjusted' efficiency scores (Chilingerian 1995). However, recent work has suggested that second-stage analyses of DEA estimates may be flawed due to assumptions concerning efficiency scores (Simar and Wilson 2004). There are technical advances underway to help compensate for this, but in the meantime analysts should proceed with caution when interpreting such analyses.

Before proceeding, it is important to note that DEA has three major limitations which require some care on the part of the analysts constructing models and interpreting results.

First, the technique is deterministic and relies on outlying observations (the most efficient DMUs). Care must be taken in interpreting results as the DEA frontier may have been influenced by stochastic variation, measurement error or unobserved heterogeneity in the data. DEA makes the strong and non-testable assumption of no measurement error or random variation in output (Newhouse 1994). Small random variation for inefficient hospitals will affect the magnitude of the inefficiency estimate for that hospital. Larger random variation may move the frontier itself, thereby affecting efficiency estimates for a range of hospitals.

Second, DEA is sensitive to the number of input and output variables used in the analysis. Overestimates of efficiency scores can occur if the number of units relative to the number of variables used is small. A general rule of thumb is that the number of units used should be at least three times the combined number of input and output variables (Cooper *et al.* 2000[1]).

Third, DEA only provides a measure of relative efficiency: a DMU which is deemed efficient using DEA is only efficient given the observed practices in the sample which is being analysed. Therefore, it is possible that greater efficiency than that observed could be achieved in the sample (since DEA does not identify the economic production function).

The Malmquist index

Since efficiency is not static, analysts may be interested in examining productivity changes over time. DEA-based Malmquist indices may be used to measure

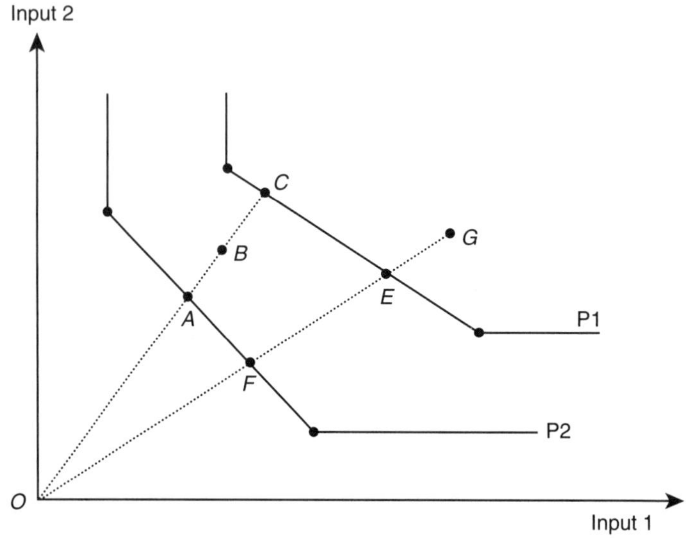

Figure 3.4 The Malmquist index.

productivity changes over time. The Malmquist productivity index (MPI) (Malmquist 1953; Caves *et al.* 1982) is defined as (with reference to Figure 3.4, a two-input, one-output model):

$$\mathrm{MPI} = \left[\frac{OE / OG}{OC / OB} \times \frac{OF / OG}{OA / OB} \right]^{0.5} \tag{3.16}$$

It is straightforward to see that the Malmquist index is itself the geometric mean of two indices. In the first, the production frontier of period 1 (P1) is taken as given and measures the distance of the two production points, G and B (representing a DMU in the two different time periods) from it. The second index is similar except the reference frontier is that of period 2 (P2). A score greater than unity indicates productivity progress as a DMU delivers a unit of output in period 2 using less inputs. In other words, the DMU in period 2 is more efficient relative to itself in period 1. Similarly, a score less than unity implies productivity regress and constant productivity is signalled by a unit score. The index can be decomposed:

$$\mathrm{MPI} = \frac{OE / OG}{OA / OB} \left[\frac{OA}{OC} \times \frac{OF}{OE} \right]^{0.5} \tag{3.17}$$

The component outside the brackets is the ratio of technical efficiency in each period and measures efficiency change when moving from period 1 to period 2

(P1 and P2 in Figure 3.4). It indicates whether the unit gets closer to its production frontier; that is, becomes more efficient (with a score greater than unity), or moves further away from the frontier; that is, becomes less efficient (with a score of less than unity), or stays the same (with a unit score). The second component of thc Malmquist index in Equation (3.16) captures technological change evaluated from both time periods; that is, movements of the actual frontier itself – the technology with reference to which a sample operates. The frontier (i.e. technology) can progress (with a score greater than unity), regress (with a score of less than unity), or stay in the same position (with a unit score). Malmquist indices are increasingly used in health care: see Hollingsworth and Wildman (2003) for a practical example, and other examples as noted in Chapter 5.

Stochastic frontier analysis

The development of SFA was, at least in part, a response to the limitations of DEA described above. SFA decomposes the error term from the classical linear regression model into two parts. The first part of a one-sided 'error' term that acts as a measure of inefficiency. By constraining this term to be one-sided, production units can only produce on or below the estimated production frontier. The second part is the 'pure error' term that captures random noise, and has a two-sided distribution. The one-sided constraint on the distribution of the inefficiency term allows a realized production frontier to be estimated, and each producer's efficiency to be measured relative to that frontier.

The use of SFA in the production of health care has received increasing attention in recent years. This is partly due to increased interest in productive efficiency issues, but also due to advances in modelling techniques and increased computing capabilities. Examples of SFA in health care include cross-sectional studies using an inefficiency term with a half-normal distribution in UK maternity hospitals (Wagstaff 1987), Spanish Ministry of Health acute hospitals (Wagstaff 1989), US hospitals (Zuckerman *et al.* 1994), and New York nursing homes (Vitaliano and Toren 1994). In a study of Spanish hospitals, a cost frontier model using panel data was also estimated, with the assumption of constant efficiency over time (Wagstaff 1989).

The stochastic frontier model of the production frontier is given by:

$$\mathrm{y_i} = \beta_i \, \mathrm{x_i} + u_i + v_i \tag{3.18}$$

where $\mathrm{y_i}$ is the vector of outputs, $\mathrm{x_i}$ is the vector of inputs, u_i is the one-sided inefficiency term ($u_i \geq 0$ for all i), v_i is the two-sided error term which is assumed to follow the usual classical linear regression model error term, and u_i and v_i have zero covariance.

In order to allow multiple outputs to be modelled (as outputs in health care are typically heterogeneous) researchers often estimate cost rather than production frontiers. Estimation of a production frontier requires that all outputs can be meaningfully aggregated into a single measure. This assumption is questionable in the health context. However, costs can be easily aggregated into a single measure using monetary units such as dollars. The estimation of the cost frontier remains a valid method for examining productive efficiency as it is the dual of the production function. The cost frontier formulation of the model is:

$$c_i = f(\mathrm{p_i}, y_i, \mathrm{z_i}) + u_i + v_i \tag{3.19}$$

where c_i is expenditure at hospital i, $\mathrm{p_i}$ is a vector of input prices, and $\mathrm{z_i}$ is a vector of producer characteristics which includes casemix variables. The inclusion of variables capturing casemix and producer characteristics in the model allows statistical testing of hypotheses concerning the relationship between these factors and producer efficiency (Evans 1971).

The stochastic frontier model is estimated by maximum likelihood and requires that the researcher specifies an appropriate distribution for the inefficiency term. The most commonly adopted approach for cross-sectional data is to assume that u_i follows a half-normal distribution (Aigner *et al.* 1977):

$$u_i^* = |u_i| \tag{3.20}$$

and

$$u_i^* \sim N(0, \sigma^2_u) \tag{3.21}$$

Other distributions suggested for cross-sectional data include the exponential and gamma distributions (Vitaliano and Toren 1994). Another approach adopted has been to use panel data which has the advantage that it requires no specific assumption about the distribution of u_i, but adds the assumption that inefficiency remains constant over time (Wagstaff 1989). However, there are no strong *a priori* theoretical reasons for choosing any of the above distributions over each other (Greene 1986). It has been argued that this has led to arbitrary and non-testable assumptions about the distribution of the inefficiency term, which is a potential source of model mis-specification (Newhouse 1994; Skinner 1994). Any conclusions about technical efficiency will depend on the accuracy of the assumption about the distribution of the inefficiency term (Wagstaff 1987, 1989).

Assumptions concerning the error term v_i in SFA may also be important. Skinner (1994) demonstrated that if the assumption of normality in the error term does not hold, and its distribution is skewed, inefficiency may be under-or over-estimated. Since the error term is assumed to show zero skewness, any skewness is attributed to the inefficiency term. For instance, periodic capital repairs to a hospital may lead to a positive skew in total cost and hence the error term. Under a stochastic cost frontier model this will result in inefficiency being detected, even if the hospitals studied are perfectly efficient. Conversely, a negative skew on the error term will bias the estimate of inefficiency downwards. Further, SFA may also reject the null hypothesis of no inefficiency too readily (Skinner 1994). Under the null hypothesis the combined error term takes a (non-skewed) normal distribution. Skinner demonstrates through simulation that the Shapiro–Wilks test of normality rejects the null less frequently than the SFA approach. This may be the result of poor power in the Shapiro–Wilks test, but may also be the result of too much power in rejecting the null under SFA.

The SFA cost frontier is often estimated using a translog functional form which allows the testing of a wide range of assumptions about the nature of the cost function, and does not impose restrictive *a priori* assumptions on its functional form (Newhouse 1994). Translog multi-product cost functions can also be used easily to test for the presence of economies of scale and scope (Butler 1995). However, this approach requires a large number of degrees of freedom (Newhouse 1994). In hospital studies, where samples are often small, this may introduce measurement error and bias in inefficiency estimates through the inappropriate aggregation of inputs and outputs. An alternative approach is to choose a functional form which is less demanding on the data (e.g. Cobb–Douglas), but this may come at the price of introducing mis-specification into the model.

Comparing frontier techniques

The main differences between SFA and DEA lie in assumptions concerning stochastic behaviour and the nature of the production/cost frontier. DEA is a non-stochastic approach and hence makes no allowance for statistical noise and random shocks, whereas SFA explicitly models random behaviour through the error term. SFA is parametric, requiring specification of the functional form for the frontier, whereas DEA is a non-parametric technique. A third but arguably less important difference is the ability of DEA to easily handle multiple outputs. SFA usually requires aggregation of outputs into a single index. This problem has led many researchers to estimate cost rather than production frontiers when using SFA as this avoids the need for a single index of output in non-monetary terms.

The SFA approach gives rise to two potentially significant problems. First, in common with OLS regression models, SFA is parametric and may place overly restrictive assumptions on the health-care production function. Specification of an appropriate functional form under regression-based approaches is often difficult as relatively little is known *a priori* about what functional form should be used. Second, the choice of the distribution for the inefficiency term is arbitrary, and is a potential source of model mis-specification (Newhouse 1994; Skinner 1994). This applies equally to both the cross-sectional formulation of the model, where there is no *a priori* reason why inefficiency should follow a half-normal distribution, and to the panel data formulation, where the assumption of constant inefficiency over time is clearly unattractive as variations in efficiency over time are a major motivation in attempting to study the production of health care (Greene 1986), although some models have been developed allowing for time-varying efficiency, this may lead to convergence problems (Greene 2004; Coelli *et al.* 2005). DEA does not require specific knowledge, or restrictive mathematical assumptions, concerning the exact ways in which inputs are transformed into health-care outputs, and can easily handle multiple inputs and outputs without the need for aggregating outputs into a single index. However, DEA does not account for random influences on provider units.

4 Measuring efficiency in health services

Introduction

This chapter will develop a framework for the practical undertaking of modelling and measurement of efficiency in health services. All practical issues will be considered, from how to specify models to how to feedback results to those who will find them the most useful.

There are a number of questions to be asked when measuring efficiency: What is to be measured? Why is this to be measured? And for whom? In most cases the answer to the first question is relatively straightforward. We could be looking at the technical efficiency of a sample of hospitals, or allocative efficiency in the delivery of primary care. The second and third questions are sometimes more difficult to answer. Usually we are concerned with increasing the amount of health care that can be delivered given certain resources, but when factors such as quality of care are introduced, analysis can become more complex. Moreover, careful consideration of a range of other factors is required, for example in examining efficiency in the hospital sector how do we account for teaching and research and its impact on the delivery of care? For whom we are measuring efficiency is also important. Is the study simply an academic exercise in order to further advance a particular technique? Has the study been commissioned by health authorities to develop a measure that can be applied practically on the ground by health service managers? Or, is the study to develop a measure to be used by commissioners of health care to promote efficiency at the health system level?

Once these questions have been addressed, an efficiency measurement study can be undertaken. There are several practical steps which need to be taken once the appropriate study perspective has been decided upon. These include data collection, model specification, sensitivity analysis of model validity and reporting of results. Efficiency measurement practitioners have tended to adopt 'rules of thumb' to guide their choices under each of these steps. We will establish why this is, and look at ways in which the researcher can validate the methods they are using in order to use the best specified model for the application in hand. This is a particular problem in non-parametric models, but one which has received scant attention to date. The feedback of results and the translation of empirical findings into policy tools are also areas that have received little attention in the literature.

We will examine how to feedback study findings to decision makers, and the critical factors in translating results from efficiency measurement studies into practical policy tools.

An important step in undertaking an efficiency measurement study is to choose the most appropriate software package for data analysis. We review the current software available to undertake efficiency measurement analysis. Software available ranges from packages that are complex to operate, but offer a wide variety of modelling possibilities and are intended for the academic user, to packages which are relatively easy to operate, but are more limited in the range of models which may be specified. Prices vary from zero for some free shareware packages, to relatively large sums for certain commercial products.

What is to be measured, why and for whom?

To answer this question, which on first impression seems quite straightforward, it is important to know what is currently measured in terms of what is thought to be 'efficiency'. This involves eliciting the type of information currently available on efficiency in health services; how this information is used; what kind of new information would be useful; the form that new information should take; and knowledge of and opinions about methods with a foundation in production economics, such as data envelopment analysis (DEA).

To help elicit information Hollingsworth and Parkin (1998) undertook a survey of relevant NHS personnel in the Northern & Yorkshire Region of the UK NHS. A postal questionnaire was sent to all hospital trusts (57 at the time) and health authorities (HAs) (14 at the time), covering each of the areas detailed above. The questionnaire was developed with the assistance of performance measurement personnel in one trust and one HA and piloted on a sample of two of each type of organization based outside of the region to assure that the most accurate and relevant information would be collected. The survey consists mainly of closed response questions seeking both factual data and attitudes towards the information.

The response rate was 70 per cent (40/57) from trusts and 93 per cent (13/14) from HAs giving an overall rate of 75 per cent (53/71). Of the respondents, 26 per cent were finance directors or assistants, 26 per cent information directors or managers, 23 per cent performance managers, 8 per cent chief-executives or assistants and 17 per cent others (including audit managers, health economists, planning directors and business development directors). The results from individual questions were as follows.

Question 1: What current use is made of efficiency measures?

Respondents were asked to rate their use (how often they are referred to) and the usefulness (beneficial or practical effect) of different efficiency measures (the NHS efficiency indexes (NHS EIs), NHS performance indicators (PIs) and indicators developed by consultancy firms), on a scale from 1 (most use or usefulness) to 5 (least use or usefulness). They were also asked for comments on each of them and about any other standard forms of analysis.

The NHS EIs measured changes in hospital and community service patient activity against changes in money allocated to services (Donaldson *et al.* 1994). A ratio was calculated expressing changes from one year to the next, this was calculated by dividing activity in the current year by activity in the previous year. Expenditure is also compared on this basis. The activity index is then divided by the expenditure index to calculate the efficiency index. It is simply a ratio of average cost in the current year compared to average cost in the previous year. PIs are a retrospective tool reporting activities in broad specialties in hospitals (Smith 1995). They provide information on: resource provision (such as staff and bed numbers); resource quality (staff training); costs (staff, maintenance, total); and process variables (length of stay, throughput per bed, waiting lists). The indicators are unrelated and intended for use at a strategic level. The main consultancy indicators used from one firm provide information concerning activity at a more detailed level linked to costs, the formulation of their indicators remaining opaque.

The following figures summarize the results. The first three compare use and usefulness ratings for each measure, measured as the percentage of respondents rating the measures very useful, that is 1 or 2, and also how these compared between HAs and trusts.

Figure 4.1 shows that few trusts make much use of the NHS EIs, and amongst those that did, few find them useful. HAs make more use of them, but again few find them to be useful. This may be due to HAs having to use EIs for certain statutory returns and that trusts see EIs as a means of control rather than as an aid to improving their own efficiency. This is reflected in comments on the use of the NHS EI and context which included: that they are a crude measure (two HAs, one trust); they are a perverse measure (one HA, two trusts); they have mandatory uses (two HAs); they have contracting or planning use (eight trusts); and they are out of date (two trusts).

Figure 4.2 shows that both the overall use of PIs and opinions of their usefulness amongst trusts is similar to those of EIs – few use them or find them useful. However, those who use PIs have a better opinion of their usefulness than the rating of EIs by those who use EIs. HAs use PIs more, although less than EIs, but their overall view of their usefulness is similar both to trusts' views of PIs and their own view of EIs. Again, those who actually use them have a higher opinion of them compared with EIs. This may be because PIs provide information at a more detailed level and to a certain extent, although not linked to each other, they may help strategically in indicating areas for improvement within organizations. The main criticism of PIs reflects their retrospective nature. Comments on the use of the NHS PIs and context included: they are out of date (two HAs, six trusts); they have service comparison use (two trusts); they are propaganda (two trusts); they have performance table use (two trusts); they are used for comparison with others (two trusts); they can be used for benchmarking (two trusts).

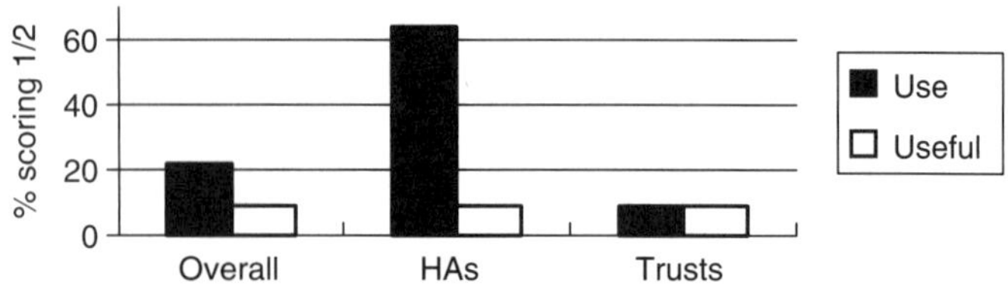

Figure 4.1 NHS efficiency indexes.

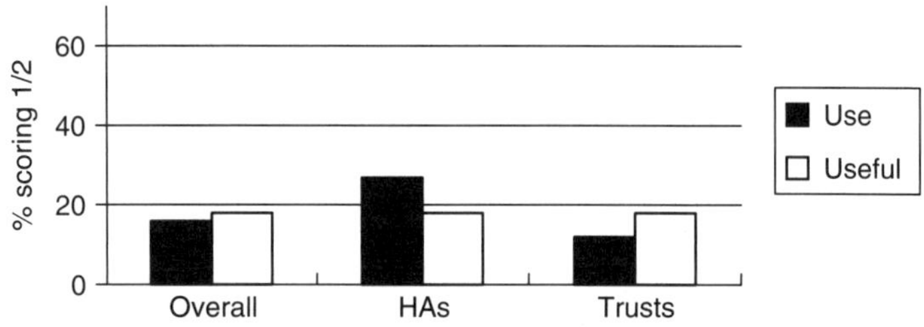

Figure 4.2 NHS performance indicators.

Some caution should be attached to the results in Figure 4.3, because not all trusts and only few HAs responded to this question. The figures are presented as percentages of the whole sample in order to avoid giving a misleading picture of the extent of use. Few HAs make use of consultancy firms' indicators, and of those who do, few find them very useful. Trusts' level in using of them is similar both to that of HAs and also to their own use of EIs and PIs. However, trusts rate their usefulness as higher than PIs and EIs. This may reflect dissatisfaction with EIs and PIs, although measures such as CHKS which do link certain activities to resource use may be of some strategic use. The main criticism of these measures is their cost.

Comments on the use of consultancy firms indicators and context include for CHKS (two HAs, eleven trusts): it is useful support information, but not used regularly; and it can provide comparative information, but overall is less useful than costs would imply. For labour-cost indicators, respondents (three trusts) are unable to compare like with like. Some mention is made of benchmarking (seven trusts), use of the York Health Economics Consortium (two trusts) and Audit Commission data (two trusts).

Figures 4.4–4.6 compare how the different measures' use and usefulness are rated within trusts, HAs and the two together.

These figures show that the pattern of use and opinions about usefulness are different between trusts and HAs: there is little relationship between level of use and ratings of usefulness; there is a clear hierarchy of level of use in HAs but not of usefulness ratings; and there is a clear hierarchy of usefulness ratings in trusts

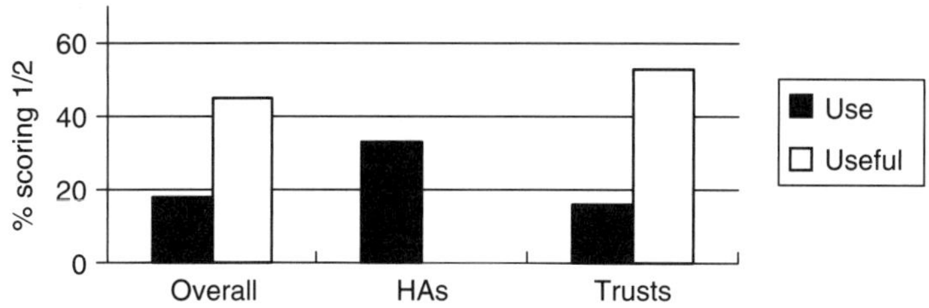

Figure 4.3 Consultancy firms' indicators.

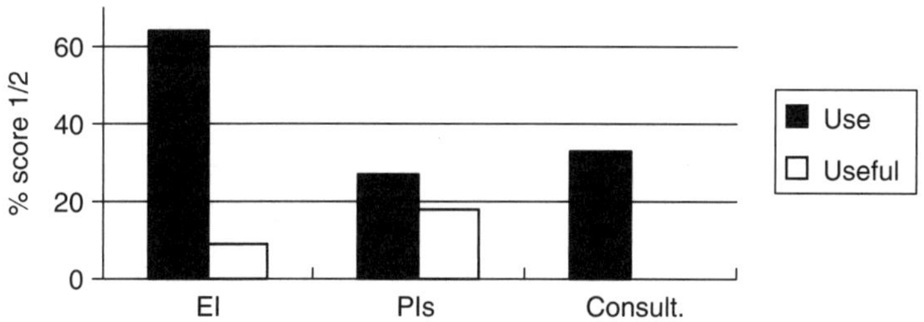

Figure 4.4 Health authorities.

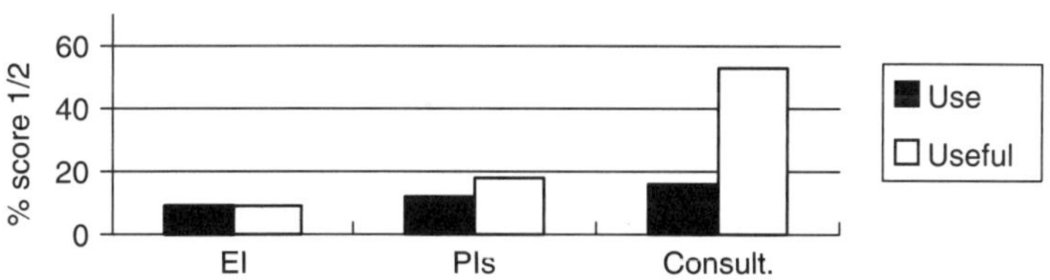

Figure 4.5 Trusts.

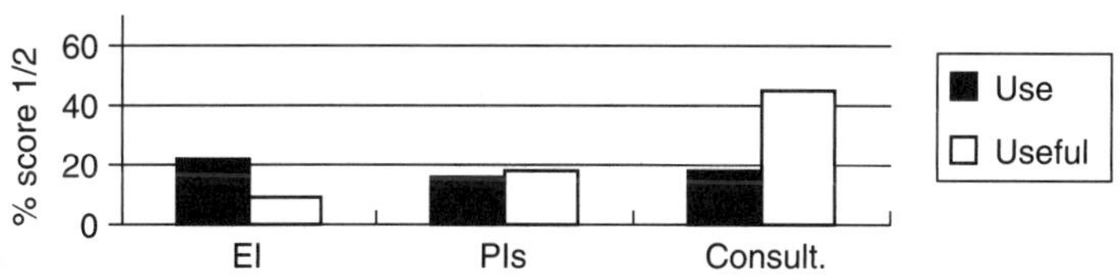

Figure 4.6 All NHS organizations.

but not of level of use. Again this clearly reflects HAs statutory use of EIs, and shows the low levels of use of any of the indicators in general by health service providers. Even when they are used they are not found to be particularly useful.

Question 2: What data are collected that are not available on a regional level?

In general, trusts and HAs do not collect data not available on a regional level. Both HAs and trusts collect data on staff and for audit purposes (one HA and five trusts each). HAs collect data on continuous care (three HAs), mental health and GP data (one HA each). Trusts collect data on outcome indicators (eleven trusts) (including gynaecology, orthopedics, community care, long-term outcomes and re-admission rates), cost data (seven trusts), output data (four trusts), asset register information, operating theatre use and health-care resource group (HRG) data (one trust each).

Question 3: Do you generate your own indicators of efficiency?

The lack of useful measures made available is reflected by the fact that 46 per cent of HAs and trusts have developed some sort of indicator of efficiency themselves (36 per cent of HAs and 49 per cent of trusts). The only common indicator developed by one HA and one Trust (separately) uses HRGs. HAs have developed indicators using price (two HAs) and GP funding allocation/population (two HAs). Trusts have developed benchmark indicators (five trusts), labour cost/service indicators (four trusts), cost of throughputs and theatre use (two trusts each). Others include output, day case and waiting list rates, management costs/revenue, assets/income, length of stay and cost/quality (one trust each). None of the indicators reported is based on any robust economic indicator of efficiency.

Question 4: What features would be desirable in any new indicator of efficiency?

Several desirable new features in indicators of efficiency are mentioned by both HAs and trusts and reflect the inadequacies of current measures. These included: comparison between trusts (four HAs, nine trusts); comparison within trusts (two HAs, nine trusts); outcome measurement (four HAs, five trusts); time trends (two HAs, six trusts); ease of use (one HA, six trusts); casemix measurement (one HA, four trusts); appropriate aggregation (two HAs, two trusts); and use of valid data (one HA, two trusts). HAs alone highlighted an interest in community service areas (four HAs), robustness of the measure (one HA), and packages of care (one HA). Trusts alone mentioned the importance of a standardized approach (five trusts), relevance (three trusts), staff information (two trusts) and ambulance information (two trusts). These desired features of any new measure are encouraging as they illustrate the need for a measure of efficiency, which reflects the production of health care within health services. A further requirement is a measure which can be used across health services in different sectors such as primary or secondary care, which is able to reflect a detailed level of activity, given costs and comparisons with the efficiency of other health-care providers.

Question 5: Who is responsible for the collection and analysis of data?

For HAs, finance and performance departments are responsible in 69 per cent of cases, contract and information departments in 25 per cent and health economists in 6 per cent. For trusts, finance and performance departments are responsible in 40 per cent of cases, contract and information departments in 23 per cent, business development in 13 per cent, human resources in 11 per cent, operations and clinical directorates (4 per cent each), audit and planning (2 per cent each). This reflects the importance with which efficiency is viewed in organizations, for contracting, financial reasons, operational reasons and for planning purposes.

The responses to question 1 on the use and usefulness of efficiency indicators demonstrate the need for a useful measure. The NHS EIs and PIs are used to a certain extent (perhaps due to mandatory requirements in the case of the NHS EI), but are not considered to be very useful, but instead are seen as crude and out of date. Indicators developed by consultancy firms are used less frequently, but are considered relatively useful, perhaps in part reflecting the dissatisfaction with standard NHS measures. In general, these consultancy indicators are seen as providing useful support information but at a high cost.

Data are not collected by individual HAs and trusts on a routine basis, although outcome indicators are collected by a number of trusts. Almost half of those surveyed generate their own indicators of efficiency, mainly benchmark indicators or a basic indicator of the relationship between cost and throughputs.

Given the level of dissatisfaction with current methods of measuring efficiency and the lack of any robust measures being developed by the HAs and trusts, it is interesting to note the features they require in a new measure. The requirement is for measures that compare between and within trusts. Measures that account for outcomes and casemix, and measure efficiency over time also rate highly. Also important are ease of use and a standardized approach, given validity and robustness. An encouraging number of those surveyed are interested in receiving feedback, both at an overall and more detailed level.

This survey confirms the need for a standardized approach to efficiency measurement in the NHS, especially given the concern expressed about efficiency in a 1997 white paper (Department of Health 1997). Any measure needs to be straightforward to use and provide a user-friendly, visible set of comparisons, useable both at hospital and sub-hospital levels. A DEA-based measure potentially provides these results in an easy to understand format, based on a robust and valid underlying methodology. These are important features. The responses to the survey confirm there is no common measure of efficiency across health services. There is a real desire for a useful measure, not perhaps in the form of a control measure used for statutory purposes (such as the NHS EIs), but a measure that is useful within health-care organizations which genuinely encourages increased efficiency. Information needs to be available at a level of detail that is useful, for example, a specialty level that relates activity to resource use, not necessarily in cost terms, but in physical resources such as numbers of staff. Measures that provide the most information indicating as to the relative efficiency of health-care organizations at a detailed level have the best chance of succeeding in increasing efficiency across the health-care sector.

How to undertake an efficiency measurement study

In general, we would advocate collecting as much data relating to economic efficiency as is practical, since data sets may contain complimentary and important information. As an example, we now show how to go about undertaking a DEA analysis drawing on an earlier study by Parkin and Hollingsworth (1997).

As described in Chapter 3, DEA is based upon a theoretical model of production, which defines the relationships between inputs and outputs. As with all empirical forms of economic modelling, in order to express theoretical relationships in quantitative terms, it is necessary to specify the model in terms of available data that represent the variables implied by the theory. Because data rarely match the requirements of theoretical models, choices must be made concerning model specification. Typically, these choices are guided both by theoretical and practical considerations.

Although DEA allows a wide choice of models, there are few criteria for choosing between them (Parkin and Hollingsworth 1997; Smith 1997). There are some practical considerations which constrain choice. For example, the greater the number of variables used, the greater the amount of information produced about inputs and outputs for inefficient units, but the fewer the number of inefficient units found. Also, if there are too many relatively inefficient units in the sample, there will be few efficient units to act as peer comparator units in the sample. Unfortunately, there are no criteria for assessing these trade-offs.

Model specifications

Because DEA is a non-parametric method, there are no standard or widely accepted statistically based validity criteria to guide model choice. To test the validity of the findings of the models, as opposed to the validity of measurement,[1] analysts employ sensitivity analysis to test the robustness of the results to changes in methods and data used. This is important in assessing the validity of the technique, both internally (do the methods employed affect results?) and externally (are the results more generally applicable?). Internal validity is important in assessing configurations of data and methods within a data set, especially given the analysts' freedom of choice in deciding these. External validity is important when DEA is intended for use as a means of improving efficiency in real-world settings. In our example, we used sensitivity analysis to test the robustness of DEA results to changes in data and methods used (Parkin and Hollingsworth 1997). Data were available for the sample for several years, and so this testing is undertaken on the data from 1994/5 and the most robust model is used for analysis from 1995/6 year. To test external validity we examine changes over time. To test internal validity of the models specified, we compare results obtained using the different models.

An important criterion for model choice is consistency with theory. All the models specified here are theoretically justified. They differ mainly in the level of aggregation of data. All models make use of the appropriate variables for the trust type with no variable omitted from the original data set. The criteria for the preferred model are: the level of aggregation of variables, the more disaggregated the data, the better; the number of efficient units, the fewer the better, except that there should not be so few that there are few peers available for comparison; the distribution of useful scores, the wider the better. If all of these criteria are met, they allow greater dissemination of information and are potentially more useful.

As an example, if we were looking at a sample of different types of hospitals, given the diverse nature of hospitals, it may be necessary to employ a model of sufficient generality and flexibility to cover all of them, at the cost of losing more detailed analysis of their differences. As a result, only one model is chosen for analysis, using data which are aggregated in order to reduce the problem of few observations for particular variables. Aggregated variables are staff other than medical, dental, nursing and midwifery, and costs other than the capital charge. The model is shown in Table 4.1.

To report results, we use the example of a sample of English trust hospitals, and ambulance trusts which undertake ambulance services.

Table 4.1 Specification of the hospital model.

	Model
Inputs	Medical and dental staff numbers
	Nursing and midwifery staff numbers
	All other staff numbers
	Capital charge
	All other costs
Outputs	Mental illness and learning disability FCE[a]s
	Maternity FCEs
	Total general and acute FCEs
	General, acute and maternity outpatient 1st attendances
	Accident and emergency attendances

[a]FCE (finished consultant episode).

Overall efficiency scores

Table 4.2 shows for each sub-sample in each year the mean, minimum and standard deviation of the efficiency scores. Priority hospitals treat mainly mental illness patients. Figure 4.7 shows ranked scores of inefficient hospitals for 1994/5. Figure 4.8 shows changes in efficiency scores between 1994/5 and 1995/6.

For the sample of hospital trusts, the low minimum scores and high standard deviations in both years suggest considerable potential for efficiency improvements in some hospitals. It is also apparent which units are outliers over the two years. Once identified these units could be examined in terms of whether their operating practices changed dramatically with the result being a large increase or decrease in efficiency. Any changes must be viewed with respect to changes of the whole sample under analysis. For example NY02 and NY36 are the two hospitals that have, respectively, the largest increase and decrease in efficiency. For NY02, an acute hospital, staff numbers fall by over 50 per cent, capital charge

Table 4.2 Summary of efficiency scores.

	No.	*Minimum*	*Mean*	*St. dev.*
All hospitals 1994/5	44	21.30	85.13	17.00
All hospitals 1995/6	44	23.68	86.15	17.60
Acute 1994/5	16	53.90	86.32	13.90
Acute 1995/6	16	72.64	90.73	11.02
Priority 1994/5	15	9.41	85.81	23.80
Priority 1995/6	15	14.60	83.79	26.36
Combined 1994/5	13	14.18	89.93	23.39
Combined 1995/6	13	3.57	83.04	33.74
Ambulance 1994/5	7	57.95	85.04	14.38
Ambulance 1995/6	7	71.94	88.73	11.74

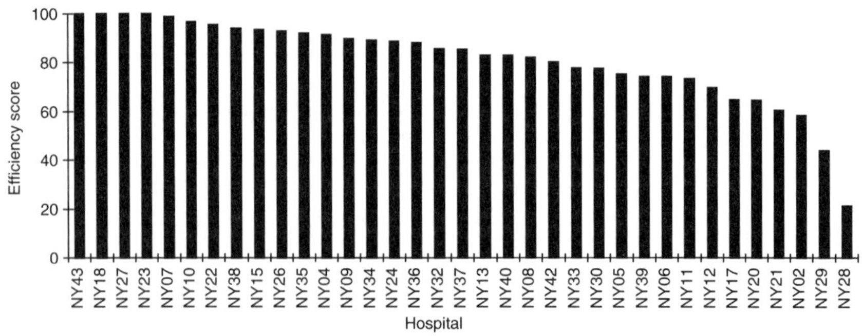

Figure 4.7 Ranked scores for all hospitals, 1994/5.

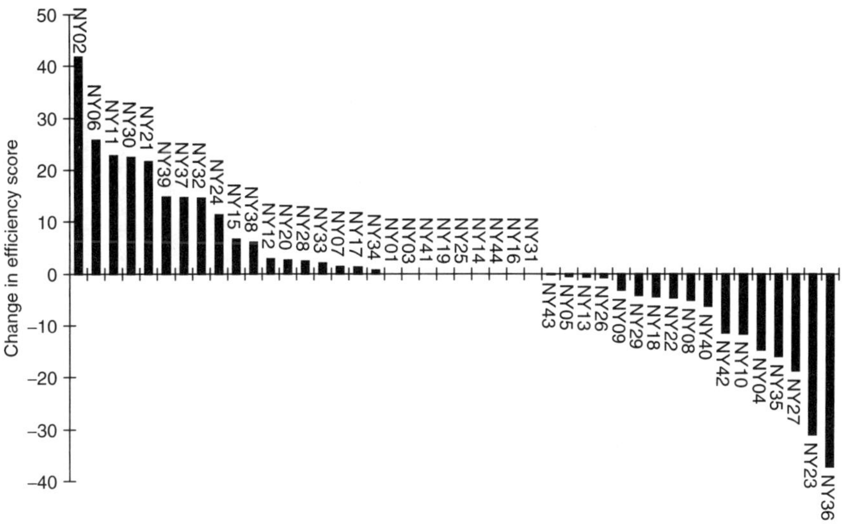

Figure 4.8 Change in efficiency scores, 1994/5 to 1995/6.

increases by 300 per cent and outputs remain fairly stable. This hospital may be in the process of moving to a new facility requiring fewer staff, or may have merged or decentralized some of its facilities with other hospitals over the course of the two years. In contrast, NY36, a combined hospital, stopped undertaking a number of outputs and concentrated on mental illness (MI) and learning difficulty (LD) patients. Although officially classified as a combined hospital, NY36 operates in 1995/6 more like a priority hospital. The lowest efficiency score is by NY28, which is a priority unit; it has 60 per cent lower costs than average, but produces significantly less output than any other unit and appears to have a low throughput of patients.

It should be noted that all units are being compared here as a pooled sample. This may not be the most appropriate, as they are different types of units undertaking different activities, therefore we assess efficiency within each hospital type, seen here as more appropriate, in terms of validity of useful comparison and usefulness of results.

Acute hospital trusts

Figure 4.9 shows ranked scores of inefficient hospitals for 1994/5. Figure 4.10 shows changes in efficiency scores between 1994/5 and 1995/6.

The minima are relatively high and the standard deviations are relatively low. Nevertheless there is potential for improvements in efficiency in some acute hospitals. There are two outliers: NY02 again may have specific reasons for increased efficiency and NY04 increases staff numbers and costs by around 8 per cent over the two years while outputs did not change significantly.

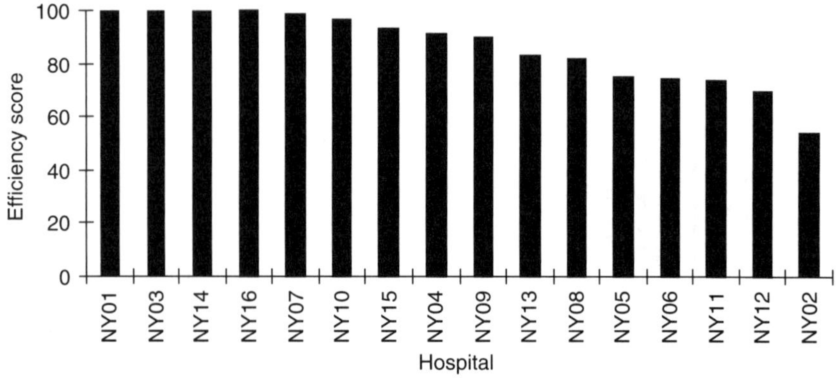

Figure 4.9 Efficiency scores for acute hospitals, 1994/5.

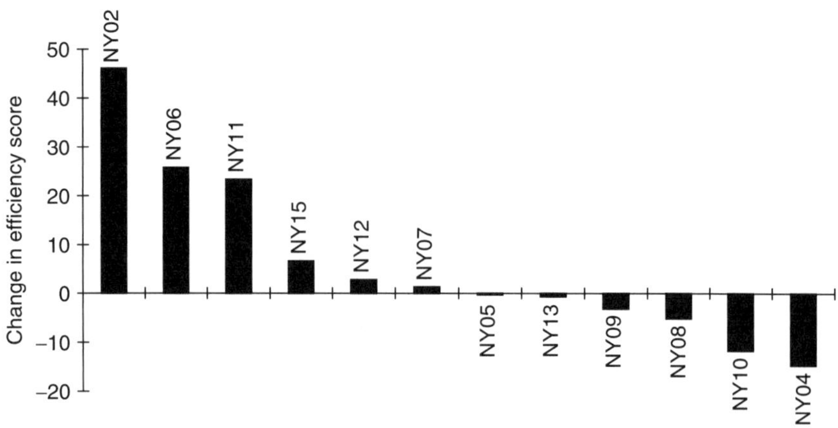

Figure 4.10 Changes in efficiency for acute hospitals, 1994/5 to 1995/6.

Priority hospital trusts

Figure 4.11 shows ranked scores of inefficient hospitals for 1994/5. Figure 4.12 shows changes in efficiency scores between 1994/5 and 1995/6.

The minima and standard deviations indicate much potential for improvements in efficiency in some priority hospitals. In particular NY28 has the lowest score (as in the all-hospitals sample), and has specific reasons for this (see all-hospitals sample). NY23 increases staff numbers by over 300 per cent, while output only increases by around 10 per cent.

Combined hospital trusts

Figure 4.13 shows ranked scores of inefficient hospitals for 1994/5. Figure 4.14 shows changes in efficiency scores between 1994/5 and 1995/6.

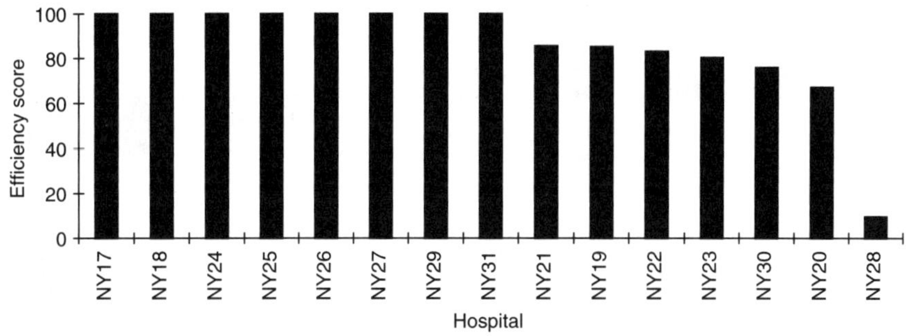

Figure 4.11 Efficiency scores for priority hospitals, 1994/5.

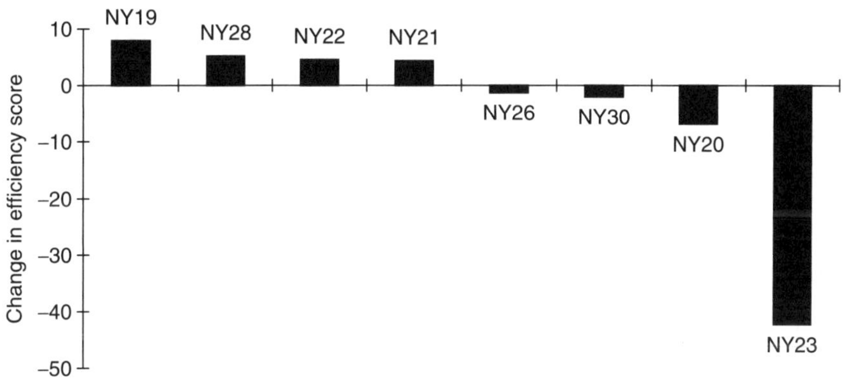

Figure 4.12 Changes in efficiency for priority hospitals, 1994/5 to 1995/6.

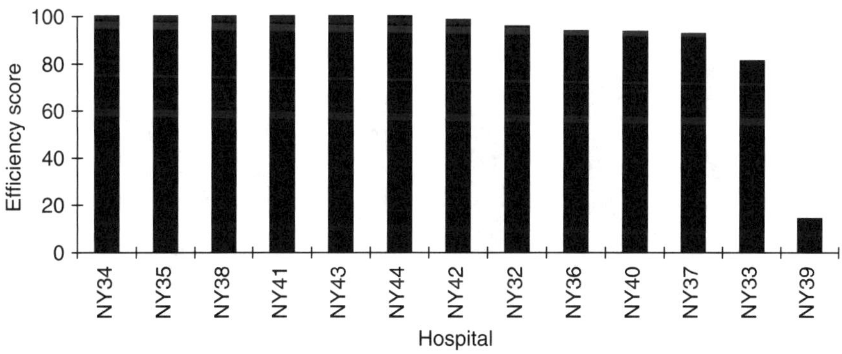

Figure 4.13 Efficiency scores for combined hospitals, 1994/5.

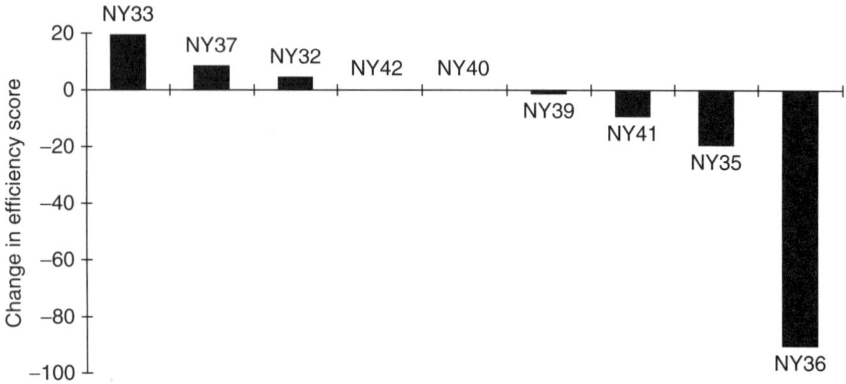

Figure 4.14 Changes in efficiency for combined hospitals, 1994/5 to 1995/6.

Again, the minima and standard deviations indicate potential for improvements in efficiency for some combined hospitals. Hospital NY39, while classified as a combined hospital operates more like a priority hospital with its main output being *MI* and *LD* occupied bed days; in addition it has costs that are 20 per cent higher than average. NY36 also has similar issues, as it, also, operates more like a priority hospital.

Ambulance trusts

Figure 4.15 shows ranked scores of inefficient trusts for 1994/5. Figure 4.16 shows changes in efficiency scores between 1994/5 and 1995/6.

The minima and standard deviations again suggest considerable potential for improvements in efficiency in some ambulance trusts. Increases in the efficiency of NY47 and NY48 can be explained by fewer staff being used to undertake more ambulance journeys.

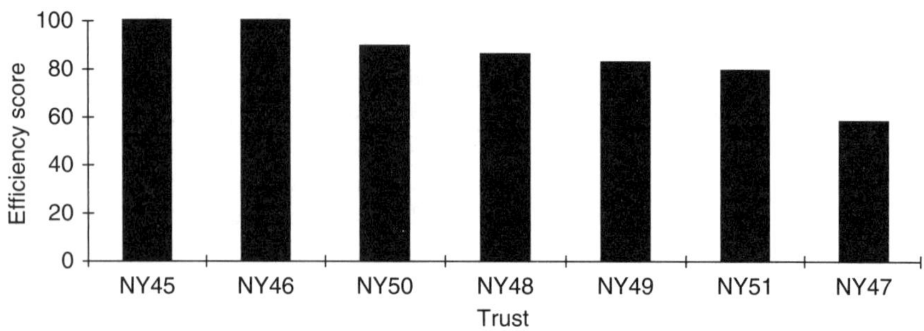

Figure 4.15 Efficiency scores for ambulance trusts, 1994/5.

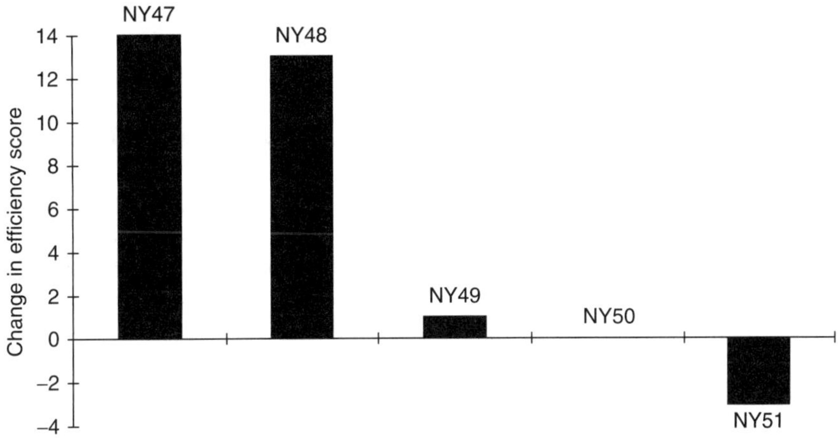

Figure 4.16 Changes in efficiency scores for ambulance trusts, 1994/5 to 1995/6.

Correlations over time

Consistency over time is a test of external validity (Parkin and Hollingsworth 1997). Although some changes over time are expected, it is unlikely that results would change dramatically over two years. Table 4.3 shows the Spearman rank and Pearson correlations between the efficiency scores for the two years. The correlations are all high and statistically significant at the 1 per cent level. This suggests that the models are robust, although the sample sizes are small.

Weights on variables

As noted in Chapter 3, DEA applies a weight to each input and each output so that they may be summed together. These weights are calculated as part of the DEA method and show each unit in the best possible light relative to the other units in the sample.[2] Summaries of the weights and their intensity related to different inputs and outputs help indicate areas that dominate others in terms of importance.[3] The weights shown are adjusted by the actual value of the variable to give an accurate reflection of their actual contribution. These are sometimes referred to in DEA as the *virtual* weights. Figure 4.17 summarizes the weights applied to variables for the

Table 4.3 Correlations over two years 1994/5 and 1995/6.

	Number	*Rank correlation*	*Pearson correlation*
All units	44	0.98	0.99
Acute units	16	0.94	0.95
Combined units	13	1.00	0.84
Priority units	15	0.97	0.94
Ambulance units	7	1.00	0.91

sample of all hospitals. For inputs, nursing staff dominate, followed by medical staff and capital charges. MI/LD attends and outpatient attendances dominate outputs. These figures reflect the performance of the trusts in our sample.

Figure 4.18 summarizes weights applied to variables for the sample of acute hospitals. For acute hospitals nursing staff and capital charge dominate input weights, but for output variables outpatient attendances and FCEs dominate, as may be expected for acute services.

Figure 4.19 summarizes weights applied to combined hospitals. Medical staff dominate the inputs to a greater degree than acute hospitals, outpatient attendances and total FCEs dominate the outputs. A&E attendances are not given such a great weighting, perhaps reflecting their random nature.

Figure 4.20 summarizes weights applied to priority hospitals. Medical and nursing staff dominate the inputs, MI and LD attends dominate the weighting to outputs for priority hospitals, as we would expect from our sample.

Figure 4.21 summarizes weights applied to Ambulance trusts. With only one output, the weights for ambulance trusts are all concentrated on the inputs, with ambulance staff dominating. Again, this is not unexpected given the activities undertaken.

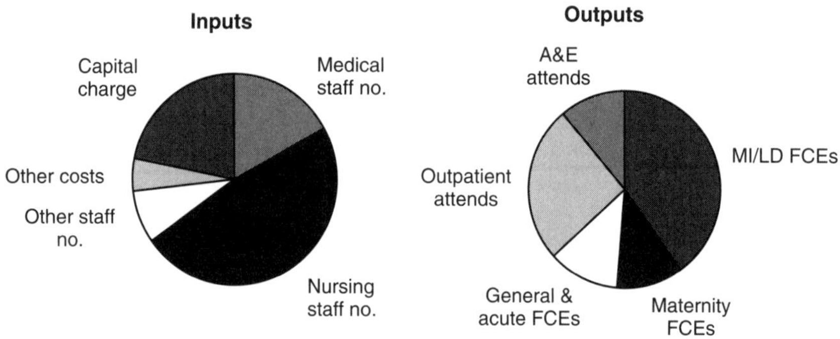

Figure 4.17 Summary of weights applied to all hospitals, 1995/6.

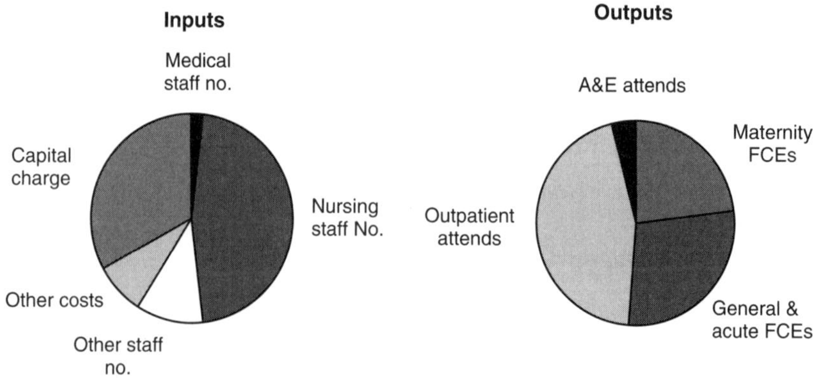

Figure 4.18 Summary of weights applied to acute hospitals, 1995/6.

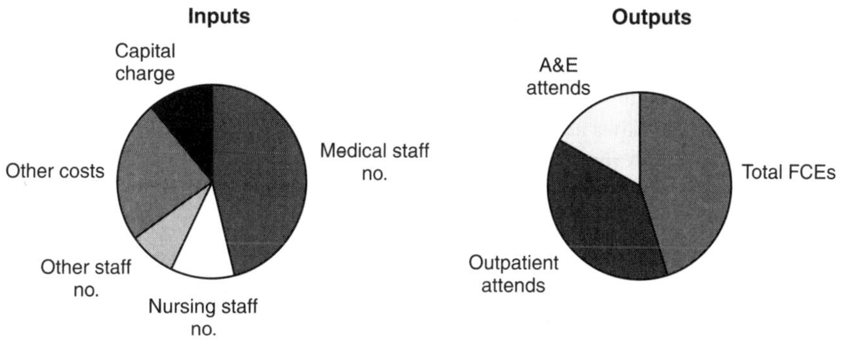

Figure 4.19 Summary of weights applied to combined hospitals, 1995/6.

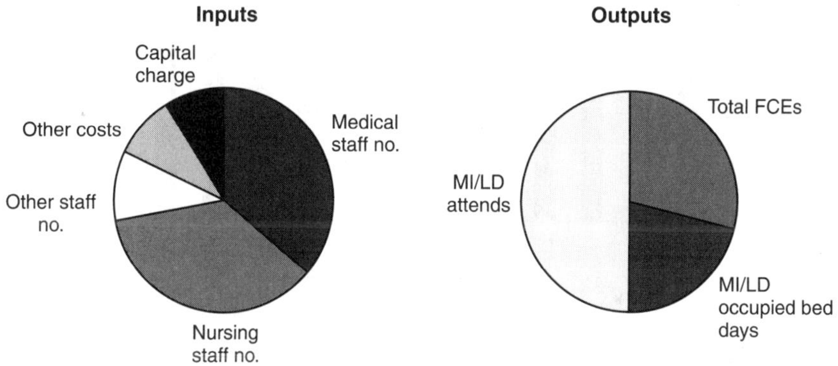

Figure 4.20 Summary of weights applied to priority hospitals, 1995/6.

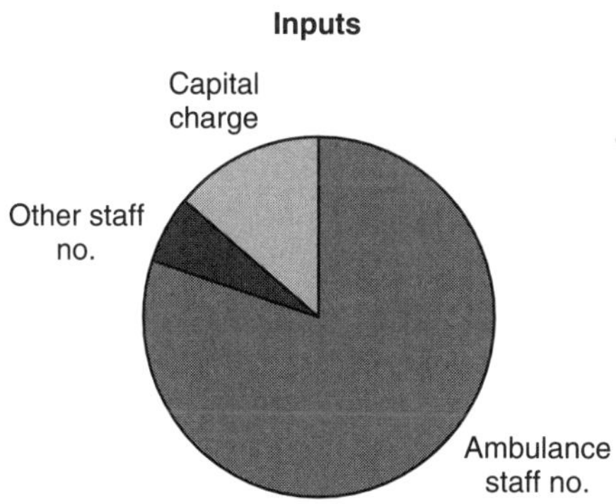

Figure 4.21 Summary of weights applied to ambulance trusts, 1995/6.

Feedback to individual units

Acute hospital NY11 is used as an example of how the DEA results might be used. Information can be fed back to hospital NY11 (highlighted) showing how it compares to the other acute hospitals in the sample.

Figure 4.22 shows that the overall efficiency of hospital NY11 was 73 per cent in 1994/5, suggesting potential for improvement. Figure 4.23 shows changes in efficiency scores between 1994/5 and 1995/6.

In hospital NY11, efficiency increased by 23 per cent between 1994/5 and 1995/6. A change in efficiency could indicate an increase in efficiency relative to

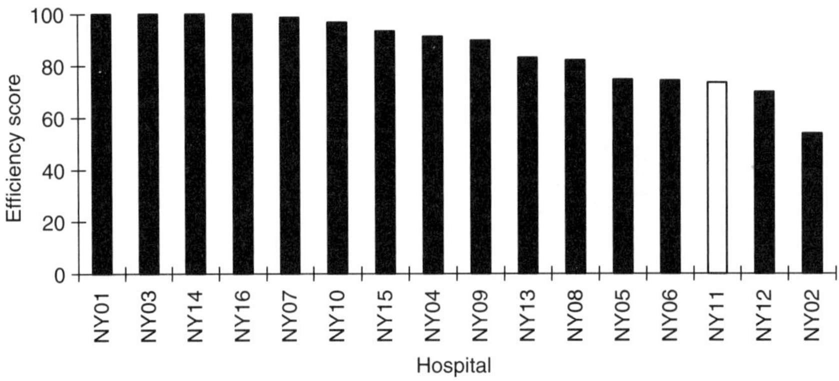

Figure 4.22 Comparison of efficiency for acute hospital NY11, 1994/5.

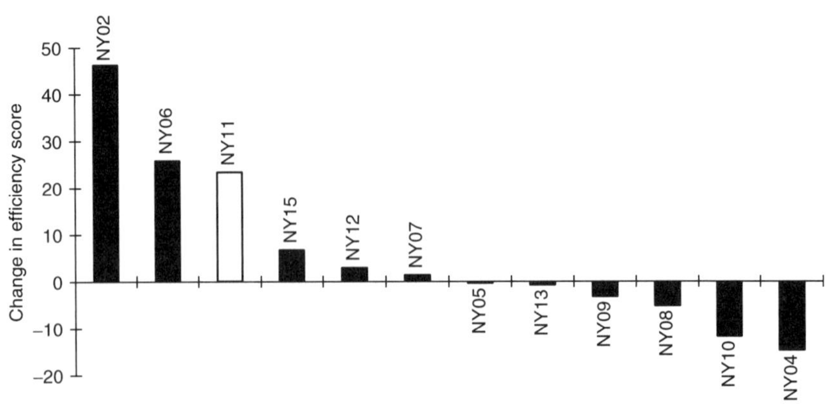

Figure 4.23 Comparison of changes over time for acute hospital NY11, 1994/5 to 1995/6.

Table 4.4 Targets for acute hospital NY11, 1994/5 and 1995/6.

Efficiency score (%)	*1994/5*	*1995/6*
	73	*97*
Variable	*To gain (%)*	*To gain (%)*
Inputs		
Capital	35	3
Other costs	29	32
Medical staff	43	3
Nursing staff	27	9
Other staff	27	3
Outputs		
Maternity FCE	0	24
General/acute FCE	0	31
Outpatient attendances	1	0
A&E attendances	13	62

the hospital's own performance or relative to that of the rest of the sample. Table 4.4 shows the amount that inputs would have to be reduced in order to produce the same output efficiently, compared to the performance of the other hospitals in the sample. For example, medical staff numbers would have to be reduced by 43 per cent in 1994/5 and three per cent in 1995/6 for this hospital to operate efficiently compared to the others in the sample. Any one of these reductions in input would lead to more efficient production, but there are many other combinations of reductions which would have the same effect. However, these target figures highlight areas within the hospital that need further investigation. Investigation may lead to the discovery of the specific circumstances which have led to the use of extra resources. For example it would appear that NY11 has increased efficiency markedly between the two years. In 1995/6, other costs would appear to be the main target for input reduction, efficiency gains having been made in the other inputs. As an alternative, processing of outputs appears to be less efficient in 1995/6 with there being some potential for improvement. This is shown graphically in Figure 4.24.

Further information can be provided concerning the inputs used by the inefficient hospitals to produce their outputs in comparison to peer hospitals. These peers are hospitals which are not only efficient with respect to their own weightings, but also with respect to those of the inefficient hospital under analysis. Comparison with efficient hospitals allows inefficient hospitals to see the areas in which efficient hospitals are using less actual quantities of inputs to produce similar or greater actual quantities of outputs. The actual quantities of inputs and outputs (scaled) for these hospitals are compared in Figure 4.25.

In this example, for 1994/5 inefficient hospital NY11 is compared to its peers, efficient hospitals NY14 and NY16. Hospital NY11 uses more of all inputs to

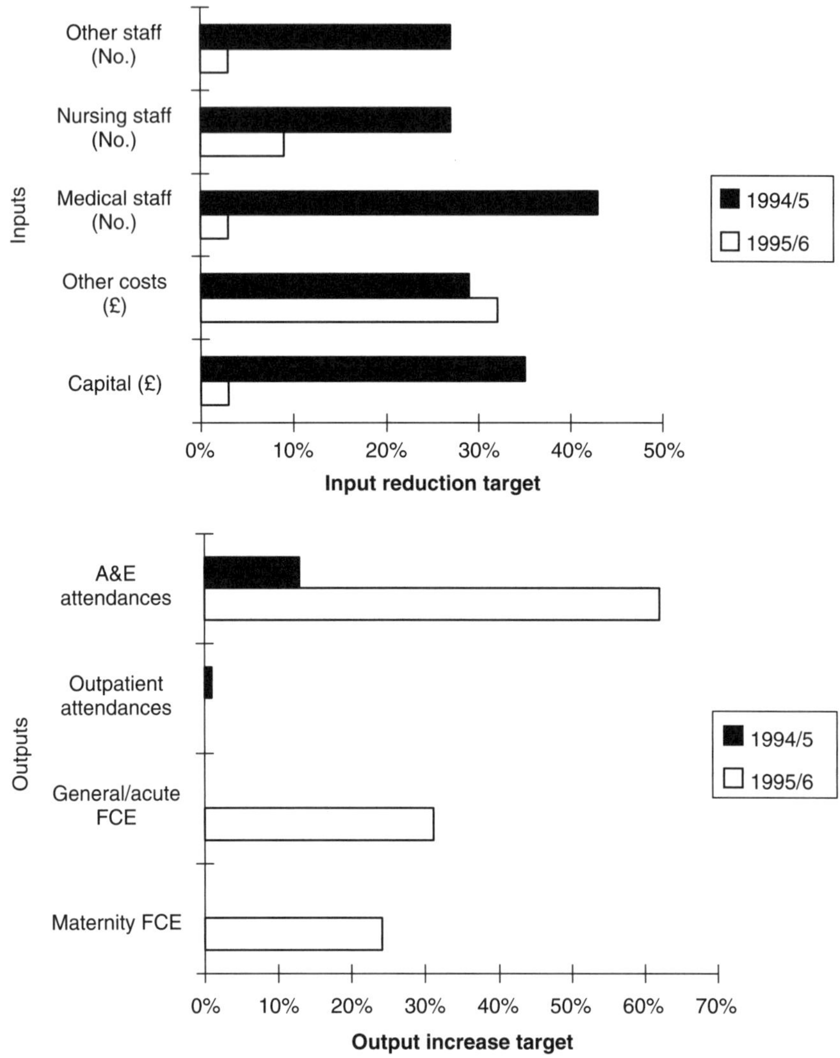

Figure 4.24 Targets for acute hospital NY11, 1994/5 and 1995/6.

produce more outputs in real terms, but in proportionate terms the difference is greater in terms of inputs, compared to its peers. In 1995/6 the proportionate difference in input use is much less. This gives a broader picture of how NY11 has improved and by relating the targets (given earlier) to this more specific information, hospital NY11 has information on those areas it may wish to concentrate on to improve efficiency.

As noted in Chapter 3, DEA applies a weight to each input and each output so that they may be summed together. These weights are calculated as part of the

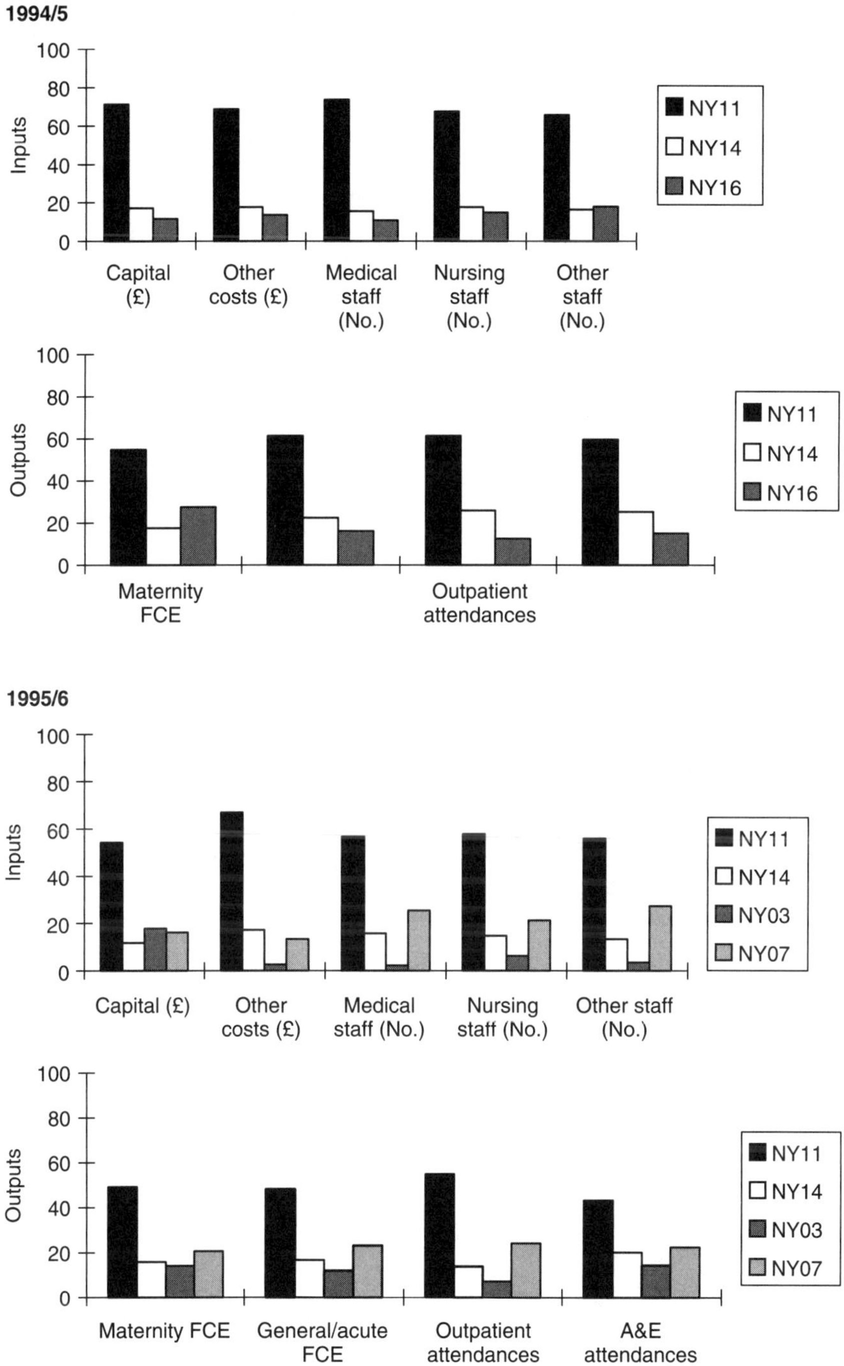

Figure 4.25 Peer comparison for acute hospital NY11, 1994/5 and 1995/6.

DEA method and show each unit in the best possible light relative to the other units in the sample. The proportion of weighting allocated to each input and output can be seen in the example given in Figure 4.26 for NY11.

All inputs and outputs receive at least a nominal weight, but what can be seen from Figure 4.26 is that some inputs and outputs dominate. This may indicate areas in which a particular unit performs well, relative to the others in the sample. If we relate these results to the targets above, nursing staff, maternity FCEs and general and acute FCEs would appear to be NY11's strongest areas in 1994/5. For 1995/6, medical staff, other staff, capital charge and outpatient attendances would appear to be the strongest areas. These correspond with the target figures in Table 6.8, where these variables have the least potential for improvement. These weights demonstrate that this hospital may not be typical of all acute hospitals, if compared to the summary of weights in Figure 6.12.

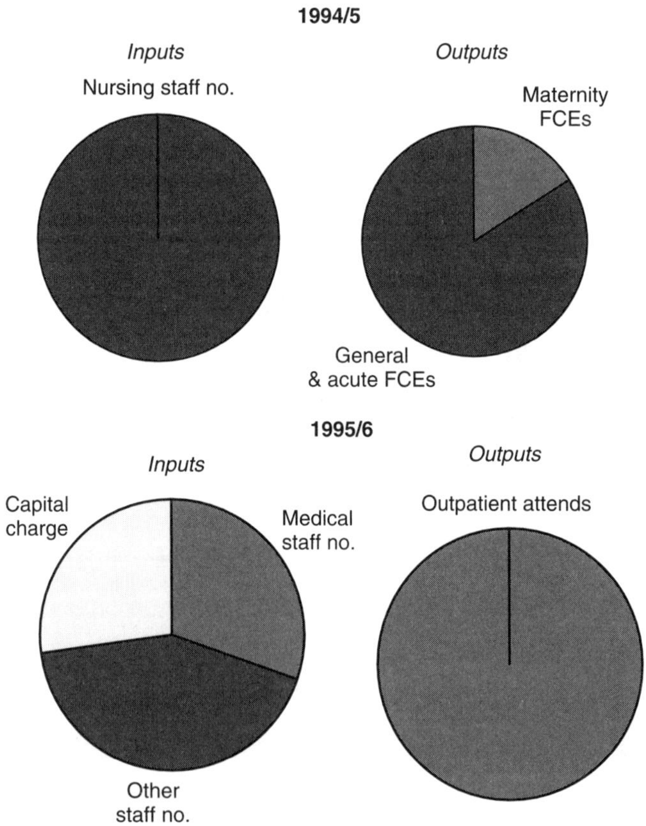

Figure 4.26 Weights for NY11.

Feedback of results

As important as the ability to calculate information concerning efficiency is acceptance of the validity of the information by those who may wish to use it. This requires that they have sufficient understanding both of its underlying basis and also of the results. Explanation is an important feature of the use of DEA as a managerial tool and Norman and Stoker (1991: 198, 205–206) suggest that previous attempts to introduce the technique in the NHS failed because of an inability to explain this to managers. Therefore a key element here is the construction of materials to explain both the technique and its products.

As an example we now show how to undertake feedback using two documents. The first is an illustrative guide, in the form of a document giving a brief guide to DEA and some summary results with explanations. This information is sent to all those participating in the study, with a questionnaire which elicited information concerning the *usefulness* of the information provided and the methods of *presentation* of the information. The second is a more detailed presentation including results. This can be used with a smaller sub-sample, representatives of which are interviewed in person.

The illustrative guide

The guide has two related purposes. The first is to test our ability to explain DEA and its products with the larger sample that a postal survey would make feasible. The second is to test a prototype of how information might be presented if it were produced on a regular basis. The guide includes an illustration of how the efficiency measure is constructed, a description of the data available, visual illustrations of the actual results generated (ranked efficiency scores, changes over time, targets and peer comparisons) and explanations of these results. A sample of a guide is contained in the Appendix.

All organizations who took part in the initial user survey were sent a copy of the guide. A single guide was initially produced, which related to one anonymous trust. However, an offer was made to produce a guide customized for a particular trust, containing data relevant to them, if they returned the feedback questionnaire which was enclosed with the illustrative guide.

Feedback questionnaire

A simple questionnaire was devised, which asks questions concerning the information provided in the illustrative guide. Respondents are asked to rate the *usefulness* of information on efficiency provided in the user guide, on a scale from 1 (useful) to 5 (not useful), and the *presentation* of information on efficiency provided in the user guide, on a scale from 1 (good) to 5 (poor). They are also asked for comments on how useful the measure is and how good the presentation is. They are asked to rate information separately concerning ranked scores, changes over time, targets and peer comparisons, and their overall impressions.

Results

As an example, we show how feedback was summarized from a real DEA application. Figures 4.27–4.31 compare for each type of information presented scores for usefulness and presentation amongst the groups of respondents, showing the percentage that rated them highly, that is 1 or 2.

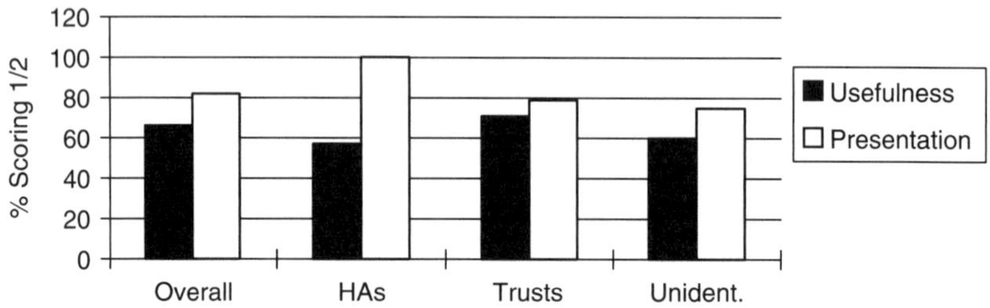

Figure 4.27 Usefulness and presentation of ranked scores.

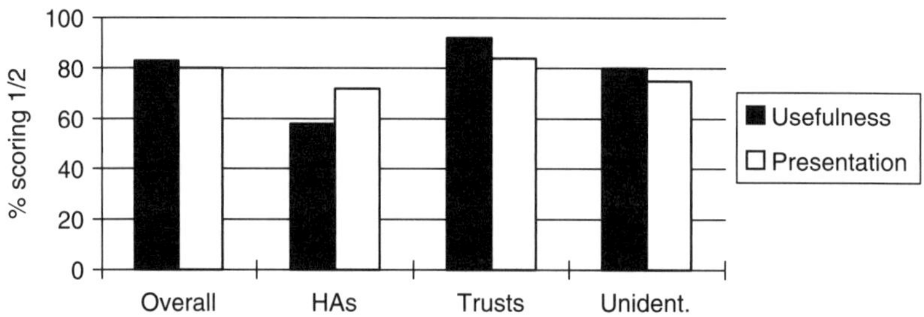

Figure 4.28 Usefulness and presentation of changes over time.

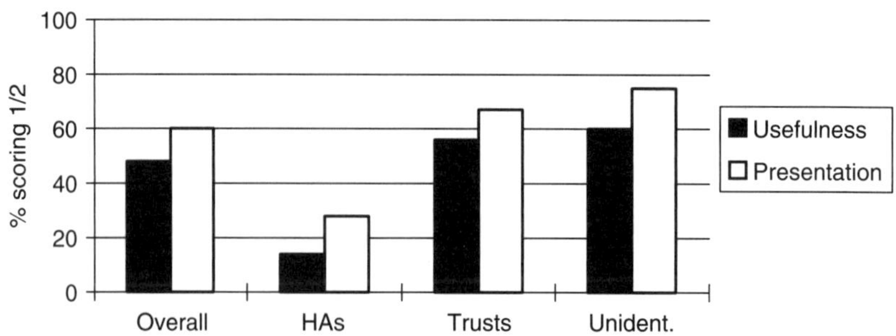

Figure 4.29 Usefulness and presentation of targets.

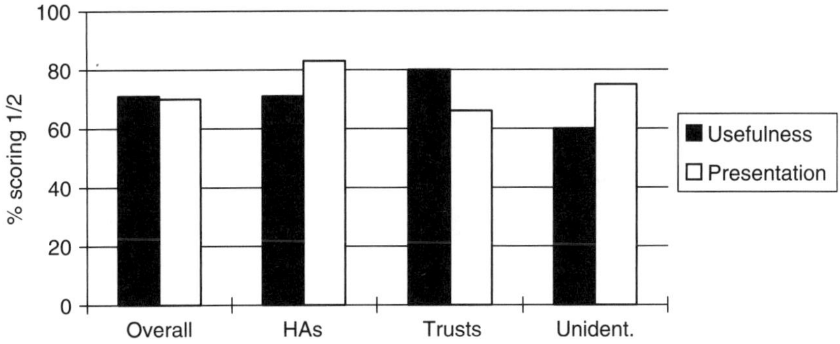

Figure 4.30 Usefulness and presentation of peer comparison.

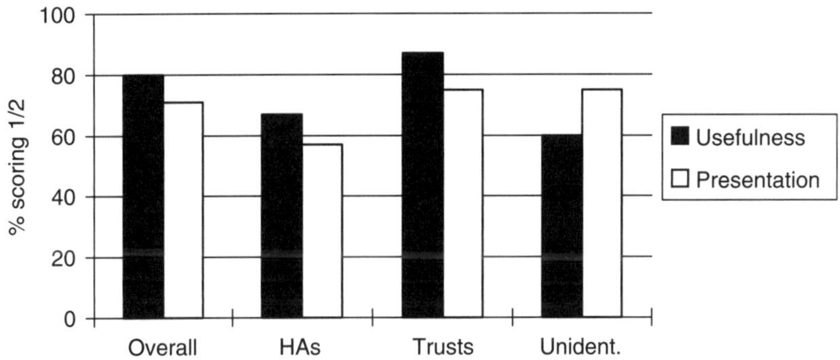

Figure 4.31 Usefulness and presentation overall.

Both the usefulness of the measure and the means of presentation rate highly in all organizations, with one exception. The exception is that the usefulness of information on targets is not rated highly by HAs, and this is matched by a lower rating for presentation. For every component of the information, as well as overall, trusts' ratings of usefulness are higher than those of HAs.

Figures 4.32–4.35 compare for each group of respondents the scores for usefulness and presentation given to the different types of information presented, showing the percentage of respondents rating them 1 or 2. This demonstrates a generally high correlation between the usefulness and presentation ratings. Amongst these ratings, target information is less highly rated, especially for HAs.

Comments on the *usefulness* of the information include comments on peers: where appropriateness is an important factor (eleven trusts); within-one District comparison would be useful (one HA); comparison across all regions would be useful (one Trust); and usefulness within hospitals may also

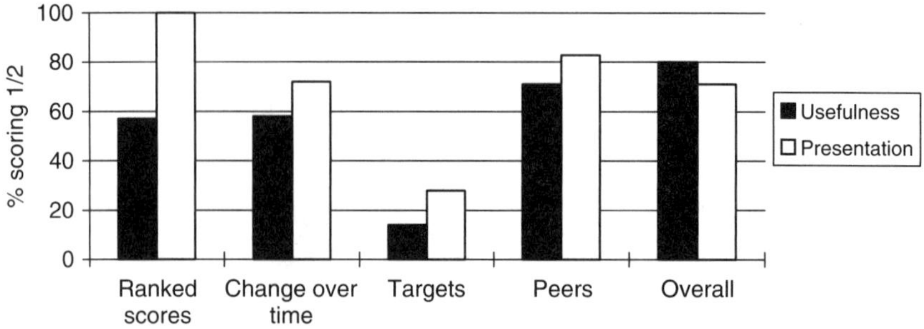

Figure 4.32 Usefulness and presentation for HAs.

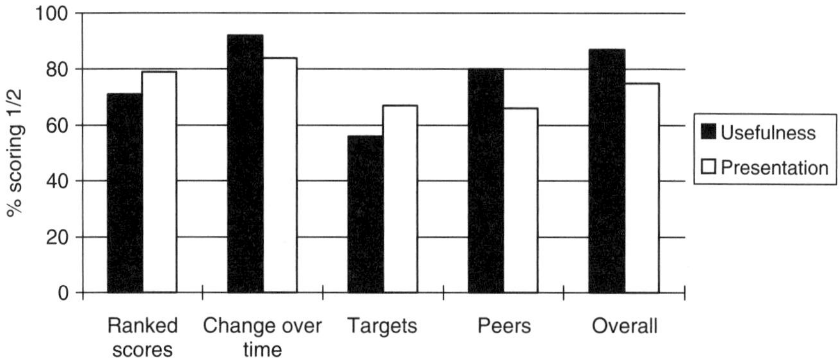

Figure 4.33 Usefulness and presentation for trusts.

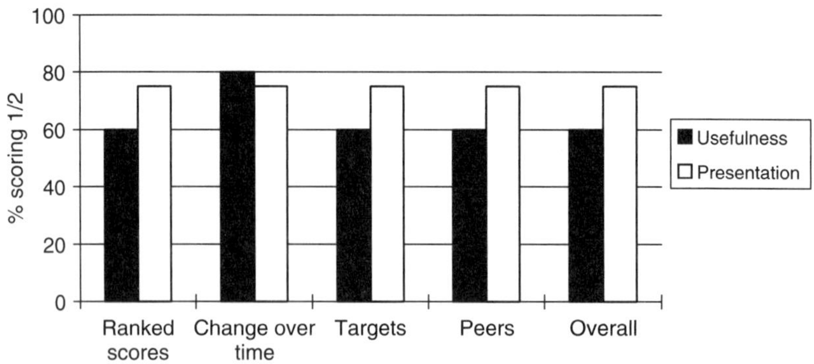

Figure 4.34 Usefulness and presentation for unidentified respondents.

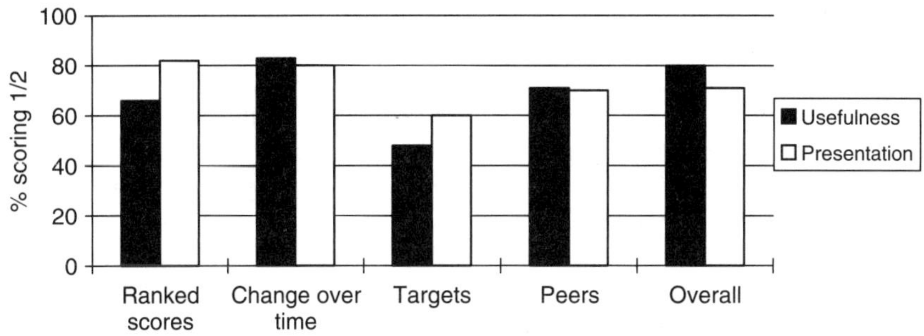

Figure 4.35 Usefulness and presentation overall.

be important (one Trust). Comments on data include: it must be relevant (four trusts, one HA); using FCEs may be a problem (three trusts, one HA); use of capital charge may be a problem (three trusts, one HA); outputs, not health outcome measures, would be useful (one Trust) and; more specialty orientation may be useful (one trust). Comments on weights include: calculation/interpretation must be explicit (two trusts, one HA) and casemix may be important (three trusts, one HA). General comments are that it may be useful if allied to other measures (one trust, one HA) and possibly too crude (two HAs).

Comments on the *presentation* of the information include on peers: information on precise numbers and size of peers may be important (two trusts) and information would be useful at specialty level (one trust). On ranked scores comments include: it would be useful if 100 per cent scores were included (one trust, one HA). On targets, comments include: precise numbers, rather than percentages, may be clearer (three trusts) and they should be changed to indicators (one HA). A general comment is they are very clear (five trusts).

More detailed studies

A representative sample was involved in closer co-operation with the study. Each participant was visited, a presentation given which contains more detail than the illustrative guide, and a semi-structured interview carried out to obtain more detailed feedback. It shows the rationale for the efficiency measure and how the analysis works, the data required, some results, potential uses for the measure and a discussion of key issues in three areas: specification of the DEA model, presentation of results and the data. The interview uses the format of the presentation as its structure. Emphasis is placed on the development of the measure and in what ways it could be improved. A large number of useful items of information and suggestions for the way forward are obtained.

Although the survey on the use and usefulness of measures already used is slightly different from the feedback survey, they may be used to compare the perceived *potential* usefulness of the new efficiency measure with the perceived *actual* usefulness of current measures. The scores for the new measure are significantly higher than for the measures already in use.

In addition, the rating for presentation is consistently high. The level of interest shown by respondents is also very strong. These results suggest that not only can the new measure be made intelligible to those who might potentially use it, but it would also likely be used because of its perceived usefulness. One aspect that emerged from the more in-depth interviews is the potential usefulness of the measurement of efficiency at a more detailed within-hospital level.

The results for all of the individual features of the new measure are also consistently high, with trusts' ratings higher than HAs. This is encouraging as it reflects that trusts may see the new measure as useful within their own organization as a means to improve their own efficiency rather than as a control mechanism to be used for statutory purposes. That HAs also find the measure of use is encouraging, as it should be more useful than measures currently available.

The flexibility of the new measure is important, especially in terms of comparison of performance relative to other providers of health services, as well as giving targets for improvement for organizations based on efficient comparators within the sample. The fact that it is a measure of relative rather than absolute efficiency makes the measure more valuable in practical terms. The responses to the presentation and feedback of the results may also reflect the crude nature of measures currently available.

The process we have used to develop and test the new measure is important. This is in itself a novel concept, especially concerning efficiency measures based on DEA. This is a first attempt in this area and as such has proved successful. However, the shortcomings of DEA should always be borne in mind: it may not be the perfect solution to measuring efficiency. As will be seen in Chapter 5 there is now a wide-ranging interest in applying DEA in health care, and areas such as the specification of models should be carefully considered. The results from DEA analysis (as with any form of economic modelling) should always be treated with caution, as the form of modelling, the specification of the model and the data used in the analysis may have an influence on the results obtained. There is always a danger that efficiency results may misguide rather than guide if these issues are not carefully considered.

Software review

An important step in undertaking efficiency measurement is deciding which software is appropriate. Here we will not review general statistical packages, but more specialist software, specifically those packages which undertake DEA, SFA and productivity analysis.

DEA packages

1. Frontier Analyst Professional, Banxia Software Ltd, Kendal, UK. Further license information available. (www.banxia.com/famain.html).
2. OnFront Version 2.0, Economic Measurement and Quality (EMQ), Lund AB, Box 2134, Lund, Sweden. (www.emq.com).
3. Warwick DEA Version Operational Research and Systems Group, University of Warwick, UK. (Note, this has recently been replaced by the PIM software package which now offers Malmquist analyses also, www.deasoftware.co.uk/aboutPIM.htm).
4. DEAP Version 2.1, School of Economics, University of Queensland, Australia. (www.uq.edu.au/economics/cepa/software.htm).
5. DEA-solver. (www.saitech-inc.com).

Test PC

Pentium II-350, 256 MB RAM, 6.4 GB hard drive, 16-bit high-colour display, Windows 98SE.

Introduction

This section not only covers DEA efficiency packages, but those which undertake Malmquist productivity analysis. It covers mainly software which is commercially available (apart from DEAP). The review updates two previous reviews in the *Economic Journal* (Hollingsworth 1997, 1999).

Three of the packages available (Warwick, DEA-solver, and Frontier Analyst) undertake DEA efficiency analysis for cross-section data. Although Frontier Analyst does come with comprehensive support information, this cannot quite match the other two packages which are supported by text books (Cooper, *et al.* 2000; Thanassoulis 2001). DEA-solver runs as part of Microsoft Excel (only the sample version distributed with the book was available for review). Warwick and Frontier Analyst run as Windows applications. All expected features are present in these two packages, for example the ability to import and export data (easier in Frontier Analyst), weights constraints and the potential of unlimited numbers of units for analysis (although this option makes Frontier Analyst relatively expensive). Both packages have an additional feature which allows the ranking of efficient units. The Warwick package offers the facility to undertake Super Efficiency (Anderson and Peterson 1993), and Frontier Analyst (as an additionally purchased add-on) offers the ability to undertake cross-efficiency analysis. While Frontier Analyst is now more useful to operations researchers and expert academic users, Warwick would be preferred by such users as it allows a wide range of models to be specified. Frontier Analyst may still be most useful for a managerial user who accepts without question the concepts of DEA on offer. Both packages offer upgrades from earlier versions, and Warwick still offer a cheaper DOS-based version.

Table 4.5 System requirements.

Software	*Windows/DOS*	*RAM*	*Hard disk space*
Frontier Analyst Professional	Windows 95 or NT, Pentium processor	16 MB (32 MB recommended)	15 MB
Warwick	Windows 3.1 or higher, IBM 386 with co-processor or higher (486 or Pentium recommended)	2 MB	2 MB
OnFront	Windows 95 or NT4.0 (Pentium recommended)	8 MB (32 MB recommended)	1 MB
DEAP	386 with co-processor, DOS 5.0 and/or Windows 3.1	4 MB	1 MB

All packages reviewed are straightforward in terms of installation, feature examples and lead the user through data preparation, all taking previously prepared data files, given some manipulation and careful reading of accompanying documentation. Models for analysis and extra features are all straightforward to set up, either in additional windows or using drop-down menus, although again sometimes this takes careful reading of the manuals (or use of the help facilities) to make the most of. All operate at a reasonable speed on the test PC, with all analysis on all packages taking less than two minutes to run. Hardware requirements are shown in Table 4.5. It is worth noting that the IDEAS software package featured in earlier reviews is now no longer available.

Productivity measurement

OnFront 2 and DEAP are available as packages which undertake DEA cross-sectional efficiency analysis and productivity analysis. It should be noted at this stage that DEAP, after initially being a commercial product is now available free of charge, this may have important consequences for users. The new version of Frontier Analyst (4), and the replacement of the Warwick software (both unavailable for testing at the time of writing) include a Malmquist option.

Ease of use

OnFront 2 is a Windows package, while DEAP runs in DOS. Documentation with OnFront 2 is as comprehensive as the previous version and includes a user guide and reference guide to productivity analysis. There is no online help available within the package, but the user guide shows how models can be specified, with technical explanations in the accompanying reference guide. Simulation is possible, which allows the user to experiment by varying actual amounts of variables to see effects on scores. The modelling of productivity scores is also straightforward and clearly explained, although as with the DEA packages above careful attention needs to be paid to the manuals.

DEAP, being DOS-based, is not as straightforward at first to get to grips with. However, once mastered it undertakes both DEA and productivity analysis effectively. Documentation is in the form of an accompanying academic paper which comprehensively reviews data preparation, analysis and results reports. The computation of results and model set up are dealt with well.

Package facilities

Data input and management in OnFront 2 is easy as spreadsheet editors are provided for both new and imported data. Data management in DEAP is not possible, data are imported as text files, and take some manipulation at first. Both packages allow analysis of any numbers of units (only restricted by the PC memory), and allow the analysis of a number of different input- or output-oriented models under conditions of either constant or variable returns to scale. Neither package allows the option of weight restrictions or any ranking of efficient units.

Performance

All software are tested on real data – a sample of 1,380 individual units of analysis with five inputs and two outputs. Cross-section analysis is undertaken on the whole sample, while for the productivity analysis, the data are split into ten sub-samples of 138 units to simulate activity over ten periods. The packages all produced accurate and identical results, for DEA and productivity measurement (DEA-solver was not tested in this way, as only the student package was available).

DEA software summary

As found in previous reviews, DEAP is the least user-friendly package reviewed here. However, it is still accompanied by clear and comprehensive documentation and produces the results, including cost efficiency, however, it does take some getting used to. OnFront 2 is straightforward to use, as are the results it produces. OnFront 2 and DEAP results can be easily subjected to further analysis in other statistical packages. Either of these packages would be appropriate for the expert to use. However, OnFront 2 may also be worth considering for straightforward managerial applications, once the appropriate DEA model for analysis has been specified, as there are a large number of model choices.

Neither of these packages produces results in a particularly user-friendly format for the non-academic user. The option of presentation of results in simple graphical form is available in OnFront 2. In fact only Frontier Analyst allows extensive graphical and tabular analysis of results.

None of these packages allows statistical analysis of results, for example correlations, analysis of distribution or more complex jackknife or bootstrapping procedures, validity testing of this type must be conducted in other packages and is not straightforward. Another problem with some packages is that they cannot handle variables which are zero, and may some replace these variables with a very small number. While this does not generally cause problems it may affect results either with very large data sets, or smaller data sets with lots of zeros. OnFront is one package that can process zero variables.

A beta testing version of OnFront 3 was reviewed. This allows the use of directional distance estimators, corresponding productivity – Luenberger productivity (Chambers *et al.* 1996; Balk 1998) – estimators are promised with future releases of version 3.

In terms of cost-effectiveness, DEAP is the obvious choice as it is free of charge. However, it should be noted that there will be little future development or product support (a degree of email support is offered). The other packages offer features that will attract different users.

Given that DEA is becoming more widely accepted in health care, it should be remembered that DEA itself is still under development, especially in terms of the choice of which DEA model is appropriate in different potential policy applications. The choice of models specified in terms of inputs and outputs, and the analytical method used (CRS or VRS, weight restrictions or not, output or input oriented, etc.) will impact upon results. Unless the model used is founded upon a robust model of production, and is tested for validity, it may produce results which are wrong. The user-friendly nature of DEA packages does allow for 'have package, will analyse' problems. This is evident from the literature, where certain applications lack any theoretical foundation, and results are therefore invalid. The danger is that some of these models and results may be interpreted incorrectly by health-care policy makers. However, a well-specified and tested model, based soundly on production theories of the area under analysis can be an important and useful guide to the efficiency of a health-care system. This is one reason that we advocate the use of (wherever possible) non-stochastic and stochastic packages alongside each other. If results are pointing in the same direction, it is more likely that they can be relied upon.

SFA software

1. Frontier 41.School of Economics, University of Queensland, Australia (http://www.uq.edu.au/economics/cepa/software.htm/).
2. LIMDEP 8 (www.Limdep.com).

These packages have been reviewed elsewhere (see the *Economic Journal* software review section: 1999; **109**, F453–F458), only a brief summary appears here.

Frontier 4.1 is like DEAP in that it is a DOS-based package that requires similar getting used to. However it is accompanied by a comprehensive working paper and produces a wide array of models and results, dealing with both cross-sectional and panel data, and cost and production functions. Although not as user-friendly as LIMDEP, it is free of charge.

LIMDEP is a widely available package and many universities carry a site licence. SFA modelling in version 8 will feature the usual distributional variations – half normal, truncated normal, exponential, and gamma for cross-sectional analysis. Panel data formulations, in terms of random and fixed effect estimators, as well as random parameters and latent class formulations.

Summary and conclusions

This chapter has demonstrated why, and how, efficiency measurement should be undertaken, using methods based on economic production theory. We show how to apply DEA to develop a system of efficiency measurement for a sample of hospitals. We subject this to validity testing in the form of sensitivity analysis of different model specifications for the different sub-samples of trusts and correlation analysis of different sets of results. The measure stands up well to these tests and proves robust and reliable. The scores obtained for the units in the sub-samples show the considerable potential for efficiency gain.

Analysis of the summaries of weights for the different hospital samples demonstrates how the weights are distributed. For example A&E attendances dominate performance for acute hospitals, reflecting the uncertain nature of their activities and for priority hospitals MI and LD occupied bed days dominate performance as expected given the nature of their activities caring for long-term mentally ill patients. An example is then given of how results could be fed back to an individual hospital to give information on their efficiency and how improvements could be made. These basic foundations of how to undertake an efficiency analysis apply equally no matter which methods are used for analysis and, as we shall go on to see, more complex methods, and means of statistical testing can all be accommodated in such a system.

We would recommend undertaking parametric and non-parametric analysis alongside each other, wherever this is possible. If results obtained are highly correlated, and point in the same directions in terms of efficiency and inefficiency, this is another means of validating such systems of efficiency measurement. Examples of this are discussed in more detail in Chapter 6, but it is an important point to keep in focus.

Appendix

Your Organization Details

Efficiency Measurement

An Illustrative Guide

Your Contact Deatils

Contents

This document is an illustrative guide to the kinds of output that can be produced by the NHS efficiency measures project, using the technique of data envelopment analysis.

Page 2 (overleaf) explains in general terms the efficiency measure on which this project is based and how it is derived from data on resource inputs and health-care outputs.

Page 3 describes the data on inputs and outputs that are currently being used in the project and gives a contact address for the project.

Page 4 gives the results for a sample hospital within the Northern and Yorkshire Region in comparison with others. (Although the data are real, the actual hospital has been made anonymous.)

Page 5 gives explanations and interpretation of the results presented on the facing page 4.

Page 6 gives a comparison of the hospital with similar hospitals and explanation and interpretation of them.

The Efficiency Measure

The basis of our approach is to regard health care as a process by which resource **inputs**, such as staff, equipment and consumable items, are turned into health-care **outputs**; in other words, how health care is produced:

The efficiency of this production process is measured by examining the relationship between the inputs and the outputs. Outputs are, in our sample, throughput measures such as episodes of care and attendances. Ideally, there would be some measure of health outcomes, but unfortunately these data are not available at present.

If efficiency is the relationship between the outputs from an activity and the amount of resources that the activity uses, a numerical measure of efficiency (E) can be defined:

$$E = \frac{Output}{Input}$$

The greater this ratio, the more output is gained for a certain amount of input.

Of course, institutions such as hospitals carry out many activities and therefore have several different outputs (for example, cases treated of different types) and inputs (for example, staff of different kinds, equipment, etc.). An overall measure of a hospital's efficiency would therefore need to take this into account, that is:

$$E = \frac{Output_1 + Output_2 + Output_3 + \ldots\ldots}{Input_a + Input_b + Input_c + \ldots\ldots}$$

The problem with this is that these inputs and outputs cannot be simply added together. A way to deal with this is to give weights to each of the inputs and outputs so that they can be added together, that is:

$$E = \frac{Output_1 * Weight_1 + Output_2 * Weight_2 + Output_3 * Weight_3 + \ldots\ldots}{Input_a * Weight_a + Input_b * Weight_b + Input_c * Weight_c + \ldots\ldots}$$

So, the indicator of efficiency is defined as the ratio of a weighted sum of the outputs of a unit to a weighted sum of its inputs.

These weights are, however, not readily observable and must be inferred. Data envelopment analysis (DEA) calculates, using linear programming methods, implicit weights for a particular hospital by looking at what they would imply about efficiency both for the hospital being considered and also all other hospitals in the sample. Specifically, it ensures that when the weights are applied to every hospital in the sample, the efficiency scores all lie between 0 and 1; and that they give the most favourable possible view of the particular hospital, that is the highest efficiency score. This identifies hospitals (so-called **peer** hospitals) which outperform the hospital under consideration even using a set of assumptions most favourable to it, and quantifies by how much they outperform it (the **efficiency score**).

This procedure is carried out for every hospital in the sample to give a score for each.

The Data

The results in this guide are derived from a data set covering every trust in Northern & Yorkshire area. The data on *inputs* are:

- capital charge
- all other costs
- medical staff numbers
- nursing staff numbers
- ambulance staff numbers
- and all other staff numbers.

The data on *outputs* are:

- maternity finished consultant episodes (FCEs)
- general and acute services FCEs
- mental illness FCEs
- attendances for A&E
- attendances for outpatients
- attendances for mental illness
- bed days for mental illness
- and ambulance journeys.

These data are currently available for 1994/5 and 1995/6.

Contact

For more information please contact:

The Results

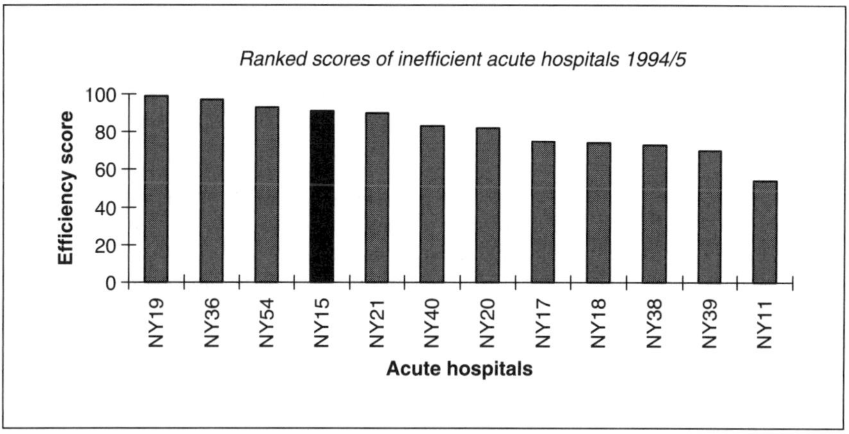
Ranked scores of inefficient acute hospitals 1994/5
Efficiency score
100
80
60
40
20
0
NY19
NY36
NY54
NY15
NY21
NY40
NY20
NY17
NY18
NY38
NY39
NY11
Acute hospitals

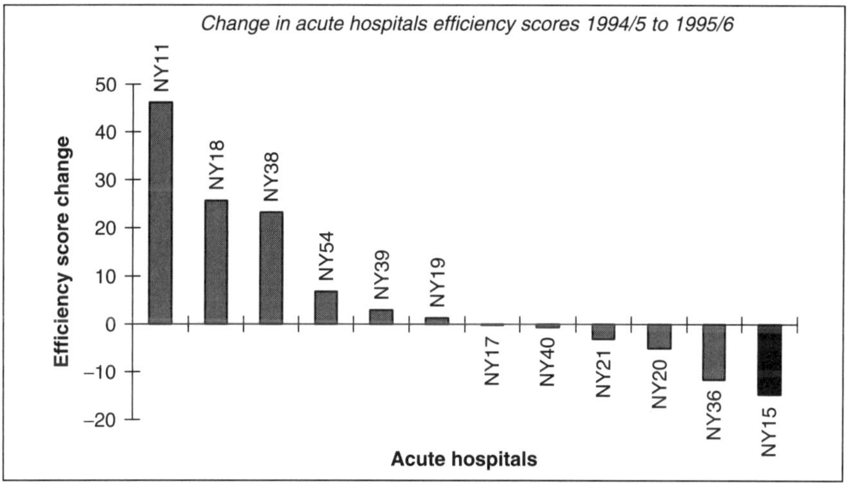
Change in acute hospitals efficiency scores 1994/5 to 1995/6
Efficiency score change
50
40
30
20
10
0
−10
−20
NY11
NY18
NY38
NY54
NY39
NY19
NY17
NY40
NY21
NY20
NY36
NY15
Acute hospitals

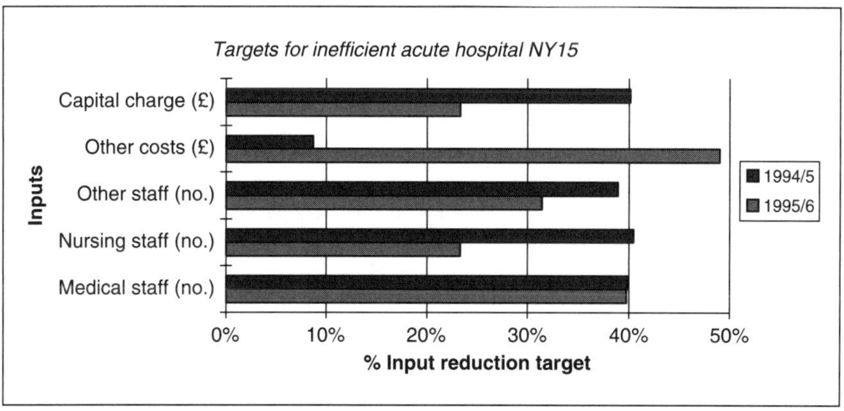
Targets for inefficient acute hospital NY15
Inputs
Capital charge (£)
Other costs (£)
Other staff (no.)
Nursing staff (no.)
Medical staff (no.)
1994/5
1995/6
0%
10%
20%
30%
40%
50%
% Input reduction target

The Results Explained

Ranked scores of inefficient acute hospitals 1994/5

The efficiency score allows comparison **between** trusts. It is constrained to lie between 0 (least efficient) and 100 (most efficient). Here the results are for a subset of 16 acute hospitals in the Northern & Yorkshire Region for 1994/5. The hospitals that scored 100 per cent efficiency are not shown.

Hospital NY15 is used as an example of how the information might be used. Information would be fed back to hospital NY15 showing how it compared to the other acute hospitals in the sample. Information concerning other hospitals is always anonymized. The overall efficiency of hospital NY15 was **91 per cent** in 1994/5, suggesting scope for improvement.

Change in acute hospitals efficiency scores 1994/5 to 1995/6

As well as comparison **between** trusts, the technique provides details concerning changes in efficiency **over time**. By tracking changes over time, hospitals will be able to monitor performance and the effects of any changes in, for example staff levels.

In hospital NY15, efficiency fell by **14 per cent** from 1994/5 and 1995/6. Any change in efficiency could indicate a fall in efficiency relative to the hospital's own performance or relative to that of the rest of the sample. This can be investigated by breaking down a hospital's own performance further.

Targets for inefficient acute hospital NY15

Information is also generated on **within** hospital performance. This shows by how much inputs would have to be reduced to produce the same output efficiently, compared to the performance of the other hospitals in the sample. Any **one** of these reductions in input use would lead to more efficient production, but there are many other combinations of reductions which would have the same effect. However, these target figures really serve to highlight areas within the hospital that need investigating further. Investigation may lead to the discovery of the specific circumstances which have led to the use of extra resources.

Target input reductions can be seen for hospital NY15 for the years 1994/5 and 1995/6. For example, medical staff numbers would have to be reduced by almost 40 per cent in 1994/5 and 1995/6 for this hospital to operate efficiently compared to the others in the sample.

Comparisons with Peers

A comparison of inputs used, and outputs produced, by inefficient acute hospital NY15 compared to its peer hospitals (NY49 & NY56) for 1994/5.

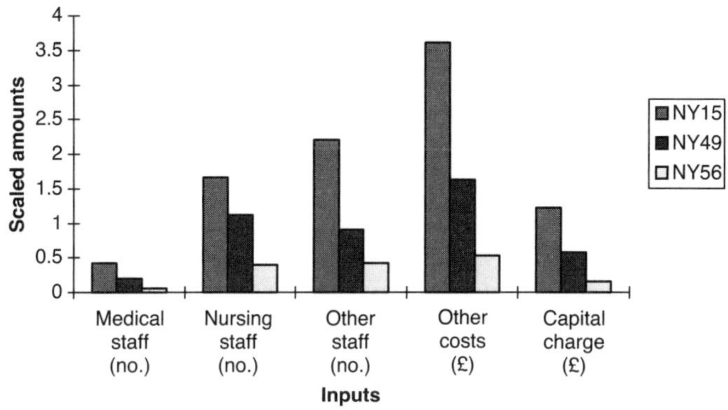

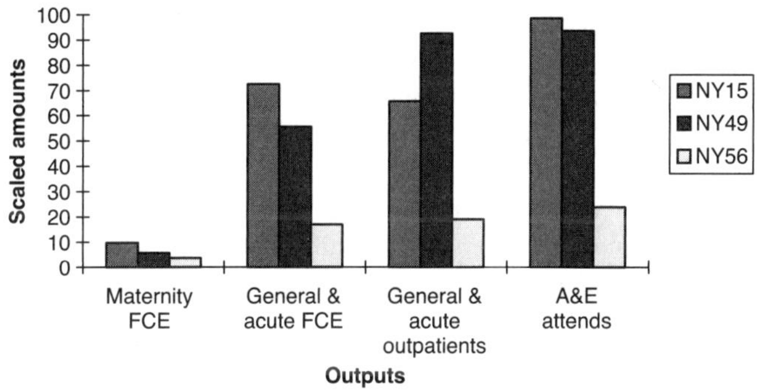

The Comparison Explained

A comparison of inputs used, and outputs produced, by inefficient acute hospital NY15 compared to its peer hospitals (NY49 & NY56) for 1994/5

Further information can be provided concerning the inputs used by the inefficient hospitals to produce their outputs in comparison to **peer hospitals.** These are hospitals which are not only efficient with respect to their own weightings, but also with respect to those of the inefficient hospital under analysis. Comparison with efficient hospitals allows inefficient hospitals to see easily the areas in which efficient hospitals are using less inputs to produce similar or greater quantities of outputs.

In this example, inefficient hospital NY15 is compared to its peers, efficient hospitals NY49 and NY56. Hospital NY15 uses more of all inputs to produce similar amounts of outputs, in scale terms, to its peers. By relating the **targets** (given on the previous page) to this more specific information, hospital NY15 has information on those areas it may wish to concentrate on to improve efficiency.

5 Application of efficiency measurement in health services

Introduction

This chapter reviews published applications of efficiency measurement in health care. This encompasses systematic searching of all available databases, as well as using contact lists such as mailbase/listserve[1] and the Productivity Analysis Research Network. Papers are reviewed with a view to determining methods used, data used, models specified, sensitivity analysis employed, validity and robustness of techniques, results and policy implications. Furthermore, results are summarized in a form of meta-analysis in order to synthesize results and draw out further implications.

An updated review in this area is important given a perceived lack of direction in the area of efficiency measurement in health (Hollingsworth and Street 2006). This is due in part to the lack of information available to researchers on what has been undertaken so far. This is always important as, until a researcher in the field can examine the directions taken by their peers, it is difficult to place one's own work in context.

Given this, it is hypothesized that much work undertaken and published in this area is of the nature of 'have software – will analyse'. This may have set a dangerous precedent, potentially leading to research that has a weak underlying basis in sound economic theory. The result may be findings on 'efficiency' being produced that lead to policy changes, where policy changes are in fact based upon invalid models and unreliable estimates of efficiency.

We draw out the consequences of the published research literature for the theory and application of efficiency measurement in health care. There is, up to the end of 2005, a published literature consisting of 289 journal papers and book chapters. This helps us to set in place robust foundations and guidelines for a research agenda for future research in this area. This will involve such important factors as statistical analysis of results, such as bootstrapping, as well as highlighting areas of analysis which require development, for example primary care, health promotion or the production of health.

As an appendix we summarize our findings, which will be a useful resource in itself for readers.

Background

In 2003, a paper was published (Hollingsworth 2003) which reviewed the literature focusing on non-parametric measurement. Up to the end of 2002, this paper found 188 published studies and concluded that evidence from Europe and the USA suggested public rather than private provision was more efficient, with the literature focusing on technical rather than allocative efficiency as health-care inputs and outputs are difficult to value. The paper notes a rapid increase in the number of studies, the first published in 1983, but 80 per cent being published between 1992 and 2002. Around 50 per cent of the studies made use of DEA alone, a fall from around two-thirds in an earlier study (Hollingsworth *et al.* 1999), but perhaps still not surprising at the time given methodological and practical developments (see the software review in Chapter 4). A fifth of studies used two-stage analysis (DEA followed by some form of regression) to attempt to identify further determinants of efficiency, even though there are doubts about the technical legitimacy of this (Simar and Wilson 2007).

In terms of area of application, almost 60 per cent were in hospitals and nursing homes in the USA. Although some papers looked at the efficiency of specific areas of secondary care, or primary care, and only in a few was an account made of the health status of individuals. The emphasis was almost always on measuring the efficiency of health care, rather than the efficiency of production of the health of the individual. Only a small number of studies tested different methods (for example weight restrictions, Malmquist techniques), or attempted validity measurement of model specification.

We build upon this review, updating all of the categories above, and add other studies using other efficiency measurement techniques, such as stochastic frontier analysis (SFA). This is increasingly used, but it is still DEA-based methods that dominate the literature.

Applications

During the last 20 years, DEA has been increasingly employed to measure and analyse the productive performance of health-care services. A health-care institution is not always expected to be efficient and there is no obvious reason why a doctor should choose to be efficient, at least in terms recognizable to an economist. In the theory of the firm, efficiency is a simple corollary of profit-maximizing behaviour, and is explicitly assumed. Firms try to maximize profits, which implies minimizing costs. However, as Evans (1971) suggests, hospitals do not adhere to maximizing/minimizing behaviour in the traditional neo-classical sense. The public health-care sector in general is often not profit-maximizing, in part due to uncertainty caused by the lack of information on prices and costs in health care. The health-care sector is a unique area of application, and one in which the measurement of efficiency has burgeoned over the past few years. This section reviews the methodologies and results of studies which measure efficiency and productivity of health services.

First, some summary statistics are provided to give an overview of the extent of the literature. The total number of studies identified up to and including 2005 is 289. Around 70 per cent of these studies publish quantifiable scores that we can analyse. The earliest is Nunamaker (1983) reflecting the contemporary nature of the techniques. Several patterns emerge when undertaking some basic analysis of the studies. The first is the rapid increase in studies over recent years, with over 70 per cent of studies having reported in the last ten years (see Figure 5.1).

Figure 5.2 shows 48 per cent of studies use DEA alone. This is not unexpected given that most methodological developments, such as using the efficiency score as the dependent variable in secondary regression analysis and applications of the Malmquist index, have occurred only recently. A fifth of studies use regression analysis in two-stage analysis, typically by regressing a series of behavioural variables on the efficiency scores in an attempt to determine influences on efficiency. Malmquist studies are used in 8 per cent of studies, and SFA and other paramatric frontier techniques are used in 16 per cent of studies.

Figure 5.3 shows that 48 per cent of applications are in hospitals. This represents a slight decrease over time, but applications are still mainly in areas of secondary care.

As far as the variables used in the analysis are concerned, they are almost entirely *output* measures of physical performance, such as inpatient days or discharges.

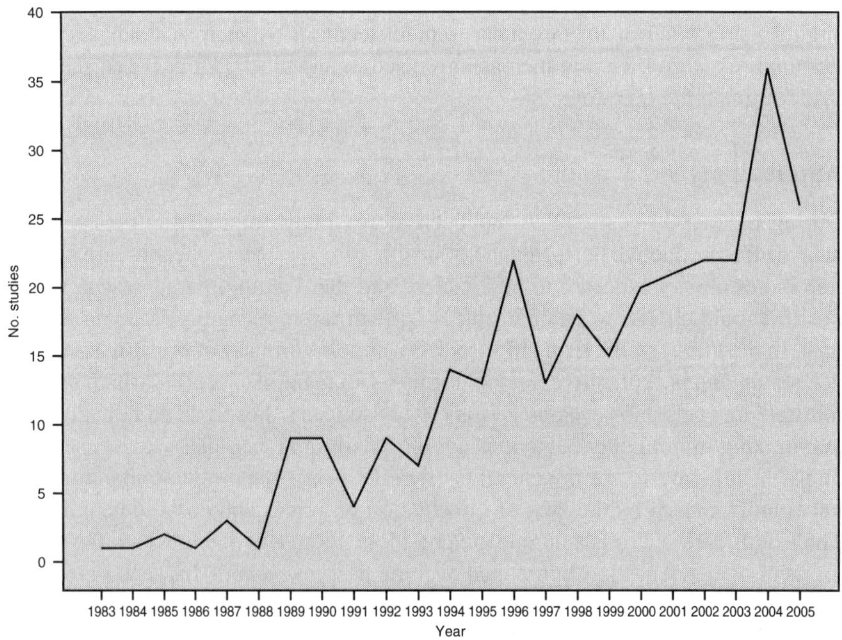

Figure 5.1 Number of efficiency studies 1983–2005.

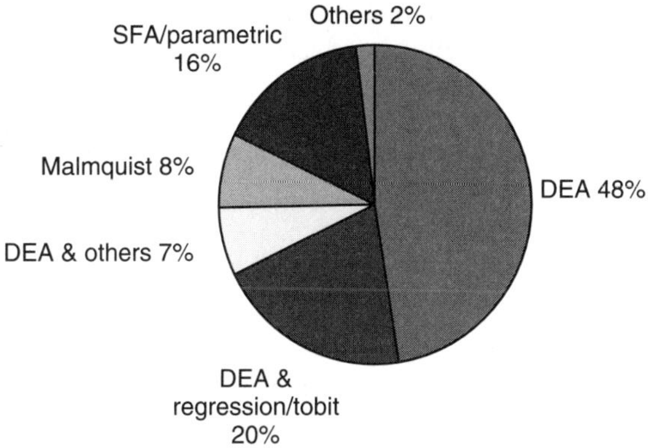

Figure 5.2 Methods used in reported studies.

There is scant (although slightly increasing) use, of *outcome* measures examining changes in health status of individuals treated. In terms of measuring output in hospitals (where it is recorded) there is an almost even split between inpatient days and inpatient cases. Input variables are mainly measures of staff and capital employed. Most of the results of the analysis are simple measures

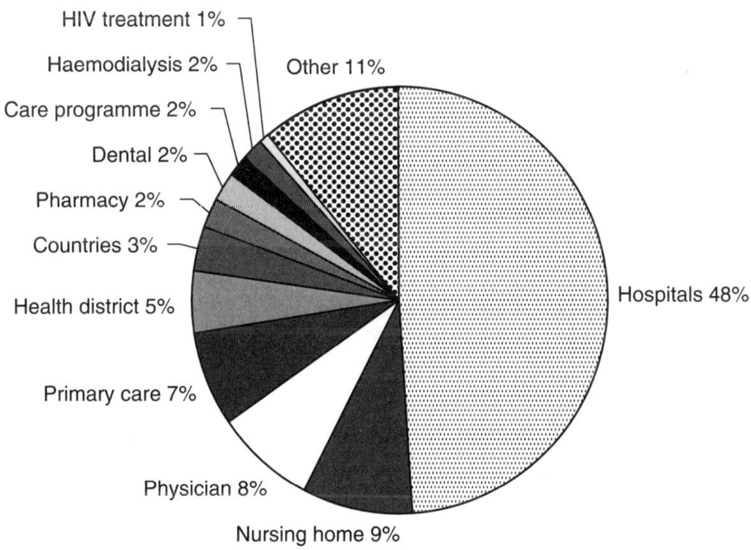

Figure 5.3 Areas of application.

of technical efficiency, although there is some analysis of studies of 'for-profit' compared to 'not-for-profit' delivery of services. More recently there have been some studies reporting on productivity changes, although these must be viewed in their individual contexts. Although most studies are straightforward applications, a small number test methods such as weight-restricted models and analysis of returns to scale. Similarly, a small number of studies perform statistical or sensitivity analysis of results.

Applications in health care

We initially concentrate on overall measures of efficiency in hospitals, before going on to examine the general health literature.

The hospital literature

Details of the hospital efficiency studies can be found in the appendix to this chapter and show the type of hospital, country, number of hospitals in the sample, author(s) and efficiency scores.[2] Most studies report results from the USA and can be categorized into different types of hospital. The main division can be made between public and private provision.[3] The public providers include Federal units, military Veteran's Administration (VA) units and Department of Defence (DoD) hospitals. Bannick and Ozcan (1995) examine 284 Federal units (158 VA and 126 DoD) finding the DoD units to be more efficient than the VA units (means 0.87 and 0.78 respectively). Burgess and Wilson (1993) look at 89 VA units with efficiency scores ranging from 0.93 to 0.97. The same authors (1996) examine the efficiency of 2,246 hospitals, finding the efficiency of VA units to be higher (0.87) than that of non-Federal, for-profit and not-for-profit units (0.82–0.83). Harrison and Ogniewski (2005) look at 131 VA hospitals in 1998, and 212 in 2001, finding an efficiency of 0.86. Ozcan and Bannick (1994) examine DoD units and find efficiency to range from 0.91 to 0.95. The private providers are mainly not-for-profit units. Bitran and Valor-Sabatier (1987) study 160 not-for-profit-units and find a mean of 0.60. Grosskopf and Valdmanis (1987) examine public and not-for-profit providers, finding means of 0.96 and 0.94 respectively. The same authors (1993) also examine solely not-for-profit units, efficiency ranging from 0.85 to 0.88. Morey *et al.* (1990) also compare public and not-for-profit units finding means of 0.95 and 0.65 respectively. Valdmanis (1990, 1992) looks at the efficiency of 41 public and not-for-profit hospitals finding the efficiency of the public units to be higher than the not-for-profit units (0.98 and 0.88 respectively). Ozcan *et al.* (1996a) examine the efficiency of 85 hospitals finding not-for-profit units to be more efficient than for-profit units (0.72 and 0.61 respectively).

Several studies examine acute/general units with some of the studies being from outside the USA. Burgess and Wilson (1998) study a sample of 132 VA and 1,413 non-VA hospitals (224 local government, 1,021 not-for-profit, 168 for-profit) hospitals in the USA from 1985 to 1988, with initial estimates put at 13.6 per cent for technical inefficiency for the whole sample in 1988. Local government hospitals had an inefficiency of 11.2 per cent, not-for-profits 15.1 per cent, for-profit hospitals 12 per cent and VA hospitals 8.2 per cent. After undertaking two-stage analysis and controlling for other factors they find ownership structure and teaching status do not affect technical efficiency. Borden (1988) examines 52 USA acute units finding efficiency to range from 0.95 to 0.99. Chirikos and Sear (1994) examine 189 USA acute units and find average efficiency to be 0.65, finding substantial variation in efficiency scores. The same authors (2000) undertake DEA and SFA on 186 acute hospitals in Florida (USA) for 1982 to 1993. Pooled panel DEA results demonstrated a mean of 0.801 (range 0.749–0.903) (see SFA section below for SFA results) with results possibly reflecting time lags.

Dittman *et al.* (1991) look at 105 USA acute units, finding efficiency to be as low as 0.49 with efficiency being dependent on the input/output mix. Ozcan (1992) also demonstrates results that are sensitive to variables being used in 40 USA acute units, finding mean efficiency to range from 0.51 to 0.92. Ozcan and Lynch (1992) examine 1,535 general hospitals in the USA finding no relationship between efficiency and closure, with a mean efficiency of 0.88. Chern and Wan (2000), in a sample of 88 non-government hospitals in the USA (for two years 1984 and 1993), saw efficiency fall from 0.80 to 0.76, with medium-sized units being the most efficient in the first year and larger units more efficient in the second year. Harris *et al.* (2000) used DEA on a sample of 20 USA hospitals (1991–1993 data) comparing pre-merger to post-merger efficiency; efficiency increases from 0.81 to 0.85, mergers seemingly increasing efficiency. Grosskopf *et al.* (1995) use output distance functions to estimate the efficiency of 99 USA hospitals in 1982 (AHA data, 18 public, 81 not-for-profit, in NY and California) and there were output substitution elasticities across ownership. This implies trade-offs on technology are similar. Although Byrnes and Valdmanis (1989) use DEA to measure the efficiency of 123 not-for-profit hospitals in California (USA) with a technical efficiency of 0.87, an allocative efficiency of 0.83, and an overall efficiency of 0.72. Ferrier and Valdmanis (1996) use two-stage analysis (DEA and tobit) to estimate efficiency for 360 rural hospitals in the USA (219 public, 95 not-for-profit, and 46 for-profit). Cost efficiency is 0.676, technical efficiency 0.787, allocative efficiency 0.861 and scale efficiency 0.893. For-profits outperform not-for-profits and public, and quality (mortality) and service mix influences performance.

Gruca and Nath (2001) use DEA to estimate the efficiency of 168 community hospitals in Canada in 1986. Secular hospitals were more efficient than religious (averaging 0.75 compared to 0.67), with government hospitals averaging 0.70. Rural hospitals were more efficient than urban (0.77 compared to 0.72), small hospitals were more efficient than large (0.77 compared to 0.69), and those with long-term care beds were more efficient (0.77 compared to 0.58). There was no significant difference across ownership types–managed care is postulated to eliminate these performance differences.

Hollingsworth and Parkin (1995a) and Parkin and Hollingsworth (1997) also demonstrate the sensitivity of results to variable model specifications for 75 UK acute units and find efficiency to be as low as 0.63. Jacobs (2001) uses methods including DEA on a sample of up to 232 UK NHS hospital trusts, estimating efficiency means between 0.645 and 0.936 for 1995/6, concluding inefficiency savings may be modest. Tsai and Molinero (2002) find a mean of 0.938 in a sample of UK hospitals. Kerr *et al.* (1999) uses two-stage analysis (DEA and tobit) to estimate the efficiency of 23 acute hospitals in Northern Ireland (NI) from 1986/7 and 1991/2 with larger units having a mean of 0.94 over the two periods and smaller units a mean of 0.91 to 0.82. Larger hospitals appear more efficient. McCallion *et al.* (1999) on a similar sample of 23 NI hospitals from 1989 to 1992 estimated cost-efficiency (CE) and allocative efficiency (AE) finding large hospitals more efficient than small (0.672 compared to 0.601 for CE, 0.715 and 0.713 for AE), the same being the case for technical efficiency (0.939 and 0.842) and for scale (0.949 and 0.913). It is concluded that there is input misallocation. McKillop *et al.* (1999), again on a sample of 23 Northern Irish hospitals from 1986 to 1992, estimate DEA super efficiency with technical efficiency ranging from 0.933 to 0.951 for larger units and from 0.842 to 0.909 for smaller hospitals. For smaller units efficiency is falling. Gannon (2005) finds efficiency ranging from 0.94 to 0.97 in Irish hospitals.

Magnussen (1996) finds 46 Norwegian units to have means of 0.93 to 0.94 with rankings depending in part on model outputs. Mobley and Magnussen (1998) use DEA to compare the efficiency of 178 USA hospitals (63 urban for-profit, 63 urban not-for-profit, 52 non-urban not-for-profit), and 50 Norwegian hospitals in 1991. Using a VRS model, technical efficiency in Norway was 0.937, in the USA for-profit urban sample, it was 0.884, in the not-for-profit urban sample 0.936, and in the not-for-profit non-urban sample 0.917. Scale efficiency was higher in the Norwegian sample, while efficiency in Norway is related to use of bed capacity. There may be physician over-utilization in the USA sample. The same authors (2002) look at 348 US hospitals, finding a technical efficiency of 0.91. Also looking at a Norwegian sample, Martinussen and Midttun (2004) find efficiency ranging from 0.83 to 0.84 in 51 hospitals. Linna (1998) uses various methods to estimate the efficiency of 43 hospitals in Finland over the period 1988 to 1994, with DEA scores ranging between 0.81 and 0.93. Linna and Häkkinen (1998) use DEA among other methods for 48 acute hospitals in 1994 in Finland, estimating DEA efficiency at between 0.84 and 0.89. Laine *et al.* (2005a) look at 114 public health centre hospitals and find a mean of 0.72. In a study of Spanish general units Lopez-Valcarel and Perez (1996) find scores to range from 0.92 to 0.95. Dalmau-Matarrodona and Puig-Junoy (1998) estimate efficiency using a two-stage model for 94 Spanish acute hospitals in 1990, finding a mean technical efficiency of 0.989, technical efficiency being influenced by the number of competitors in a market, scale efficiency being influenced by size and severity of illness. Prior (1996) looks at technical efficiency and economies of scope for 50 general hospitals in Spain, finding, overall, inefficiency of 3 per cent, and evidence of economies of scope. Prior and Solà (2000) use DEA to estimate economies of diversification for a sample of Spanish hospitals in 1987 and 1992. In 1987 there were 70 diversified and 62 specialized, and in 1992, 68 and 81 respectively. In 1987 the mean score for the diversified hospitals was 0.89 and for specialized 0.87. In 1992, the estimates were 0.93 and 0.88 respectively. It is concluded that diversification economies dominate.

Ersoy (1997) in a study of 573 Turkish acute hospitals finds 91 per cent of the sample to be inefficient. Al-Shammari (1999) finds mean scores ranging from 0.867 to 0.977 (range 0.533–1) for 15 public sector hospitals in Jordan, noting that many services are not being fully utilized. For a sample of 98 Greek public hospitals, Athanassopoulos and Gounaris (2001) find overall efficiency has a mean of 0.81 (range 0.25–1), with rural hospitals more efficient that urban (0.83 compared to 0.75). Small hospitals are generally less efficient. Athanassopoulos *et al.* (1999) for the same sample of hospitals, estimates cost-efficiency at 0.72 for rural hospitals and 0.62 for urban hospitals, and for cost-efficiency 0.86 for rural and 0.67 for urban hospitals. In a follow-up survey, a panel of 'experts' (hospital administrators) validate the methods and results. Giokas (2001), for a sample of 91 Greek hospitals (72 general, 19 teaching), uses both DEA and SFA (although there are no useable SFA results). Average efficiency for general hospitals was 0.751, and for teaching hospitals 0.847. Beguin (2001) makes use of free disposable hulls to estimate efficiency for 34 hospitals in Belgium in 1988, finding efficiency to range from 0.39 to 0.54, after outliers are removed.

Chang (1998) estimates the efficiency of six public hospitals in Taiwan from 1990 to 1994. The average efficiency scores range from 0.88 to 0.987, concluding occupancy rate has a positive impact on efficiency, and the proportion of retired patients has a negative effect on efficiency. Chang *et al.* (2004) look at over 400 hospitals in Taiwan finding efficiency ranging from 0.58 to 0.93, with private hospitals being more efficient. Liu and Mills (2005) find in a small sample of six Chinese hospitals, an efficiency decrease from 0.97 in 1978 to 0.97 in 1997. Valdmanis *et al.* (2004) find an efficiency of 0.95 in a sample of 68 Thai hospitals. Zere *et al.* (2001) look at efficiency for 86 hospitals in South Africa in 1992/3 finding an efficiency of 0.74 (range 0.518–1), with tobit analysis showing increasing outpatient attends increases efficiency. Kirigia *et al.* (2002) finds a technical efficiency of 0.96 in 54 Kenyan hospitals.

More recently, Chen *et al.* (2005) look at 89 US hospitals finding technical efficiency ranging from 0.75 to 0.80 (0.81–0.85 using variable returns models). Harrison *et al.* (2004), in a sample of over 200 USA federal hospitals, find efficiency ranging from 0.68 to 0.79. One paper which has estimated efficiency for a sample of psychiatric hospitals is Ferrier and Valdmanis (2002), finding private not-for-profit provision most efficient.

There have also been several studies that have not specified hospital type. These include: Morey and Dittman (1996); Ferrier and Valdmanis (1996); Maindiratta (1990); Nunamaker (1983); White and Ozcan (1996); and Young (1992), finding efficiency scores as low as 0.40; and Helmig and Lapsley (2001) who in a large sample of over 2,000 hospitals found efficiency ranging from 0.77 to 1. More recently, studies not specifying hospital type have included: Ferrier and Valdmanis (2004); O'Neill and Dexter (2004); Osei *et al.* (2005); Ramanathan *et al.* (2003); Steinman *et al.* (2004); and Dervaux (2004).

Table 5.1 Summary statistics for hospital efficiency scores.

	No.	*Mean*	*Median*	*St. dev.*	*Minimum*
For-profit	4	0.801	0.855	0.130	0.61
Not-for-profit	11	0.831	0.850	0.109	0.60
Public	15	0.904	0.94	0.083	0.72
Defence/VA	6	0.885	0.895	0.056	0.82
Non-teaching	2	0.742	0.742	0.046	0.71
Teaching	3	0.673	0.650	0.087	0.60
Acute/general	26	0.835	0.821	0.085	0.65
Non-specified	21	0.849	0.872	0.109	0.61
Psychiatric	1	0.47	0.47	—	0.47
All hospitals	**89**	**0.839**	**0.87**	**0.109**	**0.47**
USA Hospitals	56	0.826	0.845	0.116	0.47
Euro. Hospitals	22	0.876	0.894	0.081	0.72
Non-USA/EU	11	0.870	0.906	0.099	0.724

The summary statistics are shown in Table 5.1, and a box-plot of the efficiency scores by hospital category is shown in Figure 5.4. The mean efficiency across the whole sample is 0.84 and the median is 0.87.

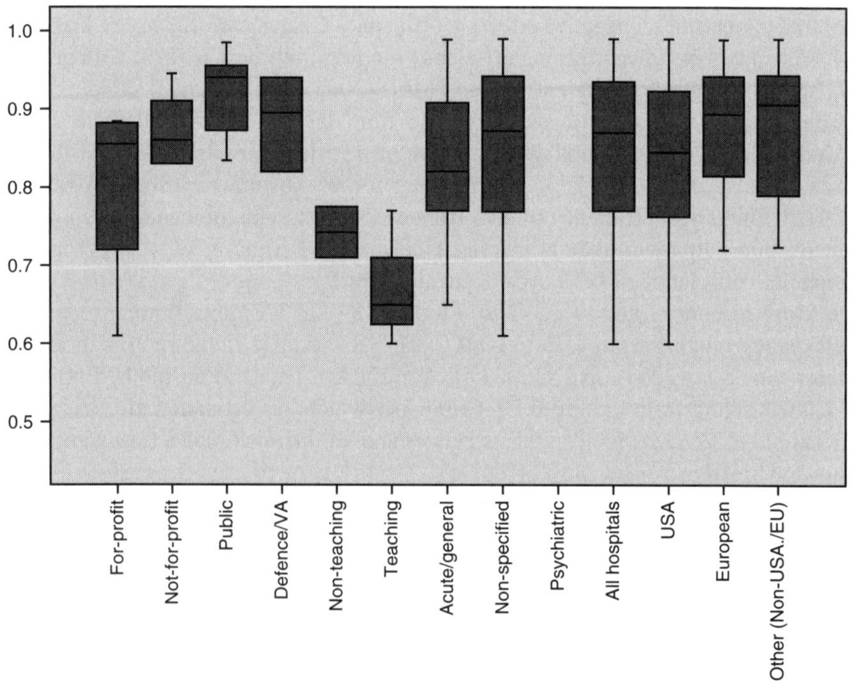

Figure 5.4 Box-plot of distribution of efficiency scores by category of hospital.

Figure 5.4 summarizes the results for each hospital type. The box-plot shows the median, quartiles and extreme values for each hospital group. This allows us to see at a glance which hospital groups are more efficient and the range of scores. Comparing efficiency across the sector, public hospitals have high mean efficiency (0.90) and the highest median score (0.94), compared with not-for-profit (generally private) hospitals which have a lower mean efficiency (0.831) and a lower median score (0.85). Defence and Veterans' Administration (VA) hospitals (which are public in nature) also have a higher mean score (0.88) and a higher median score (0.89) than not-for-profit hospitals. Not-for-profit firms care for 70 per cent of all inpatient cases in acute hospitals (Folland *et al.* 2007) and these results correlate with comparisons made in individual studies where public and private provision are compared (Grosskopf and Valdmanis 1987; Morey *et al.* 1990; Valdmanis 1990; Valdmanis 1992).[4] Examination of the standard deviation and minimum demonstrate the room for efficiency gain. For not-for-profit hospitals, the standard deviation is 0.109 and the minimum 0.60, demonstrating considerable deviation from the mean of 0.831 indicating that there is substantial room for improvement. Potential efficiency gains are less obvious for public hospitals (standard deviation 0.083, minimum 0.72 and mean of 0.90) and defence/VA hospitals (standard deviation 0.056, minimum 0.82 and mean of 0.885). There is also some potential for gain for acute/general hospitals (standard deviation 0.085 and a minimum of 0.65), deviating from the mean of 0.35.

One way to compare efficiency is to compare the efficiency of hospitals across countries. This also gives some indication as to the efficiency of different means of health-care delivery. Most results are from the USA where the average efficiency is 0.826, with a median of 0.845 and a minimum of 0.47. Here, the system is predominantly one of privately provided health-care insurance, with a safety net of Medicaid and Medicare to cover the poor and elderly respectively. This can be compared to Europe where health care is characterized by public provision or social insurance. In the European sample (including the UK, Finland, Greece, Belgium, Norway, Spain, Germany, Switzerland, Ireland and France) the average efficiency is 0.876, with a median of 0.894 and a minimum of 0.72. These results are higher than for the sample of USA hospitals, where there is greater potential for efficiency gain, with a standard deviation of 0.116 and a minimum of 0.47 for the USA sample compared to 0.081 and 0.72 for the European sample.

The results, that public provision seems more efficient and that European hospitals have higher average efficiency, would seem contrary to the perception that private market provision of services is more efficient than public provision of services. This may be because health care is an unusual economic commodity, not a tradeable good in the traditional sense.[5] A second explanation could be methodological differences between the studies, for example differences in variables used or sample sizes leading to some studies potentially being more robust than others. This means that results may be conditional upon heterogeneity of observations, rather than any real variations in efficiency. These factors mean that it may be difficult to genuinely compare results beyond looking at the overall picture.

The general health literature

There are several other health-care areas in which DEA has been applied. Details of the general health studies can be found in the appendix to this chapter, which shows the type of organization, country, number in the sample, author(s) and efficiency scores. The summary statistics are shown in Table 5.2 and a box-plot of the distribution of efficiency scores in Figure 5.5.

Cross-country analysis is undertaken, mainly using OECD data in several studies: Puig-Junoy (1998); Afonso and St Aubyn (2005); Bhat (2005); and Retzlaff-Roberts *et al.* (2004). There is some coverage in the literature of more general health-care administrative units at the most general level, with general analysis on two levels–metropolitan and health authorities and care programmes. Ozcan (1995) finds inefficiency may be due to a build up of providers in 319 USA metropolitan areas for 1990, which had an average efficiency score of between 0.79 and 0.92. Wang *et al.* (1999) use similar data on 314 metropolitan markets for the years 1989 and 1993 which demonstrated larger hospitals were more efficient, with efficiency scores ranging from 0.74 to 0.89. Ozcan and Cotter (1994) use DEA on 25 area agencies for ageing in Virginia, USA, in 1991. They found government agencies to be 0.8 efficient, joint agencies 0.5 efficient, and private not-for-profit agencies 0.57 efficient. Large and urban agencies were also more efficient.

Gerdtham *et al.* (1999) use two-stage analysis (super efficiency DEA and regression – OLS, tobit) to estimate the efficiency of 26 Swedish councils responsible for health care in 1993/4. There are no useable efficiency estimates, but it is concluded that there may be savings from switching from budget to output-based allocation of approximately 13 per cent.

Sahin and Ozcan (2000) estimate the efficiency of public hospitals in 80 regions in Turkey in 1996, with the average estimated at 0.879. Rosenman *et al.* (1997) examine the efficiency of health maintenance organizations (HMOs) in Florida, finding efficiency to be 0.65. Bryce *et al.* (2000) use DEA, among other methods, on 585 HMOs in the USA from 1985 to 1994, and although there are no useable results, they find different models give different results, with model selection influencing efficiency ranking.

In terms of primary care outside the USA, Giuffrida and Gravelle (2001) use various methods including DEA to estimate efficiency for 90 family health service authorities (FHSAs) in 1993/4 and 1994/5. DEA technical efficiency is 0.98 in both years, scores being highly correlated within the different methods (including SFA, and COLS; see SFA section below), but less highly correlated between methods.

Several UK studies estimate efficiency from the Health Authority (HA) perspective. Hollingsworth and Parkin (1995a) and Parkin and Hollingsworth (1997) estimate the efficiency of Scottish health boards (similar to HAs) using data from average hospital efficiency in each board with a view to the possibility of using the information for resource allocation decisions. Efficiency ranges from 0.72 to 1. A study by Thanassoulis *et al.* (1996) uses data from UK district health authorities looking at perinatal care. While the first study examines combining quality and quantity measures, the second compares DEA and ratio analysis, results varying with regard to individual units. Hollingsworth and Parkin (2001) look at 49 neonatal care units in the UK in 1990/91, finding an average efficiency of 0.723, and varying economies of scale. There are potential cost savings of 23 per cent for inefficient units. Salinas-Jiménez and Smith (1996) look at 85 family health service authorities, finding 51 per cent efficient.

Primary care in the USA is reviewed in several studies: Andes *et al.* (2002), Rosenman and Friesner (2004), Wagner *et al.* (2003), Wagner and Shimshak (2000), Rollins *et al.* (2001), and Draper *et al.* (2000). These studies find a wide range of inefficiency in practices. There are also studies looking at primary care outside the USA and Europe – in Sierra Leone (Renner *et al.* 2005), and Kenya (Kirigia *et al.* 2004).

A number of studies look at programmes of care and health centres. Huang and McLaughlin (1989) examine the efficiency of 77 rural health-care programmes, showing that 29 were technically efficient. Schinnar *et al.* (1990) and Kamis-Gould (1991) examine 54 American partial-care mental health programmes comparing efficiency and effectiveness, with effectiveness of care seemingly related to a mid-level of efficiency. Johnston and Gerard (2001) estimate efficiency for 64 UK breast screening units in 1996, finding a mean of 0.821, with large units having a mean of 0.921, and smaller units a mean of 0.845, concluding that the wide variation in efficiency scores may mean the size of a unit is not a significant factor related to efficiency.

American studies examine the efficiency of health centres, which can broadly be interpreted as operating at the level of *primary* care (as opposed to hospital, or *secondary* care which is discussed in the previous section). Sexton *et al.* (1989a) analyse 159 Veteran's Administration medical centres finding that 52 are inefficient, associated with potential savings of $300 million per annum.

Tyler *et al.* (1995) examine 39 mental health centres: six are efficient while those with local inpatient services are less efficient. Yeh *et al.* (1997) examine 40 community-based youth programmes, in the context of mental health, finding large programmes to be more efficient (0.69 compared to 0.55), programmes in poor areas to be more efficient (0.64 compared to 0.58) and rural programmes to be more efficient than urban (0.65 compared to 0.55). Four primary-care agencies are examined by Rosenberg (1991), comparing DEA to cost-effectiveness analysis finding that the only efficient producer has the second smallest cost-effectiveness ratio. Luoma *et al.* (1996) estimate the efficiency of 202 Finnish health centres finding that increasing resources may reduce incentives to be efficient. Pina and Torres (1992) when examining ten Spanish health centres find five to be technically efficient and four to be scale efficient. Szczepura *et al.* (1993) examine 52 UK general practices finding a range of efficiency from 0.35 to 1.

Another area where several studies have been undertaken is nursing homes. Two American studies (Chattopadhyay and Heffley 2004; Chattopadhyay and Ray 1996) find homes run for profit to be more efficient than those run on a not-for-profit basis, with mean efficiency scores of 0.94 compared to 0.81.

Kleinsorge and Karney (1992) examine 22 nursing homes in Kansas, with five of the homes being efficient for all models specified (including/excluding finances, including/excluding quality). Nyman and Bricker (1989) and Nyman *et al.* (1990) look at 184 nursing homes in Wisconsin and 296 in Iowa finding firms operating for-profit to be significantly more efficient and quality variables not to have a significant effect on results, with mean scores ranging from 0.89 to 0.93. Rosko *et al.* (1995) find a sample of for-profit homes to have a higher mean efficiency (0.82) than a sample of not-for-profit homes (0.71). Anderson *et al.* (2003) also find for-profit homes to be more efficient (0.77 compared to 0.74 for not-for-profits). Sexton *et al.* (1989b) examine 52 homes in Maine, finding that efficiency falls following the introduction of prospective reimbursement, with mean scores of 0.76–0.78. Fizel and Nunnikhoven (1993) find the efficiency of 104 for-profit homes to average 0.66, with independent homes averaging 0.62 and homes that are part of a chain 0.71. Ozcan *et al.* (1998a, 1998b) used two-stage analysis (DEA and logit) to estimate efficiency for 324 skilled nursing facilities in the USA (210 for-profit, 114 not-for-profit). The for-profit units are more efficient (0.84) compared to the not-for-profit (0.803), and the medium-sized units are more efficient than the smaller units (0.859 compared to 0.803). It is concluded that a higher percentage of Medicare patients reduced efficiency, a higher percentage of Medicaid patients increased efficiency. Fried *et al.* (1998) look at the efficiency of hospital-based nursing homes in the USA (372 skilled, 84 intermediate, 40 diversified). The skilled homes are the least production efficient (0.38), intermediate homes are more efficient (0.42), and diversified homes are the most efficient (0.46). The study fails to find significant economies of scope.

Several studies report on homes outside of the USA. Kooreman (1994) looks at 232 Dutch nursing homes, finding 50 per cent to be efficient and concluding that there may be a trade-off between labour efficiency and quality of care, with mean scores ranging from 0.8 to 0.94. Blank *et al.* (1996) examine nursing homes in the Netherlands, finding that variable costs could be reduced by approximately 30 per cent. Blank and Valdmanis (2005) look at 71 homes in the Netherlands, finding room for improvement in terms of allocative efficiency.

Capettini and Morey (1985) examine efficiency of pharmacies, and Bates *et al.* (1996) attempt to examine efficiency of prescribing, although they encounter statistical problems. Björkgren *et al.* (2001, 2004) estimate efficiency in 64 long-term care units in Finland in 1995. For two models, technical efficiency ranges from 0.85 to 0.87, cost efficiency from 0.74 to 0.77, allocative efficiency from 0.84 to 0.89 and scale efficiency from 0.92 to 0.93. Larger units appear to be more efficient.

Studies have reported on dental services. Buck (2000) uses DEA and regression to look at 100 community dental services in England in 1997/8 finding a CRS mean of 0.635, and a VRS mean of 0.673. He recognizes there is no quality adjustment, and that there may be omitted variables. Parkin and Devlin (2003) look at dental services across European countries, finding variations, and Linna *et al.* (2002) look at oral health provision in Finland. Coppola *et al.* (2003) look at dental encounters in the USA.

Table 5.2 Summary statistics for general health efficiency scores.

	No.	*Mean*	*Median*	*St. dev.*	*Minimum*
Care programme	2	0.623	0.623	0.032	0.60
Health districts Euro.	4	0.839	0.838	0.04	0.80
Health districts USA	9	0.742	0.80	0.114	0.50
Nursing homes Euro.	6	0.821	0.83	0.114	0.70
Nursing homes USA	19	0.765	0.81	0.158	0.38
Primary care Euro.	6	0.821	0.815	0.104	0.675
Primary care USA	8	0.681	0.781	0.223	0.39
Primary care (non-USA/EU)	2	0.79	0.79	0.014	0.78

Ozcan *et al.* (1999) in looking at 64 organ procurement organizations, found larger organizations to be more efficient (0.948) compared to smaller units (0.789) in terms of organs recovered. Renal care appears to be a growing area for analysis, with studies in the USA (Ozgen and Ozcan 2002), and Europe (Gerard and Roderick 2003; Kontodimopoulos and Niakas 2005).

Examination of the statistics in Table 5.2 and the box-plot of the distribution of scores in Figure 5.5 demonstrates there is potential for efficiency gain. For health districts there is room for improvement, both in Europe and the USA (means of 0.839 and 0.742 and minimums of 0.80 and 0.50 respectively). There is also scope for efficiency gain in primary care. In Europe the mean is 0.821 compared to the USA mean of 0.681 where there is more potential for improvement (standard deviation 0.223 and minimum of 0.39). However, this may simply reflect the diverse nature of primary-care delivery in the USA and Europe. A more valid comparison is of nursing homes which in the USA seem less efficient compared to those in Europe (means of 0.765 and 0.821, and medians 0.81 and 0.83, respectively, demonstrate scores may be more similar as there would appear to be an outlier problem; analysis in this way is one way to isolate this problem as DEA is sensitive to outliers), whereas both demonstrate potential for improvement, with the minimum scores of 0.70 for the European homes, and 0.38 for the USA homes, and standard deviations of 0.114 and 0.158.

Malmquist productivity applications

A summary of Malmquist-based productivity studies is provided in the appendix. Färe *et al.* (1997) examine changes in productivity between 19 countries between 1974 and 1989. Two models are used, one using intermediate outputs (days and discharges), which shows little evidence of productivity growth, and one using health outcomes (life expectancy and infant mortality), which demonstrates some evidence of growth. Hollingsworth and Wildman (2003) re-estimate the WHO measures of cross-country efficiency (World Health Report 2000), finding the

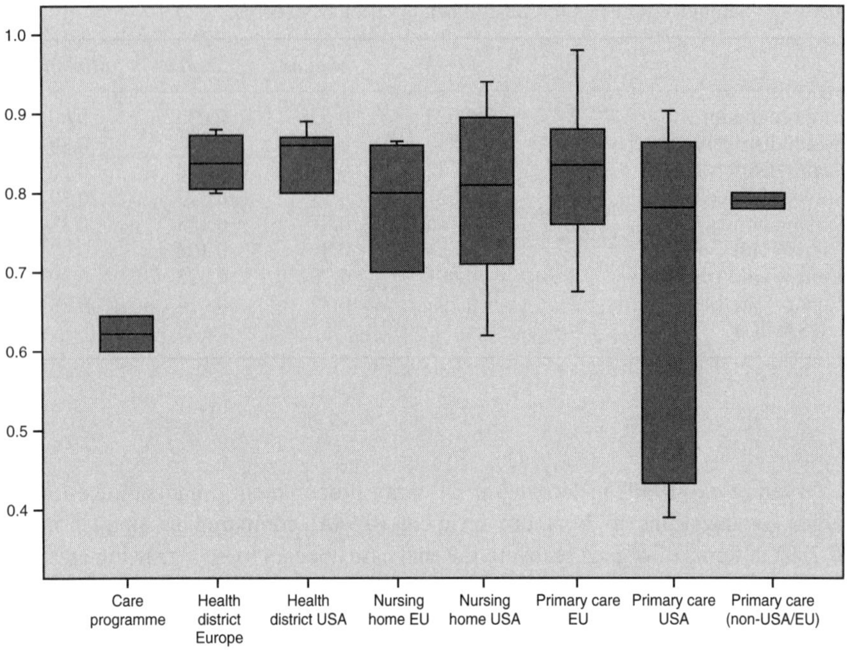

Figure 5.5 Box-plot of distribution of efficiency scores by general health category.

use of Malmquist (and SFA) may result in a greater breadth of information being available.

Giuffrida (1999) uses Malmquist indices to estimate productivity changes for 90 UK FHSAs for the years 1990/1 to 1994/5. For the full model, productivity change is 1.01, technical efficiency is 0.996, pure technical efficiency change is 1.003, technical change is 1.005, and scale change is 1.003. It is concluded there is a small productivity improvement due to technical and scale efficiency, not technology change. There is seen to be limited scope for productivity gain.

Burgess and Wilson (1995) look at USA hospitals finding Federal hospitals to demonstrate a significant amount of technical regress while there are small changes in non-Federal units.

Färe *et al.* (1994a) examine 17 Swedish public hospitals and find considerable variation in productivity across hospitals and time. Linna (1998) uses Malmquist analysis alongside SFA on 42 hospitals in Finland (1988 to 1994) finding an annual average increse in productivity of 3 to 5 per cent, due equally to cost efficiency and technical change.

Maniadakis *et al.* (1999) use data from 75 Scottish acute hospitals from 1991/2 to 1995/6 and apply Malmquist indices to estimate productivity and quality changes, finding there was a productivity slowdown in the first year following NHS reforms, but productivity progress in subsequent years. Changes are dominated by technological change, with hospital efficiency changing little, and quality may have suffered at the expense of productivity. Maniadakis and Thanassoulis (2000) look at the same 75 Scottish acute hospitals from 1991/2 to 1995/6 reporting productivity progress (0.928), and cost efficiency progress (0.912), made up of allocative efficiency progress and technological regress, with overall gains being small. The same authors (2004) use data on 30 Greek hospitals to decompose a cost Malmquist index. Hollingsworth and Parkin (2003) look at changes in 44 UK hospitals, finding an overall productivity increase. McCallion *et al.* (2000) look at hospitals in Northern Ireland from 1986 to 1992 finding larger hospitals increase productivity by 2.31 per cent, and smaller ones by 22.53 per cent. Technological increase is outweighed by a decline in efficiency change for small hospitals. Scale efficiency falls. Sommersguter-Reichmann (2000) looking at 22 Austrian hospitals from 1994 to 1998 (17 public non-profit, 5 private non-profit) finds an increase in productivity in the final two years (1.093 to 1.038) due to technology improvement and due to financing a new system. Zere *et al.* (2001) look at productivity for 86 hospitals in South Africa in 1992/3 finding it declined by 12 per cent due to technology regress, while the efficiency change was marginal.

Dismuke and Sena (1999) used Malmquist indices (alongside SFA) on Portuguese district and central hospital diagnostic technology from 1992 to 1994 (for cerebrovascular disorders and heart failure), finding productivity is related to the diagnosis related group (DRG) system. Tambour (1997) looks at 20 ophthalmology departments in Sweden from 1988 to 1993 concluding that overall the productivity change for the sector is positive and significant in all but one period. Average change in efficiency is positive but not significant, technology change is generally positive, with overall productivity change being driven by change in technology, for example medical technology or administrative systems.

Löthgren and Tambour (1999) estimate productivity using both a standard model and a network model for Swedish pharmacies. The standard model finds productivity progress at 0.914, efficiency change at 0.979, technology change at 0.934 and technical efficiency at 0.872. Färe *et al.* (1992, 1995) examine the productivity of Swedish pharmacies, the second of the two studies with the novel inclusion of quality variables.

SFA and other applications

A summary of studies using SFA and other parametric techniques is provided in the appendix. Gravelle *et al.* (2003) re-estimate the WHO cross-county estimates, not finding a satisfactory model. Bryce *et al.* (2000) use SFA and fixed effects regression (as well as DEA) on 585 HMOs in the American on an unbalanced panel from 1985 to 1994, concluding that different models lead to different results and model selection can influence efficiency ranking. Defelice and Bradford (1997) use SFA on 1984 and 1985 data on American primary-care physicians from solo practices to large HMOs. They conclude that differences in efficiency are not due to solo or group practice, levels of inefficiency are similar.

Giuffrida and Gravelle (2001) use SFA, corrected ordinary least squares (COLS), and canonical regression (as well as DEA) on 90 UK FHSAs. COLS scores range from 0.868 to 0.915, stochastic frontier scores range from 0.872 to 0.982 and canonical scores range from 0.80 to 0.81 (DEA scores range from 0.904 to 0.994). They conclude scores are correlated within the different methods, but not as highly between the methods. Another interesting application is that by Kathuria and Sanker (2005) of Indian state public health systems, who find a range of inefficiencies.

Folland and Hofler (2001) use SFA on a sample of 791 US hospitals in 1985 concluding that group mean inefficiencies are robust to variations in methods, and that individual hospital ranks are not highly correlated, however, not-for-profit hospitals were more efficient than for-profit. Li and Rosenman (2001) use SFA on a panel of 90 USA (Washington State) hospitals between 1988 and 1993 finding average inefficiency of 33 per cent, with hospitals with a higher casemix index, or more beds, being less efficient, while for-profit hospitals were more efficient. Mobley (1998) uses SFA (results used as part of tobit regression) on 1984 and 1990 data on 455 and 404 Californian (USA) hospitals serving Medicaid patients, commenting that distributional effects led to efficiency gains post-reform (the 1982 California Medicaid Reform Act increased competition and awarded contracts to more efficient providers), however, costs rose for public hospitals, as uncompensated care burdens rose. Zuckerman *et al.* (1994) apply SFA to 1,600 USA hospitals in 1986/7 (28 per cent public) finding, for pooled data, an inefficiency of 0.132 for teaching, 0.135 for non-teaching, 0.141 for public, 0.144 for proprietary and 0.129 for private not-for-profit. This means potential inefficiency costs of $31 billion.

Rosko (1999) uses SFA then tobit on 1994 data on 3,262 USA hospitals, using three error distribution terms. He finds mean inefficiency ranging from 0.202 to 0.255, depending on the distribution of the error. It is concluded that inefficiency scores are robust with respect to assumptions regarding the distribution of the error term, and that for-profit status is associated with increased inefficiency, with for-profits being less efficient than not-for-profits. Rosko (2001a), using SFA and fixed effects models on an unbalanced panel of 1,631 hospitals over the period 1990 to 1996 and found a mean inefficiency score of 0.153 (range 0.125 to 0.175). Efficiency increased over the period, with an inverse relationship between HMO penetration and inefficiency; the same was the case with industry concentration. Inefficiency was positively related to for-profit status. Rosko and Chilingerian (1999) run SFA on 195 Pennsylvania (USA) acute-care hospitals in 1989, finding inefficiency ranges from 3.5 to 17 per cent. X-Efficiency increases with regulatory and payment pressure, but declines with competitive pressure. Inefficiency is also associated with industrial concentration. Rosko (2001b) uses SFA on 1,966 USA short-term community hospitals, finding inefficiency of 12.96 per cent. Increases in managed-care penetration, dependence on Medicare and Medicaid, being in a multi-hospital system, location in a competitive area, and the pool of uncompensated care being greater are all associated with decreased inefficiency. Not-for-profit ownership increased inefficiency.

Chirikos (1998, 1998/9) uses SFA on 186 Florida hospitals (USA) from 1982 to 1993 and estimated that efficiency rose 1.6 per cent per year, stating that inefficiency levels are high with costs exceeding the frontier by 15 per cent. SFA is seen as yielding plausible estimates of efficiency, but caution needs to be exercised, not only in modelling inputs and outputs, but specifying the structure of the cost model (for example the distribution of the efficiency term). SFA is most useful in tandem with other techniques. Chirikos and Sear (2000) using the same sample of hospitals found SFA results ranging from 0.75 to 0.85, concluding that DEA and SFA yield convergent results overall, but divergent results for individual hospitals. Vitaliano and Toren (1996) applied SFA to 219 general-care hospitals in New York (USA) in 1991 (85 per cent not-for-profit, 10 per cent government, 5 per cent for-profit). Average inefficiency is 18 per cent. Hospitals with larger Medicare populations are more efficient, hospitals with more than 300 beds are more efficient, and reimbursement restrictions may help. Unionization seems to contribute to inefficiency. Butler and Li (2005) found inefficiency and decreasing returns to scale in 57 US rural hospitals, and McKay *et al.* (2002/3) in a very large sample of over 4,000 USA hospitals found not-for-profits to be most efficient (14 per cent inefficiency), and for-profits least efficient (16 per cent inefficiency). Rosko (2004) found inefficiency increased with for-profit status and Medicare share, and fell with HMO penetration, for 616 American hospitals. Rosko and Proenca (2005) found mean inefficiency of just under 15 per cent in a large sample (1,368) of urban general hospitals.

Jacobs (2001) uses SFA, OLS (and DEA) on a sample of up to 232 UK NHS hospital trusts. The OLS mean ranges from 0.541 to 0.611, the SFA mean from 0.645 to 0.936, and the DEA mean from 0.831 to 0.876. The author concludes differences across methods may be due to noise and data deficiencies, with actual inefficiency savings being modest. Street (2003) uses SFA on 226 acute hospitals in the UK finding efficiency ranging from 0.87 to 0.90. Linna (1998) uses SFA (and Malmquist indices) for 43 hospitals in Finland from 1988 to 1994. SFA scores were between 0.88 and 0.90, finding a moderate correlation with Malmquist scores. Linna and Häkkinen (1998) use SFA (and DEA) on a sample of 48 acute hospitals in Finland in 1994 finding SFA scores between 0.86 and 0.93, and DEA scores between 0.84 and 0.89, concluding that the choice of modelling affects results. A weight-restricted DEA model was correlated with a parametric model. There was broad agreement across the models, that they should be used together.

Wagstaff (1989) uses SFA on 49 Spanish public hospitals from 1977 to 1981 estimating inefficiency on a cross-section (1979) at 28 per cent, stating it is likely that only 10 per cent of this was actually inefficiency, and this may not be significant. Panel data suggests that a third of the variation may be inefficiency which may be as high as 42 per cent of average costs. It is concluded that more than one estimation technique should be applied. Wagstaff and López (1996) using 1988 to 1991 data on 43 Spanish public and private hospitals find average inefficiency of 58 per cent, with public hospitals having a higher level of inefficiency (75 per cent) than private hospitals (56 per cent). This is potentially due to the fact that private hospitals can vary hours of work, and negotiate pay.

There was mild evidence of economies of scope. Paul (2002) uses data on 208 Australian hospitals finding higher results in large urban facilities.

Hofler and Rungeling (1994) use SFA on 1985 data on 1,079 nursing homes in the USA. They estimate allocative and technical inefficiency using homothetic production and cost frontiers. They find for-profit homes to have lower costs, and in allocative inefficiency terms staff and capital are overcapitalized. Costs are 5.8 per cent higher than efficient. Technical inefficiency is estimated at 2 per cent, giving overall inefficiency of approximately 8 per cent. They conclude potential gains to be small. Nursing home-type applications in Europe include that by Crivelli *et al.* (2002) who found ownership was not related to inefficiency, and Farsi and Filippini (2004) who found private homes were more efficient.

Dismuke and Sena (1999) use SFA (and Malmquist indices) on Portuguese district and central hospital diagnostic technology from 1992 to 1994, for cerebrovascular disorders and heart failure, with live and deceased discharges as outputs. Technical efficiency increased for computerized axial tomography use, echocardiogram use had declining technical efficiency in districts and increasing technical efficiency in central hospitals, and electrocardiogram use was stable for central hospitals and declining for districts. It is noted that technical efficiency increases have not been accompanied by increases in quality. Bosmans and Fecher (1995) use SFA and OLS on 1990 to 1991 data on Belgian inpatients affiliated with two main insurance organizations in 85 to 185 hospitals (depending on specialty). Efficiency by specialty was 0.778 for ear, nose, and throat, 0.615 for respiratory, 0.536 for circulatory, 0.621 for digestive, 0.713 for musculoskeletal, and 0.711 for gynaecology. It is noted that public care is more efficient than private, and non-teaching more efficient than teaching, and regression shows size, area, ownership and management are all related to efficiency.

Grytten and Rongen (2000) use SFA (compared to a deterministic frontier) for Norwegian dental services from 1986 to 1992, with inefficiency ranging from 0.05 to 0.11 in the SFA model and 0.14 to 0.49 in the deterministic model.

Giuffrida *et al.* (2000) use random and fixed effects models on 1989/90 to 1994/5 UK FHSA (primary care) data. Both models suggesting economies of scale, but little evidence of economies of scope. Although inefficiency is treated cautiously in the paper, they estimate one high-cost authority to be significantly above the mean. Puig-Junoy and Ortún (2004) look at 180 primary-care teams in Spain finding public teams more efficient than contracted-out teams. Gaynor and Pauly (1990) estimate the efficiency of 6,353 primary care physicians in the USA, using traditional and behavioural functions and estimating technical efficiency at 0.66, with coefficients similar across specifications. Incentives may affect quantity produced, but not technical efficiency. Relating compensation to productivity does not increase production.

Grosskopf *et al.* (1990) use maximum likelihood estimation to estimate a frontier and nurse productivity in 91 community health facilities (not-for-profit, non-teaching hospitals) in California in 1983. Their results suggest overemployment of registered nurses relative to licensed practical nurses, and also evidence of monopsony power.

Summary and conclusions

Recently, the number of studies which seek to measure health service efficiency and productivity have increased dramatically and there is already an extensive literature that reflects this growing interest (Hollingsworth and Street 2006). However, because of the distinct features of the health-care industry, research in this field should be reviewed cautiously and the results of different studies should be interpreted and used carefully. The inability to measure the *real* output of the health-care industry, changes in health status and the low quality of available data lead to problems. As Newhouse (1994) notes, these techniques work better when the product is homogeneous and unidimensional (for example kilowatts per hour in the electricity industry) and not multiple and heterogeneous as in health care. In addition, as the same author notes, it is almost certain that health industry studies suffer from omitted variable bias. The techniques used to overcome these problems have been often criticized. To complicate matters, the estimated results may be sensitive to changes in the basic assumptions or specifications of the models used and the characteristics of the environment in which the units operate. Thus, the results may only be valid for the units under investigation and consequently may be difficult to generalize.

This review of results should be treated with caution and it is suggested that most useful in identifying trends. In the studies reviewed here, little sensitivity analysis or statistical testing has been undertaken. This is due to the fact that, unlike econometrics, there are no accepted methods for proceeding (for example formulating model specification) and no standard statistical tests for results, although these are under development (Cooper *et al.* 2004).

It may be most productive in health services performance measurement to use disaggregated observational data and concentrate on homogeneous and small segments of the health-care system. In this case, the input–output number decreases and inputs as well as outputs are better defined and more accurately measured. Thus, it is more likely that the proxies used for inputs and outputs will be closer to the actual values and the calculated efficiency measures will be more accurate.

The accuracy of the estimated performance measures depends on the use of an appropriate and well-specified model, the inclusion of the relevant inputs and outputs and the use of accurate data. The choice of an appropriate model is an important methodological issue. Different approaches have advantages and disadvantages and the choice of the most appropriate estimation method should depend on the type of organizations under investigation, the perspective taken and the quality of the available data.

DEA is a non-parametric method and does not assume a functional form for the frontier. Hence, it can accommodate wide-ranging behaviour in applications. However, measurement errors can bias results. Thus, DEA may be best employed for applications having relatively small potential measurement errors. A further line of enquiry is the impact of sample size on efficiency scores and the effects of model mis-specification (Smith 1997), and also, of more advanced DEA techniques which allow for the ranking of efficient, as well as inefficient, units. Given the limitations of DEA and SFA, it may be that they are best employed together, when possible. If both methods suggest similar directions for results then the validity of such findings is enhanced.

Because of the special features of health services provision, these methods must be tested and developed further in order to provide reliable results that can be utilized in management and policy making. At present, they are most useful in identifying general industry trends, investigating the association of performance with managerial and organizational characteristics and in testing general hypotheses, rather than in providing final statements about individual organizational efficiency. This is the context in which we interpret the results from studies reported here and it should be noted again that results implying that public rather than private provision of health-care is more efficient should be viewed in the context that the studies in our sample may not be genuinely comparable. Nevertheless the results may have policy implications and may reflect the organizational structure of health-care delivery in different countries. In the USA, an important finding is that public hospitals in general outperform private hospitals, and it may also be important that European hospitals outperform USA hospitals. The implication of both of these findings may be that the public provision of health care is more efficient. This may have important policy implications.

There is a danger that the analysis of particular sectors is undertaken without due attention to the problematic areas highlighted here, such as specification of the model and the sensitivity of results to changes in assumptions, as well as taking account of statistical developments. There is a need for research to be undertaken both at methodological and applied levels. Although a few studies make use of state-of-the-art methods, too many studies simply report the efficiency scores of health-care institutions. There is potential for futher work on market structure, concentration and the scope of production.

Appendix

Summary of studies on nonparametric hospital efficiency

Hospital type	*Country*	*Number*	*Author(s)*	*Efficiency scores*
Federal/Defence/ Veterans' administration	USA	284	Bannick and Ozcan (1995)	Defence mean: 0.87 VA mean: 0.78
	USA	89	Burgess and Wilson (1993)	Range: 0.93–0.97
	USA	2,246	Burgess and Wilson (1996)	Efficiency scores, mean: VA 0.87 Non-Fed 0.82 FP 0.83 NFP 0.83
	USA	132 VA, 1413 non-VA	Burgess and Wilson (1998)	Inefficiency: Overall 13.6%; local govt 11.2%; non-profit 15.1%; profit 12%; VA 8.2%
	USA	93	Hao and Pegels[6] (1994)	Range: Teaching: 0.54–1 Non-teaching:0.55–1
	USA	131 hospitals in 1998, 121 in 2001	Harrison and Ogniewski (2005)	1998 0.86 (s.d. 0.11) 2001 0.86 (s.d. 0.11)
	USA	3,780	Ozcan and Bannick (1994)	Means: Army: 0.94 Air Force: 0.96 Navy: 0.91 Dept. of Defence: 0.95
For-profit/Not-for-profit	USA	160	Bitran and Valor-Sabatier (1987)	NFP Mean: 0.60
	USA	360	Ferrier and Valdmanis (1996)	CE: 0.676 TE:0.787 AE:0.861 SE: 0.893
	USA	123	Byrnes and Valdmanis (1994)	AE: 0.73 TE: 0.84 SE: 0.94
	USA	82	Grosskopf and Valdmanis (1987)	Pooled, means: Public: 0.94 NFP: 0.91 Separate, means: Public: 0.96 NFP: 0.94
	USA	108	Grosskopf and Valdmanis (1993)	Range: Casemix adjusted: 0.86–0.88

(Continued)

Hospital type	*Country*	*Number*	*Author(s)*	*Efficiency scores*
				Casemix un-adjusted: 0.85–0.86
	USA	60	Morey *et al.* (1990)	Public mean: 0.95 NFP mean: 0.65
	USA	85	Ozcan *et al.* (1996a)	Overall mean: 0.65 FP: 0.61 NFP: 0.72
	USA	41	Valdmanis (1990)	Public: 0.98 NFP: 0.88
	USA	41	Valdmanis (1992)	Means, range: Public: 0.97–1 NFP: 0.83–0.94 Scale efficiency: Public: 0.79–1 NFP: 0.92–0.97
Acute	USA	52	Borden (1988)	Mean scores range: 0.95–0.99
	USA	89	Chen *et al.* (2005)	VRS TE: 0.81–0.85 CRS TE: 0.75–0.80 SE: 0.93–0.94
	USA	348	Mobly and Magnussen (2002)	TE: 0.908
	USA	186	Chirikos and Sear (2000)	Mean: 0.801
	USA	189	Chirikos and Sear (1994)	Mean: 0.65
	USA	105	Dittman *et al.* (1991)	Range: 0.49–1
	USA	40	Ozcan (1992)	Mean range: 0.51–0.92
	UK	75	Hollingsworth and Parkin (1995)	Range: 0.63–1
	UK	23	Kerr *et al.* (1999)	Means: Larger: 0.94 Smaller: 0.82–0.91
	Norway	46	Magnussen (1996)	Mean range: 0.93–0.94
	Spain	94	Dalmau-Matarrodona and Puig-Junoy (1998)	Mean: 0.989
	Finland	48	Linna and Häkkinen (1998)	Efficiency scores between 0.84 and 0.89. Broad agreement with DEA models
	UK	75	Parkin and Hollingsworth (1997)	Mean range: 0.85–0.91
Public	Taiwan	1996–483 1997–473	Chang (2004)	Efficiency range: 0.58–0.93. Private hospitals more efficient, may be down to casemix or quality

(Continued)

Hospital type	*Country*	*Number*	*Author(s)*	*Efficiency scores*
	Ireland	33	Gannon (2005)	Efficiency range: 0.94–0.97
	USA	1998–280 2001–245	Harrison *et al.* (2004)	Means: 1998: 0.68 2001: 0.79
	Kenya	54	Kirigia *et al.* (2002)	TE: 0.956 SE: 0.968
	Finland	114	Laine *et al.* (2005a)	Mean: 0.72
	China	6	Liu and Mills (2005)	1978: 0.97 1997: 0.73
	Norway	51	Martinussen and Midttun (2004)	1999: 0.827 2000: 0.835 2001: 0.841
	Thailand	68	Valdmanis *et al.* (2004)	Mean: 0.954 (s.d. 0.69)
	UK	44	Hollingsworth and Parkin (2003)	Mean: 0.85–0.86
	South Africa	56	Kirigia *et al.* (2000)	TE: 0.906
General	USA	1,535	Ozcan and Lynch (1992)	Mean: 0.88
	USA	80	Chern and Wan (2000)	Range: 0.76–0.8
	USA/Norway	190/50	Mobley and Magnussen (1998)	TE: Norway: 0.937 USA FP urban: 0.884 USA NFP urban: 0.936 USA NFP non-urban: 0.917
	Taiwan	6	Chang (1998)	Range: 0.88 – 0.987
	Greece	98	Athanassopoulis (1999)	Production efficiency: means 0.67–0.86 Cost-efficiency means: 0.62–0.72
	Greece	91	Giokas (2001)	Mean: 0.751
	UK	232	Jacobs (2001)	Mean range: 0.645 – 0.936
	UK	23	McCallion *et al.* (1999)	Means: CE: Large: 0.672 Small: 0.601 AE: Large: 0.715 Small: 0.713 TE: Large: 0.939 Small: 0.842 SE: Large: 0.949 Small: 0.913

(Continued)

Hospital type	*Country*	*Number*	*Author(s)*	*Efficiency scores*
	UK	23	McKillop *et al.* (1999)	Range: Large: 0.933–0.951 Small: 0.842–0.909
	UK	27	Tsai and Molinero (2002)	Mean: 0.938
	Turkey	—	Sahin and Ozcan (2000)	Mean: 0.879
	Spain	75	Lopez-Valcarcel and Barber Perez (1996)	Overall range: 0.92–0.95 Overall scale: 0.96–0.98
Non-specific	USA	360	Ferrier and Valdmanis (1996)	CE: 0.68 TE: 0.79 AE: 0.87 SE: 0.89
	USA	254	Grosskopf *et al.* (2004)	TE: CRS 0.6, VRS 0.71 SE: 0.85
	USA	123	Byrnes and Valdmanis (1989)	NFP: TE: 0.87 AE: 0.83 OE: 0.72
	USA	27	Morey *et al.* (2000)	Mean: 0.906
	USA	27	O'Neill (1998)	Non-teaching SPE: 1.25 Teaching SPE: 1.15
	USA	7	Sherman (1984)	Range: 0.88–1
	USA	55	Maindiratta (1990)	Efficiency range: 0.51–1 Scale efficiency range: 0.51–1
	USA	105	Morey and Dittman (1996)	Mean: 0.95
	USA	16	Nunamaker (1983)	Range: 0.91–1
	USA	170	White and Ozcan (1996)	Church: 0.81 Secular: 0.76
	USA	20	Harris (2000)	Range: 0.81–0.85
	USA	236 teaching, 556 non-teaching	Grosskopf *et al.* (2001)	Non-teaching: 0.71 Teaching 0.65
	USA	22	Young (1992)	Range: 0.40–1
	Canada	168	Gruca and Nath (2001)	Means: Secular: 0.75 Religious: 0.67 Govt: 0.70 Rural: 0.77 Urban: 0.72 Small: 0.77 Large: 0.69.
	Belgium	34	Beguin (2001)	Range: 0.39–0.54 (FDH)

(Continued)

Hospital type	*Country*	*Number*	*Author(s)*	*Efficiency scores*
	Spain	132 & 149	Prior and Solà (2000)	Means: Diversified: 0.89 & 0.93 Specialized: 0.87 & 0.88
	Spain	50	Prior (1996)	Inefficiency: 3%
	USA	38	Ferrier and Valdmanis (2004)	1996: OE 0.79 TE 0.88 SE 0.9 1997: OE 0.8 TE 0.88 SE 0.87
	USA	53	O'Neill and Dexter (2004)	Median: 0.99
	Ghana	17	Osei *et al.* (2005)	VRS TE: 0.61 (s.d. 0.12) SE: 0.81 (s.d. 0.25)
	Oman	20	Ramanathan (2005)	CRS mean: 0.872 VRS mean: 0.926
	Botswana	13	Ramanathan *et al.* (2003)	Mean: 0.99
	Germany and Switzer-land	105 German and 251 Swiss	Steinmann *et al.* (2004)	German range 0.79–0.828, Swiss range: 0.719–0.752
	Germany	2,020–2,145	Helmig and Lapsley (2001)	Range: 0.769–1
	France and USA		Dervaux (2004)	France inefficiency: 19.8% (SE 9.5%, TE 7.1%, congestion 3.2%) US inefficiency 23.7% (SE 6.3%, TE 14%, congestion 3.4%). Direct comparison difficult.
	Jordan	15	Al-Shammari (1999); Sarkis and Talluri (2002)	Means: 0.867–0.977 [117]; 0.688–0.884 [169]
	South Africa	86	Zere *et al.* (2001)	Mean: 0.74
Psychiatric	USA	506	Ferrier and Valdmanis (2002)	Mean: 0.47 Private NFP: 0.65 Private FP: 0.57 Public: 0.23–0.28

VA	Veterans Administration
LG	Local government
FP	For-profit
NFP	Not-for-profit
Non-Fed	Non-Federal
CE	Cost-efficiency
TE	Technical efficiency
AE	Allocative efficiency
SE	Scale efficiency
SPE	Super efficiency

Summary of studies on non-parametric general health organization efficiency

Organization type	*Country*	*Number*	*Author(s)*	*Efficiency scores*
Cross-country	OECD	—	Puig-Junoy (1998a)	TE: increases 0.59 to 0.72
	OECD	24	Afonso and St Aubyn (2005)	CRS: 0.815 VRS: 0.832–0.946
	OECD	24	Bhat (2005)	Mean: 0.901
	OECD	27	Retzlaff-Roberts *et al.* (2004)	Mean: 0.89–0.958
	Developing countries	51	Alexander *et al.* (2003)	Effic: 1.033–1.036
Health Districts	USA	319	Ozcan (1995)	Range: 0.72–1
	USA	314	Wang *et al.* (1999)	Range: 0.74–0.89
	USA	298	Ozcan *et al.* (1996b)	Range: 0.79–0.90
	USA	25	Ozcan and Cotter (1994)	Govt: 0.8 Joint: 0.5 Private NFP: 0.57
	USA	28	Rosenman *et al.* (1997)	Mean FP: 0.68 Mean NFP: 0.66
	Sweden	26	Gerdtham *et al.* (1999)	Inefficiency: 13%
	UK	15	Hollingsworth and Parkin (1995)	Range: 0.76–1
	UK	15	Parkin and Hollingsworth (1997)	Range: 0.72–1
	UK	189	Thanassoulis *et al.* (1996)	Range: 0.60–1
	UK	85	Salinas-Jiménez and Smith (1996)	Range: 0.73–1
Care Programmes	USA	54	Schinnar *et al.* (1990)	Range: 0.62–0.67
	USA	40	Yeh *et al.* (1997)	Overall mean: 0.60
Primary care	USA	159	Sexton *et al.* (1989a)	Range: 0.66–1
	USA	115	Andes *et al.* (2002)	Mean: 0.39
	USA	156	Roseman and Friesner (2004)	TE: 0.736 AE: 0.913 CE: 0.75 SE: 0.876
	USA	27	Wagner *et al.* (2003)	Range: 0.65–1
	USA	21	Wagner and Shimshak (2000)	Score: 0.903
	Sierra Leone	37	Renner *et al.* (2005)	TE: 0.72 SE: 0.82
	Austria	591	Staat (2003)	Mean: 0.84
	Kenya	32	Kirigia *et al.* (2004)	Mean: TE: 0.8 SE: 0.9
	USA	39	Tyler *et al.* (1995)	Mean: 0.44
	Finland	202	Luoma *et al.* (1996)	Mean: 0.88
	Spain	10	Pina and Torres (1992)	Range: 0.58–1
	USA	36	Rollins *et al.* (2001)	0.801–0.994
	USA	249	Draper *et al.* (2000)	Mean: 0.427

(Continued)

Organization type	*Country*	*Number*	*Author(s)*	*Efficiency scores*
	UK	90	Giuffrida and Gravelle (2001)	TE: 0.98
	Greece	133	Zavras *et al.* (2002)	Range: 0.66–0.808
	UK	52	Szczepura *et al.* (1993)	Range: 0.35–1
Nursing homes	USA	140	Chattopadhyay and Heffley (1994)	Mean: 0.90
	Finland	10	Björkgren *et al.* (2004)	Mean: 0.86–0.87
	Netherlands	71	Blank and Valdmanis (2005)	TE: 1 SE: 1 AE: 0.95 CE: 0.95
	USA	487	Anderson *et al.* (2003)	Mean: 0.72 FP: 0.77 NFP: 0.74
	USA	140	Chattopadhyay and Ray (1996)	Mean NFP: 0.81 Mean FP: 0.94
	USA	372	Fried *et al.* (1998)	Skilled home: 0.38 intermediate: 0.42 diversified: 0.46.
	USA	22	Kleinsorge and Karney (1992)	Range: 0.71–1
	USA	184	Nyman and Bricker (1989)	Mean: 0.89
	USA	296	Nyman *et al.* (1990)	Mean: 0.93
	USA	52	Sexton *et al.* (1989b)	Means range: 0.76–0.78
	USA	324	Ozcan *et al.* (1998ab)	Means: FP: 0.84 NFP: 0.803
	USA	104	Fizel and Nunnikhoven (1993)	Means (all FP): Overall: 0.66 Chain: 0.71 Independent: 0.62
	USA	461	Rosko *et al.* (1995)	Means: FP: 0.82 NFP: 0.71
	USA	990	Fried *et al.* (2002)	With SFA as 3-stage method, mean 0.905.
	Netherlands	232	Kooreman (1994)	CRS Mean: 0.80 COD Mean: 0.94
	Netherlands	—	Blank *et al.* (1996)	Mean: 0.70
	Norway	471	Erlandsen and Førsund (2002)	Input saving 0.76; output increase 0.78; Technical productivity 0.70; scale 0.90–0.93.
	Finland	64	Björkgren *et al.* (2001)	Means: CE: 0.74–0.77 TE 0.85–0.87 AE 0.84–0.89 SE 0.92–0.93

(Continued)

Organization type	*Country*	*Number*	*Author(s)*	*Efficiency scores*
Organ Procurement	USA	64	Ozcan *et al.* (1999)	Overall mean: 0.843
stroke treatment	USA	214	Ozcan (1998b)	Means: More experience: 0.81 Less experience: 0.59–0.61
Mechanical ventilation	USA	62 hospitals, 7,961 patients	O'Neal *et al.* (2002)	IPD: 0.527 Discharges: 0.491
Sinusitis treatment	USA	178 physicians	Pai *et al.* (2000)	Inefficient physicians: 0.71 (metropolitan 0.75, rural 0.66)
	USA	176	Ozcan *et al.* (2000)	Inefficient generalists: 0.71 Inefficient specialists: 0.73
Dental services	UK	100	Buck (2000)	CRS mean: 0.635 VRS mean: 0.673
	USA	279,999 patient encounters	Coppola *et al.* (2003)	Mean: 0.788 (s.d. 0.13)
	Finland	228	Linna *et al.* (2002)	Primal efficiency: mean 0.72–0.81 Cost-efficiency: mean 0.62–0.79
	EU	6 countries	Parkin and Devlin (2003)	Health-care median: 0.848 Oral health median: 0.483
Neonatal care	UK	49	Hollingsworth and Parkin (2001)	Mean: 0.723
Vaccination	Bangladesh	117 sites/ clinics	Valdmanis *et al.* (2003)	CRS TE: 0.33 (s.d. 0.26) VRS TE: 0.50 (s.d. 0.29) SE 0.64 (s.d. 0.27)
Renal care	USA	791 facilities	Ozgen and Ozcan (2002)	TE of inefficient facilities: 0.79
	UK	70 haemodialysis units	Gerard and Roderick (2003)	Mean: 0.9
	Greece	118 haemo-dialysis	Kontodimopoulos and Niakas (2005)	Overall mean: 0.704 (s.d. 0.139)

(Continued)

Organization type	*Country*	*Number*	*Author(s)*	*Efficiency scores*
		Units		Public: 0.65 Private: 0.82
Screening	UK	64	Johnston and Gerard (2001)	Mean: 0.821
Immunization	Australia	23 local authorities	Hollingsworth *et al.* (2002)	Cost-efficiency: 0.689 (rural), 0.816 (urban) Productive efficiency: 0.706 (rural), 0.804 (urban)
Pharmacies	USA	68	Capettini *et al.* (1985)	Range: 0.44–0.98

FP For-profit
NFP Not-for-profit
CRS Constant returns to scale
COD Constant or decreasing returns

Summary of studies on productivity (Malmquist) analysis

Organization type	*Country*	*No. of units*	*Author(s)*	*Results*
General health	International	19	Färe *et al.* (1997)	Some evidence of productivity growth when using outcomes rather than outputs
	International	140	Hollingsworth and Wildman (2003)	Examination of sub-samples may be most useful
Primary care	USA	585	Bryce *et al.* (2000)	Different models lead to different results
	UK	90	Giuffrida (1999)	There is a small productivity improvement, but little scope for more
Opthalmology	Sweden	20	Tambour (1997)	Positive changes in productivity
Hospital	USA	1545	Burgess and Wilson (1995)	Technical regress in Federal units
	Greece	30	Maniadakis and Thanassoulis (2004)	Malmquist: 0.97 Cost Malmquist: 0.96
	Spain	20	Sola and Prior (2001)	Malmquist: 1.3, change in quality 0.98, TE change 0.98, technology change 1.36.

(Continued)

Organization type	*Country*	*No. of units*	*Author(s)*	*Results*
				Technology driving global fall in index
	Spain	68	Ventura *et al.* (2004)	TE: 0.829 Pure TE: 0.89 SE: 0.93
	USA	186	Chirikos and Sear (2000)	Convergent results to DEA for industry, divergent for individual hospitals
	UK	44	Hollingsworth and Parkin (2003)	Overall change: 1.07, technology change dominated for acute sub-sample
	UK	232	Jacobs (2001)	Differences across methods (DEA and OLS) may be due to noise/data deficiencies Inefficiency savings may be modest
	UK	75	Maniadakis *et al.* (1999)	Productivity progress is dominated by technological change
	UK	75	Maniadakis and Thanassoulis (2000)	There is cost-efficiency and allocative efficiency progress
	UK	—	McCallion *et al.* (2000)	Smaller hospitals increase productivity more than large hospitals
	Austria	22	Sommersguter-Reichmann (2000)	Productivity increases due to technology improvement
	Finland	43	Linna (1998)	Scores are moderately correlated with Malmquist scores
	Sweden	17	Färe *et al.* (1994)	Variation in productivity
	South Africa	86	Zere *et al.* (2001)	Productivity declined 12%, driven by technology regress
Diagnostic technology	Portugal	62,136 dis-charges	Dismuke and Sena (2001)	Prospective payment systems have positive impact on productivity, where a measure of quality is included
Ophthalmology	Sweden	20	Tambour (1997)	Overall productivity change is driven by changes in technology

(Continued)

Organization type	*Country*	*No. of units*	*Author(s)*	*Results*
	Sweden	34 departments	Roos (2002)	
Dental	Norway	14	Grytten and Rongen (2000)	Inefficiency ranges from 0.05 to 0.11
Pharmacy	Sweden	—	Löthgren and Tambour (1999)	Productivity progress
	Spain	80	Gonzalez and Gascon (2004)	CRS: 0.68 VRS: 0.84 SE: 0.81 Technology change minimal
	Sweden	74	Färe *et al.* (2002)	Improvement overall, consumer satisfaction can affect results
	Sweden	42	Färe *et al.* (1992)	Over nine time periods, there were seven periods of improvement and two of regress
	Sweden	257	Färe *et al.* (1995)	Quality matters when measuring productivity change.
Dialysis	USA	140	Ozgen and Ozcan (2004)	Mean: 0.918 Technology regress, efficiency increase, may mean increase in quality
Primary care	Austria	591	Staat (2003)	Productivity index 1.05, individual efficiency improves (0.98), technology falls (1.08)

Summary of studies using SFA/parametric techniques

Organization type	*Country*	*No. of units*	*Author(s)*	*Results*
Cross country States	WHO	141 countries (1993–1997), 50 more in 1997	Gravelle *et al.* (2003)	It is premature to reach conclusions on the production of health, given available methods
	India	16 state public	Kathuria and Sanker (2005)	Inefficiency range: 0.686–1 in fixed

(Continued)

Organization type	*Country*	*No. of units*	*Author(s)*	*Results*
		health systems		effects, 0.725–1 in random effects, 0.719–1 in maximum likelihood
Hospitals	USA	90	Li and Rosenman (2001)	Average inefficiency 33%
	Holland	General hospitals in 27 health care regions	Blank and Eggink (2004)	TE: 0.86 AE: 0.92 There is technical regress through time
	USA	57 rural hospitals	Butler and Li (2005)	42% inefficient 23% decreasing returns to scale
	Ireland	33	Gannon (2005)	Various models, including time-varying, and compares with DEA, concluding that DEA is not controlling for certain factors
	USA	4,075	McKay *et al.* (2002/3)	Inefficiency: All: 0.141–0.148 NFP: 0.135–0.141 FP: 0.163–0.167 Govt.: 0.147–0.156
	USA	616	Rosko (2004)	1990 inefficiency: 14.35% 1999 inefficiency: 11.78% Decreases associated with HMO penetration and time; increases associated with FP status and Medicare share
	USA	1,368 urban general hospitals	Rosko and Proenca (2005)	Mean inefficiency: 0.148. Network/system users were more efficient
	UK	226	Street (2003)	COLS: 0.694 SF: 0.874–0.903. COLS overstates inefficiency if hospitals are prone to random events, and choice of technique affects ranking

(Continued)

Organization type	*Country*	*No. of units*	*Author(s)*	*Results*
	USA	382	Koop *et al.* (1997)	Mean effic: 0.85 NFP: 0.86 FP: 0.79 Govt: 0.87 Model specification is robust (Bayesian SFA)
	USA	186	Chirikos (1998a, 1998b)	Inefficiency: 15%
	USA	91	Grosskopf *et al.* (1990)	Evidence of monopsony power
	USA	3,262	Rosko (1999)	Mean inefficiency: 0.202–0.255
	USA	1,631	Rosko (2001a)	Mean inefficiency: 0.153
	USA	1,966	Rosko (2001b)	Inefficiency: 12.96%
	USA	195	Rosko and Chilingerian (1999)	Inefficiency range: 3.5–17%
	USA	455 & 404	Mobley (1998)	Distributional effects led to post-reform efficiency gains
	USA	219	Vitaliano and Toren (1996)	Average inefficiency: 18%
	USA	1,600	Zuckerman *et al.* (1994)	Inefficiency: 0.132 for teaching, 0.135 for non-teaching, 0.141 for public, 0.144 for proprietary, 0.129 for private NFP
	Spain	49	Wagstaff (1989)	Inefficiency: 28% (only 10% actual inefficiency)
	Spain	43	Wagstaff and López (1996)	Inefficiency: 58%, public more inefficient than Private
	Finland	48	Linna and Häkkinen (1998)	Efficiency scores between 0.86 and 0.93. Broad agreement with DEA Models
	USA	791	Folland and Hofler (2001)	Not-for-profit more efficient than for-profit
	Australia	208	Paul (2002)	Higher results for larger facilities and acute facilities in urban areas.

(Continued)

Organization type	*Country*	*No. of units*	*Author(s)*	*Results*
				Efficiency higher with greater capital base, and lower with higher levels of personal care
	Finland	43	Linna (1998)	Scores are moderately correlated with Malmquist scores
Nursing homes	USA	1,079	Hofler and Rungeling (1994)	Allocative inefficiency 5.8%; technical inefficiency 2%
	USA	653	Anderson *et al.* (1999)	Bayesian SFA Overall effic.: 0.69 Indep: 0.784 FP: 0.901 NFP: 0.725
	Switzerland	886	Crivelli *et al.* (2002)	Median inefficiency: 13%. Ownership not significantly related to inefficiency
	Switzerland	36	Farsi and Filippini (2004)	Private NFP are more efficient than public by 3%. There are potential scale economies
	Finland	122 Institutional care wards for the elderly	Laine *et al.* (2005b)	Technical inefficiency: 16%
Primary care	USA	—	Defelice and Bradford (1997)	Levels of inefficiency are similar between solo and group Practices
	Spain	180 primary care health teams	Puig-Junoy and Ortun (2004)	Overall effic: 0.92 Public: 0.928 Contracted out: 0.837
	USA	6,353	Gaynor and Pauly (1990)	TE: 0.66
	UK	90	Giuffrida and Gravelle (2001)	Stochastic scores are correlated within methods, but not highly between methods (COLS and DEA)

(Continued)

Organization type	*Country*	*No. of units*	*Author(s)*	*Results*
Diagnostic technology	Portugal	—	Dismuke and Sena (1999)	SFA and Malmquist, with SFA results finding differing efficiency levels for differing technologies
Pharmacy	USA	—	Okunade (2001)	Biased and pure technical change Effects
specialties	Belgium	—	Bosmans and Fecher (1995)	Public care is more efficient, non-teaching hospitals more efficient than teaching

6 Advanced applications and recent developments

Introduction

This chapter will highlight certain areas in which there may be a deficit of research. Based on our in-depth knowledge of current practice in this area, our literature review in Chapter 5, and our own research in progress, we can postulate the following areas that seek to address some of these areas of deficit.

1 *Comparison of the different methods of analysis and their policy implications:* Should, as indicated in Chapter 5, different methods be used alongside each other as a means of validating analysis? Here stochastic frontiers and DEA methods are compared in their application to both cost and production frontier analysis using data we are currently analysing. This will include testing alternative model specifications, and examination of the robustness and properties of the efficiency measures generated. Critically, we will explore the appropriateness of alternative techniques under alternative study assumptions, settings and perspectives. This data set extends over a number of time periods, so we will also present and discuss alternative approaches for time-series productivity analysis in health services, and the relative merits of those alternatives.
2 *Economies of scale and scope:* We will examine the impact on efficiency of the size of operation of a health-care 'provider unit', and the scope of different services offered – is it more efficient to specialize in a particular service, or diversify and jointly produce a number of different outputs?
3 *Weight restrictions:* Within the modelling of efficiency it is possible that different variables may be perceived to be more important than others, for example within a hospital it may be that teaching is seen as more important than providing a minor injury service. If so, there are means of restricting the weights given to variables within the analysis so that differing levels of importance are attached to different variables. We will explore whether the methods of doing this are valid, their basis in theory and whether results can inform policy choices.
4 *The efficient production of health:* Applications of efficiency measurement to date have, in the main, estimated the efficiency of the production of

health care. As discussed in Chapter 2, health care is just one input into the production of health. We will look at the efficiency of the production of health using data on oral health and health care in order to establish what the impact of the efficient production of oral health care is on the efficient production of oral health. Consequent modelling issues will also be discussed.

5 *Analysis of different health-care measures:* Most applications of efficiency modelling to date have been in the hospital sector. We will extend the application of efficiency measurement techniques, introducing quality-adjusted health-care *outcome* variables into analysis that has in the main previously made use of *output* variables.

Comparison of the different methods of analysis and their policy implications

As discussed in Chapter 4, the choice of model used can be critical to the results obtained. Within, as well as between methods, there are a wide range of configurations for models. Unfortunately, when using non-stochastic methods there are no standard means of assessing if a model is correctly specified. To some extent this can be overcome using extensive sensitivity analysis (Parkin and Hollingsworth 1997) as described in Chapter 4. However, even when the appropriate model has been specified there are several methods of analysis which can then be undertaken: DEA is just one means of analysis.

Even within methods there are many different options, for example should the model have constant returns to scale (CRS) or variable returns to scale (VRS)? The underlying model may help us decide; for example, VRS may be appropriate for estimating the relationship between country-level health indicators and Gross Natural Product (Gravelle *et al.* 2001) and it is generally assumed the relationship between health-care expenditure and health is concave (Culyer and Wagstaff 1993; Hollingsworth and Wildman 2003).

There is also the choice of whether to use an output maximization or input minimization model. Conceptually health outcomes are endogenous to a system or an individual, countries (or individuals) may therefore wish to maximize health, and an output maximization model would be appropriate for a *production of health* model. This contrasts with a *production of health-care* model, where outputs, for example, for a hospital, can be assumed to be exogenously determined (or for an emergency department may be randomly determined). Therefore you would be justified using an input minimization model.

When are weight restrictions justified? Again, this depends on what is being modelled. Restricting weights in DEA takes away what many think of as its major benefit, the freedom of units to allocate their own weights to maximize their performance. However, there may be certain circumstances where a unit may wish to ensure a certain service is seen as vital by, for example, hospital managers does not receive a near-zero weight, something that can happen in DEA. Weight restrictions will be discussed in more detail below.

An example is useful in illustrating how different methods can be used in tandem to validate efficiency measurement. The following is from Hollingsworth and Wildman (2003) where the WHO efficiency indices of 140 countries health are re-estimated. Parametric models, non-parametric models and stochastic frontier models are run in tandem and compared.

Parametric models

The WHO league tables of countries ranked by efficiency indices provides no information as to how countries have changed over time; that is, they are time invariant. An extension of their modelling using a time-variant parametric model, using the estimator of Cornwell *et al.* (1990), demonstrates how efficiency changes over time (see Table 6.1). It can be seen that average efficiency increases over time but countries with the lowest levels of efficiency have lower efficiency over time, as illustrated by the increase in the standard deviation.

Stratification of samples can produce insights into trends and indicate what is actually driving efficiency. Hollingsworth and Wildman (2003) estimate the OECD and non-OECD subsamples, which may be more appropriate than examining the whole sample in terms of like comparisons. Even though it is found that

Table 6.1 Parametric efficiency estimation.

	Min.	*Max.*	*Mean*	*Std. dev.*
Time-invariant				
All	0.468	1	0.815	0.137
OECD	0.823	1	0.919	0.05
non-OECD	0.466	1	0.784	0.139
Time-varying				
All				
1993	0.479	1	0.812	0.134
1994	0.475	1	0.813	0.135
1995	0.468	1	0.815	0.136
1996	0.455	1	0.815	0.138
1997	0.443	1	0.819	0.14
OECD				
1993	0.819	1	0.917	0.052
1994	0.821	1	0.917	0.051
1995	0.822	1	0.918	0.051
1996	0.824	1	0.918	0.05
1997	0.826	1	0.919	0.049
Non-OECD				
1993	0.476	1	0.783	0.136
1994	0.472	1	0.783	0.137
1995	0.467	1	0.784	0.139
1996	0.454	1	0.785	0.141
1997	0.442	1	0.788	0.143

the OECD model is mis-specified, the non-OECD model is not mis-specified and descriptive statistics are presented in Table 6.1. It is evident that the OECD countries appear more efficient over all five years. Stratification of this sample suggests that the relationship between health service expenditure and health is different for OECD countries. This is a good example of the reasons for undertaking meaningful analysis of meaningful data – the most valid techniques used on inappropriate data samples may produce meaningless results, and similarly, invalid techniques used on robust data will produce an equally meaningless set of results.

Non-parametric results

Parametric estimation ensures that at least one country lies on the efficiency frontier but it gives no information as to movements of the frontier, something that DEA-based Malmquist indices measure.

Malmquist indices show that productivity regresses over the panel (see Table 6.2) by 5 per cent overall. Decomposing the indices shows that technological change (i.e. the movement of the frontier itself) drives these overall changes. The individual countries are actually moving closer to the frontier. For the full sample there is efficiency gain in most years, with an overall efficiency gain of 4 per cent. In contrast, the technology to which the samples are comparing themselves (the frontier itself) is regressing by 9 per cent.

Table 6.2 Descriptive statistics – Malmquist – DALE – all countries, n=140.

	Min.	*Max.*	*Mean*	*Std. dev.*
1993–4	0.66	2.67	1.02	0.18
Efficiency				
Technology	0.94	1.06	0.99	0.02
Productivity	0.65	2.61	1.00	0.17
1994–5				
Efficiency	0.26	2.42	1.01	0.15
Technology	0.95	0.99	0.98	0.01
Productivity	0.25	2.35	0.99	0.14
1995–6				
Efficiency	0.58	1.21	0.99	0.06
Technology	0.98	1.05	0.99	0.02
Productivity	0.60	1.25	0.98	0.06
1996–7				
Efficiency	0.65	1.54	1.04	0.09
Technology	0.81	0.98	0.95	0.06
Productivity	0.57	1.31	0.98	0.06
1993–7				
Efficiency	0.75	2.24	1.04	0.16
Technology	0.80	0.93	0.91	0.04
Productivity	0.62	1.93	0.95	0.14

Table 6.3 Descriptive statistics – Malmquist – DALE – OECD, $n=30$.

	Min.	*Max.*	*Mean*	*Std. dev.*
1993–4	0.86	1.02	1.00	0.04
Efficiency				
Technology	0.99	1.06	1.00	0.02
Productivity	0.91	1.02	0.99	0.02
1994–5				
Efficiency	0.68	1.02	0.99	0.06
Technology	0.99	1.01	0.99	0.01
Productivity	0.69	1.00	0.98	0.06
1995–6				
Efficiency	0.99	1.22	1.02	0.04
Technology	0.84	0.99	0.97	0.04
Productivity	0.89	1.02	0.99	0.03
1996–7				
Efficiency	0.99	1.07	1.01	0.01
Technology	0.95	0.99	0.98	0.01
Productivity	0.96	1.01	0.99	0.01
1993–7				
Efficiency	0.60	1.11	1.02	0.09
Technology	0.85	0.95	0.94	0.03
Productivity	0.54	1.02	0.96	0.09

As with the parametric analysis, stratifying samples into potentially more useful sub-samples can highlight differences. Here, OECD and non-OECD and countries patterns can be interpreted (Tables 6.3 and 6.4). It would appear that technologically the OECD countries are not regressing at the same rate as non-OECD countries (6 per cent compared to 10 per cent), with more specific change in the non-OECD countries in 1996/7. Individual country efficiency increases by 2 per cent in the OECD sample and 4 per cent in the non-OECD sample. Productivity is down 4 per cent and 6 per cent in the two samples, respectively. As with the parametric results, it appears the non-OECD countries are driving changes.

The cross-section DEA results (Table 6.5) show a mean efficiency over the five years of around 0.89 for the full sample, 0.97 for the OECD countries, and 0.87 for the non-OECD countries, reflecting the parametric results. Super efficiency models are made use of as a means of differentiating between the efficient countries.

Stochastic frontier results

For the full sample, efficiency was 0.84 (see Table 6.6). Again, when the sample is stratified, the OECD countries have higher efficiency than the non-OECD sample.

Table 6.4 Descriptive statistics – Malmquist – DALE – Non-OECD, $n=110$.

	Min.	*Max.*	*Mean*	*Std. dev.*
1993–4	0.66	2.67	1.02	0.20
Efficiency				
Technology	0.94	1.06	0.99	0.02
Productivity	0.65	2.61	1.01	0.19
1994–5				
Efficiency	0.26	2.43	1.01	0.17
Technology	0.95	0.99	0.98	0.01
Productivity	0.25	2.35	0.99	0.16
1995–6				
Efficiency	0.59	1.21	0.99	0.07
Technology	0.98	1.05	0.99	0.02
Productivity	0.60	1.25	0.98	0.06
1996–7				
Efficiency	0.65	1.54	1.05	0.10
Technology	0.81	0.98	0.94	0.06
Productivity	0.57	1.31	0.98	0.07
1993–7				
Efficiency	0.75	2.25	1.04	0.18
Technology	0.80	0.93	0.90	0.04
Productivity	0.62	1.93	0.94	0.16

Table 6.5 Descriptive statistics – cross-section DEA.

	Min.	*Max.*	*Mean*	*Std. dev.*
All, $n=140$				
Standard DEA				
1993	0.542	1	0.890	0.11
1994	0.544	1	0.886	0.11
1995	0.527	1	0.888	0.11
1996	0.510	1	0.890	0.12
1997	0.491	1	0.892	0.12
Super efficiency				
1993	0.543	1.198	0.893	0.12
1994	0.544	1.357	0.892	0.13
1995	0.527	1.353	0.893	0.12
1996	0.515	1.365	0.894	0.13
1997	0.491	1.309	0.894	0.13
OECD, $n=30$				
Standard DEA				
1993	0.902	1	0.967	0.03
1994	0.912	1	0.968	0.02
1995	0.916	1	0.969	0.02
1996	0.915	1	0.972	0.02
1997	0.914	1	0.971	0.02
Super efficiency				
1993	0.902	1.045	0.969	0.03
1994	0.912	1.040	0.970	0.03

Table 6.5 (continued)

	Min.	*Max.*	*Mean*	*Std. dev.*
1995	0.916	1.038	0.972	0.03
1996	0.915	1.029	0.974	0.03
1997	0.914	1.025	0.973	0.03
Non-OECD, $n=110$				
Standard DEA				
1993	0.542	1	0.874	0.12
1994	0.544	1	0.869	0.12
1995	0.527	1	0.872	0.12
1996	0.510	1	0.872	0.12
1997	0.490	1	0.874	0.13
Super efficiency				
1993	0.542	1.197	0.876	0.13
1994	0.544	1.357	0.875	0.14
1995	0.527	1.353	0.876	0.13
1996	0.511	1.365	0.876	0.14
1997	0.491	1.309	0.876	0.13

Model validity

Spearman rank correlations are used to validate the models in terms of internal (within method) and external (across method) validity, in the same sense as Parkin and Hollingsworth (1997). Correlations between parametric models are high and statistically significant (0.994 and 0.999), which is illustrative of the internal validity of the models. Correlations between non-parametric models are high and significant (between 0.922 and 0.944), suggesting internal validity.

Table 6.6 Descriptive statistics – SFA.

	Min.	*Mean*	*St. dev.*
All, $n=140$			
1993	0.53	0.846	0.116
1994	0.52	0.846	0.116
1995	0.52	0.845	0.117
1996	0.52	0.844	0.117
1997	0.52	0.844	0.118
OECD, $n=30$			
1993	0.86	0.948	0.032
1994	0.86	0.949	0.031
1995	0.87	0.951	0.030
1996	0.87	0.952	0.029
1997	0.88	0.954	0.028
Non-OECD, $n=110$			
1993	0.54	0.833	0.119
1994	0.54	0.832	0.120
1995	0.53	0.830	0.122
1996	0.53	0.828	0.123
1997	0.52	0.827	0.124

Table 6.7 Spearman rank correlation coefficients[a].

	1993	*1994*	*1995*	*1996*	*1997*
	Parametric1	*Parametric 2*	*Parametric 3*	*Parametric 4*	*Parametric 5*
All					
DEA SE	0.8	0.84	0.82	0.82	0.83
SFA	0.65	0.66	0.66	0.66	0.67
Non-OECD					
DEA SE	0.83	0.87	0.85	0.84	0.83
SFA	0.71	0.72	0.72	0.72	0.72
OECD					
DEA SE	0.69	0.7	0.65	0.56	0.58
SFA	0.46	0.5	0.5	0.51	0.49

[a] All coefficients are significant using a 99 per cent confidence interval

Correlations between the parametric and non-parametric models can be seen in Table 6.7. Correlations between methods are high, implying the models specified are externally valid, as are the methods used to analyse the data. For the stochastic frontier models, results are highly correlated in terms of both internal validity and external validity. Correlations for the OECD models are significant, but generally lower than the non-OECD and full sample correlations. This reflects potential mis-specification of the OECD model, demonstrating the need for alternative models for different stratifications of the data.

All of the above gives us a wealth of information on what is actually happening in this sample of 140 countries over five years in terms of the movements of individual countries, and the sample as a whole. Also the efficiency of subsamples can be examined. The high correlations between different methods confirms the validity of modelling and the robustness of results overall. If the methods were not correlated it may indicate underlying problems with the models specified. Trends from all techniques point us in the same direction when analysing this sample of data, validating the techniques we are using. However, although the techniques are valid, as argued by Hollingsworth and Wildman (2003) and others, the data collected by WHO are questionable therefore drawing policy conclusions will depend on better data. However, as data collection is expected to improve and broaden, it is important that models are developed to usefully analyse such data.

Economies of scale and scope

As noted in Chapter 5, several studies have made use of measures of economies of scale using non-parametric analysis, making use of the Banker, Charnes, and Cooper (1984) model. As discussed in Chapter 3, this method places an extra constraint in the DEA model, allowing the estimation of whether a unit has increasing, constant or decreasing economies of scale.

Ferrier and Valdmanis (1996) use two-stage analysis to estimate efficiency for 360 rural hospitals in the USA finding a scale efficiency of 0.893. McCallion *et al.* (1999) for 23 UK hospitals from 1989 to 1992 find large hospitals more efficient than small (0.949 and 0.913). Mobley and Magnussen (1998) use DEA to compare the efficiency of 178 USA hospitals and 50 Norwegian hospitals in 1991. Scale efficiency was higher in the Norwegian sample. Dalmau-Matarrodona and Puig-Junoy (1998) estimate efficiency using a two-stage model for 94 Spanish acute hospitals in 1990, finding scale efficiency being influenced by size and severity of illness. Hollingsworth and Parkin (2001) look at 49 neonatal care units in the UK in 1990/91, finding varying economies of scale. Pina and Torres (1992) when examining ten Spanish health centres find four to be scale efficient. Björkgren *et al.* (2001) estimate efficiency in 64 long-term care units in Finland in 1995. Scale efficiency ranges from 0.92 to 0.93. Larger units appear to be more efficient. Giuffrida (1999) uses Malmquist indices to estimate productivity changes for 90 UK FHSAs for the years 1990/91 to 1994/5 concluding there is a small productivity improvement due to scale efficiency, not technology change. McCallion *et al.* (2000) look at hospitals in Northern Ireland from 1986 to 1992 finding larger hospitals increase productivity by 2.31 per cent, and smaller ones by 22.53 per cent. Scale efficiency falls. Giuffrida *et al.* (2000) use random and fixed effects parametric models on 1989/90 to 1994/5 UK FHSA (primary care) data, both models suggesting economies of scale.

As the use of economies of scale analysis is relatively common, we now turn to understanding the analysis of economies of scope. A number of microeconomics text books define economies of scope (e.g. Gravelle and Rees 1992). Economies of scope analyses the way a firm operates in terms of the range of production, rather than the scale or size of production (see Chapter 2). Economies of scope exist when outputs can be produced using fewer inputs when produced jointly as opposed to when produced separately. This may explain the existence of multi-product firms. In particular, the presence of multi-product firms (like large hospitals) is the product of the exploitation of both excess capacity and shareable inputs. If the costs of any shared input are 'sub-additive' (that is, less than the costs of providing these inputs separately), then there are potential economies of scope. Examples of shared inputs are buildings, heating, lighting and labour which may be used for the production of more than one output. So far, the existing literature has concentrated on cost issues of economies of scope and production using econometrics, which excludes important aspects of the production of care such as the contributions of different types of staff (Scott and Parkin 1995). However, as Panzar and Willig (1981) note, application of this concept to production costs alone may not encapsulate all significant factors that may influence the presence of economies of scope.

Here, we examine how DEA can be used to measure economies of scope, which allows the use of several inputs (physical units or costs) producing several outputs and relates efficiency to the scope of production to analyse whether joint production or specialization is more efficient.

Theory of economies of scope

Economies of scope, described in Chapter 2, describe an aspect of production where cost savings may be a function of the scope of production and exist when it costs less to combine two or more product lines in one firm, rather than produce the products separately (Panzar and Willig 1975, 1981). Thus, it is possible that cost savings may result from joint production of several outputs in one productive unit, in contrast to the outputs being produced in isolation in specialized units. As cost is not the only determinant of the structure of a firm (Bailey and Friedlaender 1982), there may be other important factors, such as the division of labour or demand for services.

In health care, there is no need for the provision of different services in a hospital if the entire hospital could be utilized by just one demanded service, for example maternity services. However, given that this is unlikely, any spare capacity is potentially most efficiently used by providing additional services (Bailey and Friedlaender 1982). In such cases, it is important to determine the efficiency of the different production options – specialized or joint production of outputs. If two or more outputs can be produced at less cost by one firm than by two or more firms, then joint production constitutes the most efficient means of supply. This may especially be the case if inputs are indivisible, such as large buildings or equipment (for example, a scanner in a hospital). It also applies to intangible inputs, such as research activities or business 'know-how' (Bailey and Friedlaender 1982). Further, it may reduce information transaction costs to have the management function, that is co-ordination and supervision, of delivering health care in one organization rather than being diversified over several specialist organizations. In this case it is more efficient to negotiate contacts with a single multi-product health-care organization rather than with several specialists. Overall, there may be economies from administering a multi-product hospital, in contrast to specialization.

Few papers look at economies of scope (sometimes referred to as diversification). Prior (1996) looked at economies of scope for 50 general hospitals in Spain, finding evidence of economies of scope. Prior and Solà (2000) use DEA to estimate economies of diversification for a sample of Spanish hospitals in 1987 and 1992. In 1987 there were 70 diversified and 62 specialized, and in 1992, 68 and 81, respectively. In 1987 the mean score for the diversified hospitals was 0.89 and for specialized, 0.87. In 1992, the estimates were 0.93 and 0.88, respectively. It is concluded that diversification economies dominate.

Fried *et al.* (1998) look at the efficiency of hospital-based nursing homes in the USA (372 skilled, 84 intermediate, 40 diversified). The skilled nursing homes are least production efficient (0.38), intermediate homes are more efficient (0.42), and diversified homes are most efficient (0.46). The study reports not finding significant economies of scope. Wagstaff and López (1996), using 1988 to 1991 data on 43 Spanish public and private hospitals, find average inefficiency of 58 per cent. There was mild evidence of economies of scope. Giuffrida *et al.* (2000) find little evidence of economies of scope.

The most promising methodological advancement here is considered to be that developed by Färe *et al.* (1985, 1994b) which they refer to as economies of diversification. Economies of diversification, and the more specialized case of economies of scope, are traditionally defined with reference to sub-additivity of the cost function. However, duality theory shows that sub-additivity of the cost function is the equivalent of super-additivity of the input set. As a result, not only can economies of scope be estimated by comparing cost frontiers, but also an extension to this approach, based on Koopmans technology, permits the technical efficiency consequences of diversification to be investigated (see Färe *et al.* (1985), for an exposition of this). There is still much work left to be undertaken in this area in health care, but the theoretical foundations have been established, and practical applications are possible for both single-input multiple-output, and multiple-input multiple-output modelling (Parkin and Hollingsworth 2005) where this method is used to demonstrate this non-parametric measure of detecting diversification economies, both in terms of a single-input, multiple-output model, and a multiple-input, multiple-output model. Results suggest evidence of economies of scope in the UK hospital sector. This means that multi-service hospitals appear to be more efficient at producing services, this is after correcting for technical and cost inefficiency, meaning it is the combination of services they offer which is the cause of their dominance in terms of the production of health care.

Weight restriction in DEA

An oft-cited advantage of the standard DEA model is its total weight flexibility. The advantage of this being that it does not impose a set of weights which potentially misrepresent the real values of inputs and outputs for a particular unit (Dyson and Thanassoulis 1988). However, it has the disadvantage that it may produce results that permit some of the inputs and outputs to be virtually ignored. Although weights are technically restricted to be larger than an Archimedian infinitesimal, in practice they can have zero impact (Allen *et al.* 1997; Thannassoulis *et al.* 2004). Imposing restrictions on weights may overcome these disadvantages without seriously affecting the advantages, but because the weights in DEA models do not have a distinct interpretation, constraining them is considered largely arbitrary (Luoma 1996).

Dyson and Thanassoulis (1988) describe a method of restricting weights within a single resource-input model. In such a model, the weight on each output reflects the amount of that resource used per unit of that output. Where the single input is cost, then the weight reflects the cost per unit of output. Given such economic interpretations, it may be desirable to place lower bounds on them, in order to ensure that the optimal solutions do not represent unrealistically low resource requirements for some outputs. These lower bounds can be set using regression analysis to estimate average values (Allen *et al.* 1997). The input is regressed on the outputs, giving regression coefficients which are interpreted as the average resource use per unit of output. The weight restrictions are set at some percentage of the coefficient reflecting a minimum resource level. Such a percentage should be based on knowledge of the process of producing the outputs.

However, often the production process is not fully understood, so one way forward is to undertake sensitivity analysis to determine the effects of choice over a range of possible percentages. Also, weight restrictions often lead to infeasible solutions in DEA models and it should be noted when weight restrictions are imposed switching from input minimization to output maximization models can have an impact on estimates.

As an example, using this method, a comparison is made of a weight-restricted set of estimates compared to unrestricted for the 75 acute Scottish hospitals in Parkin and Hollingsworth (1997). A version of the inpatient day model was used. It is not possible to report weight-restricted models using inpatient cases as the output, as none produced feasible solutions. In addition, only weight restrictions of less than 20 per cent of the coefficient produced feasible solutions for every year for the inpatient day model, and as this level produces the largest impact on results, it is the only model reported. Compared over time, the weight-restricted model results look very different to those of the non-weight-restricted model (see Table 6.8). The two models produced similar results for 1992–3, but were very different for the other two years. Compared to that year, the weight-restricted model was similar for 1991–2 and different for 1993–4. The reason for this is the use of different minimum weights for each year. The minimum weights for 1991–2 and 1992–3 were similar to each other and acted to smooth out the differences produced by the unrestricted model. However the weights for 1993–4 were very different and produced very different results which were not apparent in the unrestricted model (the example is from Hollingsworth and Parkin (1995).

Correlations were low but significant between the models indicating some model validity. In summary, if a non-arbitrary weighting system can be specified, it can be seen that restricting the weights can have a potentially significant impact upon efficiency estimates. This may have distinct policy implications. However, the understanding of the production relationship is important in deciding upon weight restrictions, otherwise they are largely arbitrary, see also the section on the analysis of different health-care measures in this chapter.

Table 6.8 Weight-restricted estimates.

	Mean	*St. dev.*	*Minimum*	*Number efficient*
Unrestricted				
1991/2	58.24	20.83	22.08	6
1992/3	82.07	12.94	50.66	12
1993/4	80.67	15.38	37.70	17
Weight-restricted				
1991/2	74.37	18.65	6.24	9
1992/3	74.33	15.33	31.66	9
1993/4	41.76	18.08	17.88	2

The efficient production of health

Most studies in efficiency measurement have concentrated on estimating the efficiency of the production of health care, rather than the production of health by individuals (see Chapter 5). Measuring the production of health raises several issues, especially when trying to estimate the impact of health care on an individual's health. There have been international comparisons of health system performance (recent examples include the World Health Report (2000) where the data and framework for analysis have been criticized (Hollingsworth and Wildman 2003).

Parkin and Devlin (2003) and Parkin and Hollingsworth (1999) present a model comprised of two linked production processes: the production of health care and of health. The model builds upon Grossman's (1972b) demand for health model and the health determinants approach of Evans and Stoddart (1990). The application for this, oral health, is an area for which the measurement of outcomes and health status is relatively straightforward.

There are two production processes: the production of health care and the production of health (Figure 6.1, from Parkin and Devlin 2003). Professional oral health care is produced from the formal health-care system, using inputs such as dentists' and other oral health workers' time, equipment, premises and consumables. Oral health is produced by individuals who combine the output of oral health care with their own determinants of health.The two processes are linked by recognizing that the *output* of the oral health-care production function is an *input* to the oral health production function. The two models together form an overall system.

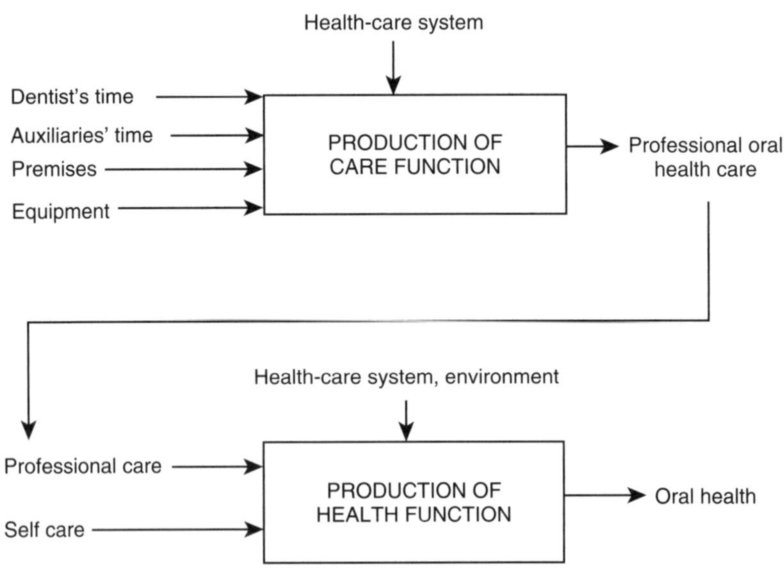

Figure 6.1 A model of the production of oral health and dental health care.

Data from seven EU countries are used to illustrate the application. The data had a multilevel structure, comprising seven countries, 287 dental practices and 1,392 patients. Some, though not all, of the data could be linked between patients and their dentists.

For the DEA health-care model, inputs were: dentists chairs, equipment age, years of experience, dentist hours and staff hours; While the output was average number of patients per hour. For the sub-sample of dentists whose data could be linked to patient data, two indicators of the quality of their patients' oral health were included: the mean number of sound teeth and the number of patients reporting their state of teeth and gums as excellent or good.

For the DEA health model, inputs were included brushing teeth, check-ups, consulted non-dentist and employed, and outputs included: sound teeth and state of teeth. Because the latter is a categorical variable, the two-stage DEA procedure devised by Banker and Morey (1986) was used. First, a frontier was estimated for the sub-sample of those assessed to be in a poor state of oral health using numbers of sound teeth as the output. The resulting efficiency scores are relative to those with a similarly poor health state and are not dominated by those with a good state. Secondly, a DEA frontier was estimated for the *whole* sample. The final efficiency scores for those in poor oral health are those from stage 1 and for those in good health are those from stage 2.

Both of the models used pooled data to estimate a single cross-country production function. Spain's system is largely an extraction-only service, in contrast to the comprehensive services provided elsewhere. Efficiency comparisons with respect to the production of health care therefore may be confounded by the fact that the output in Spain is much less complex. The same applies to the production of health, not because the inputs or outputs differ from other countries, but because the mixture of cases seen within the system may be different. Therefore, estimates were made with and without the data from Spain. There was no linked data from Denmark, so it is excluded from the quality-adjusted health-care production model.

DEA results, including median efficiency scores and the number of efficient practices within each country, are shown in Table 6.9. For the production-of-care model, the UK has the highest average score and UK dentists form a large majority of the best-practice frontier. Germany has the lowest average score, with no practices on the best-practice frontier.

When Spain was included, it had the highest median efficiency score, which is consistent with the relative ease of obtaining output for a given set of inputs in an extraction-only service. All of the median scores were much lower reflecting the existence of apparently highly efficient Spanish practices. However, other countries' rankings were not affected, suggesting that the DEA analysis for them was not affected by the inclusion of an irrelevant alternative.

The quality-adjusted model produced identical rankings. However, the absolute values cannot be compared with the previous model because of the smaller numbers of practices included. To check the robustness of these findings, the non-quality adjusted models were re-estimated without Denmark, but this had no impact on the remaining countries' rankings.

Table 6.9 Comparative efficiency of six European Union countries in the production of oral health care, quality-adjusted oral health care and oral health.

	Oral health care				*Quality-adjusted oral health care*				*Oral health*		
	Number	*Median efficiency score*	*Number efficient*		*Number*	*Median efficiency score*	*Number efficient*		*Number*	*Median efficiency score*	*Number efficient*
UK	44	67.93	14	UK	19	100	13	UK	234	53.33	10
Ireland	38	48.53	3	Ireland	19	93.61	5	Denmark	72	53.21	1
Netherlands	44	40.22	1	Netherlands	9	84.48	3	Ireland	228	50.00	6
France	35	35.36	3	France	29	75	5	Netherlands	227	50.00	2
Denmark	27	29.79	1	Germany	12	44.52	0	France	201	43.75	4
Germany	42	24.08	0	—	—	—	—	Germany	231	41.94	3
All	230	38.62	22	All	88	84.88	26	All	1,193	48.31	26

For the production of oral health model, there is relatively little variation between countries, but the UK again has the highest average efficiency score, while France and Germany have the lowest. UK patients also supply the largest number of those on the health production efficiency frontier, however, the numbers reflecting efficiency in each country do not follow the efficiency score rankings. When Spain was included, it had the highest average score and the most efficient patients, but other countries' rankings were unaltered.

Overall, the DEA results demonstrate a strong correlation between the efficiency with which dentists in a country produce oral health care and the efficiency with which their patients produce oral health. As such we can conclude DEA appears a valid means of measuring the overall efficiency of health systems.

Analysis of different health-care measures

Most applications of efficiency modelling to date have been in the hospital sector. As noted in Chapter 5 there have been limited attempts to introduce quality-adjusted health-care *outcome* variables into this area of analysis that has previously consisted of using *output* variables.

Outcome variables, which accurately reflect changes in health status, are still unused for efficiency measurement in health care. At the present time, proxy variables such as readmission rates are becoming widely available. Hollingsworth and Parkin (1995) note that due to small sub-samples avaliable in outcome data, there are restrictions on what can be done from a practical level. The raw numbers for clinical outcomes may not include enough numbers and may be overshadowed by the large number of cases when analysis is undertaken. A further problem noted, is when the clinical outcome indicators are in the form of percentages which are not suitable for inclusion in DEA. Having raw numbers of inpatient cases, inpatient days and clinical outcome percentages in the same model leads to perverse results. To solve this problem Hollingsworth and Parkin (1995) suggest that instead of using total costs as the input into the model to use cost per case, and the Banker, Charnes and Cooper (1984), output maximizing DEA formulation. This means that feasible and meaningful results are obtained using ratios (Fernandez-Castro and Smith 1994; Hollingsworth and Smith 2003).

With production of health models, using the individual or groups of individuals as the units of production, it is feasible to use health outcome measures, for example see the earlier section in this chapter on oral care.

Summary

This chapter has not sought to encompass all statistical developments currently being made in the rapidly evolving area of efficiency measurement. Instead we have shown how developments can usefully be applied in the measurement of health and health care. We have compared and contrasted why different means of measuring efficiency may be best used in parallel and how analysing cross-sectional data also may be insufficient. Analysing time series or panel data may be required in order to get a true picture of how organizations or systems are performing over time.

It is worth noting that quality of data may also be an issue. Using the WHO performance index as an example, we show how state-of-the-art techniques of analysis can be applied. However, these are only of use in policy terms if the data are of a high quality. We assume that data in general (the WHO report being a case in point) will improve and that the whole spectrum of efficiency analysis will become more policy oriented as suitable data are allied to well-specified models analysed by state-of-the-art techniques.

We then summarize how economies of scale *and* scope should be accounted for whenever possible. Not only can size have an impact on performance, so can the scope of operations – is it more efficient for health-care providers to specialize or be more general in their approach to providing services? Evidence at present is inconclusive and this is an important area for future research.

Weight restrictions in health-care models are a problematic area. In most areas, it is not really possible to estimate a true relationship (and therefore respective importance) between different factors of production. However, there may be some interest in testing removing the near-zero weighting attached to some interest in efficiency analysis and the difference this makes to results.

Most studies have looked at the efficiency of health-care organizations. The emphasis may be moving gradually to examining how individuals efficiently determine their own health. We look at the example of how a whole system approach may be useful, linking health and health care to analyse the efficiency of the overall system. Modelling health-care outputs and health outcomes together may lead to methodological and practical problems. Modelling the two separately, within an overall systems model, may be a better alternative.

7 Future directions

In this, the final chapter, we comment on progress to date in efficiency measurement in health and health care, and suggest a research agenda for the future. Given the rapid growth in research in the area in the last ten years we summarize why efficiency measurement has gained in popularity, despite some criticisms of the efficiency measurement tools available to researchers. Some of this popularity may be attributed to the relative ease with which researchers can now employ DEA and SFA methods. However, much of it may also be attributed to the potential uses of efficiency measurement in decision making.

Potential uses of efficiency measurement techniques in health and health care include:

- target setting for health service providers, for example determining input/output mix, estimating the effects of service substitution on input and output, and exploiting economies of scale and scope;
- monitoring/benchmarking performance, for example filtering of complex information and identifying outlying providers;
- evaluation of performance, for example estimating inefficiency from managerial practices and from different levels of the organizational structure within the provider;
- determining efficient reimbursement rates, for example estimating cost-minimizing case payment rates.

The extent to which efficiency measurement techniques have been successfully used for these purposes is dubious. Areas of further research are many and varied. In particular, research is required as to the potential for efficiency measurement to inform reimbursement policy in the future.

Two key issues in the context of the health sector are of particular importance: quality of care and health outcomes. Efficiency measurement techniques that properly account for quality and health outcomes are important. However, a range of further health-related issues are equally important. For example, how can measures of capital utilization be advanced? How robust are measures of casemix, the potential for endogenous outputs in modelling and the potential impact of measurement error and omitted variables on efficiency estimates? Recent advances from the productivity analysis and statistics literature and their potential for application in the health sector, including stochastic DEA, bootstrapping techniques and hierarchical modelling, may be of use here but are still under methodological development.

Another problem, as summarized in Hollingsworth and Street (2006), is the issue surrounding the market for efficiency analyses. The supply side of the market in efficiency analysis is flourishing. The increase in papers is exponential (see Chapter 5 and Sommersguter-Reichmann 2005).

One reason for the growth in academic output is that the barriers to entering the research field have been lowered, because both the raw materials (i.e. data) and technological processes (i.e. DEA and SFA) are increasingly accessible to researchers. Software is increasingly available or generic computer packages are incorporating procedures allowing researchers to apply these techniques relatively easily to their data (see Chapter 4).

There is also intense pressure to publish for academics, which has encouraged innovation and product differentiation among researchers, who are exploiting the longitudinal nature of many datasets (Greene 2004; Farsi *et al.* 2005), applying increasingly sophisticated analytical techniques in order to extract as much information from the data as possible. All this has led to an increase in both the volume and quality of academic publications. This increase in supply has not been matched by demand. There are markets for efficiency analysis. Academics need to keep up to speed with the latest technological breakthroughs and advances in any area, and many papers and conferences are available for this explicit purpose. However, two other markets are relatively untapped: policy makers and the units under analysis.

Efficiency analyses has been undertaken which was intended to ultimately impact on policy, the most high profile being the WHO world rankings (World Health Report 2000). Although these ultimately failed, some policy makers are using efficiency studies to inform their decision making. Three concrete examples are the use by Queensland Health in Australia, where DEA is used on a sample of hospitals, among a suite of performance indicators (see www.health.qld.gov.au/quality/mq_reports.asp), in Norway where efficiency analyses were used in 1995 as one argument for moving to DRG-based financing (Biørn *et al.* 2003) and are currently used by some regional Health Enterprises to inform their internal resource allocation (Magnussen 2005 – see, in Norwegian only: www.tidsskriftet.no/lts-pdf/pdf2005/3300-2.pdf), and in New Zealand where DEA has been used since 1997 to identify efficiency in expenditure terms (see Rouse and Swales 2006). Yet these policy applications are few and far between. So why are efficiency studies not made use of?

Efficiency analyses should address key concerns of policy makers including relevance, timeliness and reliability. In most health systems, the pursuit of efficiency remains a central preoccupation, arising from concern about the healthcare expenditure and the need to structure incentives such that production units (e.g. hospitals) are encouraged to pursue the objective of efficient behaviour.

These incentives are taken as given in markets where competition is the norm: short-term inefficiency erodes profit margins, long-term inefficiency predicts exit from the market. Markets for health care are rarely competitive so, in the absence of policy intervention, inefficiency may persist. Techniques such as DEA and SFA appear to offer policy makers insight into the variation in efficiency among DMUs and, thereby, of where efficiency gains might be considered. Efficiency analyses are retrospective in nature, but this is not unique – most performance monitoring relies on historical data. The ease with which DEA and SFA can be applied implies that only the speed of the information flow impedes the timeliness of analysis, and so potential feedback and usefulness.

One concern for policy makers may be reliability. DEA and SFA estimate the efficiency frontier and calculate distances from this frontier in different ways, and the estimates of relative efficiency produced by each technique often differ, sometimes dramatically. Estimates are also often sensitive to choices in model specification (as discussed in Chapter 3), particularly so when analysing complex production modalities such as in health care. This undermines confidence in whether the analytical tools can estimate organization-specific inefficiency in a reliable manner. Policy based on unreliable evidence is undesirable. Until fundamental issues such as this are resolved, marketing efficiency analyses to policy makers will be ineffective.

So, what might efficiency analysts offer organizations to encourage their participation in the efficiency analysis market? What limits organizations' participation now? Incentives to pursue efficient behaviour, incentives to participate in comparative benchmarking type exercises and specificity of any information. Publicly-funded health systems in general have moved from historical budgeting to some form of case-related payment scheme and as patients are given greater choice about where to receive treatment, the health-care market has become somewhat more competitive. These competitive pressures should spur organizations to pursue greater efficiency and expand market share. The take-up of efficiency analyses might increase in consequence.

Efficiency analyses are comparative and depend on accurate information. Where there is limited disclosure of required information, any benchmarking exercise will be partial, and offer limited policy-relevant insights. In competitive settings, an organization would like to know about their competitors without yielding much information about themselves. More informative analysis may be feasible in regulated industries where organizations might be obliged to provide the requisite information; mandatory disclosure does not, however, preclude inaccurate reporting (Smith and Street 2006). Participation in such exercises might be secured if they are conducted by independent organizations and the results are anonymized (Hollingsworth and Parkin 2003).

Even if there were accurate disclosure, efficiency analyses may not provide organizations with the requisite information to make decisions and take action. Efficiency analyses tend to focus on the organization as the unit of analysis, but this may provide them with little insight about where and how actual technical improvements could be made. This is a particular problem for health-care providers, as they have multiple products. Specific information is required about the efficiency of these different production processes, which presents an interesting challenge to users of frontier measurement techniques.

If health-care markets were perfectly competitive, efficiency measurement would be unnecessary. They aren't, and DEA and SFA have been developed to identify the extent of inefficient behaviour. The supply of efficiency analyses is impressive and growing. However, the demand-side of the market for efficiency analysis is under-developed. Most analyses appear to be targeted at academic users, and are little utilized by either policymakers or organizations. To be more useful, the analytical techniques need further development. There needs to be greater confidence that the results are reliable. This means greater attention to model construction (as well as underlying theory), especially better understanding of the nature of production of health care and of production constraints. Also, analysis needs to be more specific. Instead of merely quantifying the extent of inefficiency, analyses need to identify the nature and form of inefficiency; and therefore what can be done about it. These challenges are not straightforward and academic researchers need to work more closely with policy makers and organizations in order to meet them.

In this book we have discussed in detail the rationale for efficiency measurement, undertaken a detailed rationalization of the concepts and definitions of efficiency, and explained the techniques for undertaking measurement. We have given a practical framework for undertaking measurement of efficiency for health-care organizations, and for how to translate this into practical, user-friendly information for policy makers. The increasingly vast literature in this area is summarized, showing the breadth of supply of efficiency studies. We then go on to identify the potential for future research, and why supply has so far outstripped demand in terms of research on efficiency measurement.

In the end, as good researchers should (we believe), we ask as many questions as we answer, and so we conclude as we are almost obliged to: Further research in this area is recommended.

Notes

3 Efficiency measurement techniques

1 They provide a rule of thumb: $n \geq \max \{m \text{ x } s, 3(m + s)\}$, n = number of DMUs, m = number of inputs, s = number of outputs (p. 252).

4 Measuring efficiency in health services

1 See Parkin and Hollingsworth (1997) for a more detailed explanation of validity of *measurement* and *findings*.
2 For a taxonomy of weights in DEA see Pedraja-Chaparro *et al.* (1997).
3 Summaries are shown for 1995/6. Weights for 1994/5 show similar trends.

5 Application of efficiency measurement in health services

1 The email list DEA-health (http://www/jiscmail.ac.uk/lists/dea-health.html) proved very useful.
2 References to within hospital efficiency are summarized in Hollingsworth (2003).
3 Ownership definitions used here are: public–state owned/run firms; for-profit – privately run; not-for-profit – in some cases are voluntary/charity run firms which serve the poor. However, health-care not-for-profit firms obtain 90 per cent of revenue from sales and receipts, are privately run, are entitled to many tax exemptions and advantages, make a residual surplus and compete with for-profit hospital firms. For a discussion of the roles of not-for-profit, for-profit and public delivery of health care, see Folland et al. (1997): 409–435.
4 For an in-depth explanation of the roles of not-for-profit, for-profit and public delivery of health care see Folland *et al.* (2007).
5 See McGuire *et al.* (1988) for an in-depth discussion of health care as an economic commodity.
6 Reported in teaching statistics rather than VA/defence.

Bibliography

Afonso, A. and St Aubyn, M. (2005) 'Non-parametric approaches to education and health efficiency in OECD countries', *J Appl Econ*, **8**: 227–246

Aigner, D.J., Lovell, C.A.K. and Schmidt, P. (1977) Formulation and estimation of stochastic production function models', *J Economet*, **6**: 21–37

Alexander, C.A., Busch, G. and Stringer, K. (2003) 'Implementing and interpreting a data envelopment analysis model to assess the efficiency of health systems in developing countries', *IMA J Manage Math*, **14**: 49–63

Allen, R., Athanassopoulos, A., Dyson, R.G. and Thanassoulis, E. (1997) 'Weight restrictions and value judgements in data envelopment analysis: evolution, development and future directions', *Ann Oper Res*, **73**: 13–34

Al-Shammari, M. (1999) 'A multi-criteria data envelopment analysis model for measuring the productive efficiency of hospitals', *International J Oper Prod Man*, **19**: 879–890

Anderson, P. and Peterson, N.C. (1993) 'A procedure for ranking efficient units in data envelopment analysis', *Man Sci*, **39**: 1261–1264

Anderson, R.I., Lewis, D. and Webb, J.R. (1999) 'The efficiency of nursing home chains and the implications of non-profit status', *J Real Est Port Man*, **5**: 235–245

Anderson, R.I., Weeks, H.S., Hobbs, B.K. and Webb, J.R. (2003) 'Nursing home quality, chain affiliation, profit status and performance', *J Real Est Res*, **25**: 43–60

Andes, S., Metzger, L.M., Kralewski, J. and Gans, D. (2002) 'Measuring efficiency of physician practices using data envelopment analysis', *Man Care,* **11**: 48–54

Athanassopoulos, A. and Gounaris, C. (2001) 'Assessing the technical and allocative efficiency of hospital operations in Greece and its resource allocation implications', *Eur J Oper Res*, **133**: 416–431

Athanassopoulos, A., Gounaris, C. and Sissouras, A. (1999) 'A descriptive assessment of the production and cost efficiency of general hospitals in Greece', *Health Care Man Sci* **2**: 97–106

Auster, R.D., Leveson, I. and Sarachek, D. (1969) 'The production of health, an exploratory study', *J Hum Res*, **4**: 411–436

Bailey, E.E. and Friedlaender, A.F. (1982) 'Market structure and multi-product industries', *J Econ Lit*, **20**: 1024–1048

Balk, B.M. (1998) *Industrial Price, Quantity and Productivity Indices*, Massachusetts: Kluwer Academic

Banker, R.D. and Morey, R.C. (1986) 'Efficiency analysis for exogenously fixed inputs and outputs', *Oper Res* **34**: 513–521

Banker, R., Charnes, A. and Cooper, W. (1984) 'Some models for estimating technical and scale inefficiencies in data envelopment analysis', *Man Sci*, **30**: 1078–1092

Banker, R.D., Conrad, R. and Strauss, R. (1986) 'A comparative application of data envelopment analysis and translog method: an illustrative study of hospital production', *Man Sci* **32**: 30–44

Bannick, R.R. and Ozcan, Y.A. (1995) 'Efficiency analysis of federally funded hospitals: comparison of DoD and VA hospitals using data envelopment analysis', *Health Serv Man Res*, **8**: 73–85

Barrow, M. and Wagstaff, A. (1989) 'Efficiency measurement in the public sector: an appraisal', *Fisc Stud*, **10**: 72–97

Bates, J.M., Baines, D. and Whynes, D.K. (1996) 'Measuring the efficiency of prescribing by general practitioners', *J Oper Res Soc*, **47**: 1443–1451

Beguin, C. (2001) 'Nonparametric frontier model as a tool for exploratory analysis of hospital stays', *Meth Inf Med,* **40**: 241–247

Bhat, V.N. (2005) 'Institutional arrangements and efficiency of health care delivery systems', *Eur J Health Econ*: 215–22

Biørn, E., Hagan, T., Iverson, T. and Magnussen J. (2003) 'The effect of activity based financing on hospital efficiency: a panel data analysis of DEA efficiency scores 1992–2000', *Health Care Man Sci*, **6**: 271–283

Birch, S. and Gafni, A. (1992) 'Cost effectiveness/utility analyses: do current decision rules lead us to where we want to be?', *J Health Econ*, **11**: 279–296

Bitran, G.R. and Valor-Sabatier, J. (1987) 'Some mathematical programming based measures of efficiency in health care institutions', *Adv Math Prog Financ Plann*, **1**: 61–84

Bjorkgren, M.A., Hakkinen, U. and Linna, M. (2001) 'Measuring efficiency of long-term care units in Finland', *Health Care Man Sci,* 4: 193–200

Bjorkgren, M.A., Fries, B.E., Hakkinen, U. and Brommels, M. (2004) 'Case-mix adjustment and efficiency measurement', *Scan J Pub Health*, **32**: 464–471

Blank, J.L. and Eggink, E. (2004) 'The decomposition of cost efficiency: an empirical application of the shadow cost function model to Dutch general hospitals', *Health Care Man Sci*, **7**: 79–88

Blank, J.L. and Valdmanis, V. (2005) 'A modified three-stage data envelopment analysis', *Eur J Health Econ*, **6**: 65–72

Blank, J.L.T., Eggink, E. and de Graaff, A.I. (1996) 'Een empirisch onderzoek naar de productiestructuur van verpleeghuizen in Nederland', *Zuinig op zorg* September 3–5 (in English)

Borden, J.P. (1988) 'An assessment of the impact of diagnosis-related group (DRG)-based reimbursement on the technical efficiency of New Jersey hospitals using data envelopment analysis', *J Acc Public Pol,* **7**: 77–96

Bosmans, N. and Fecher, F. (1995) 'Performance of Belgian hospitals: A frontier approach', *Health Econ*, **4**: 389–397

Boussofiane, A., Thanassoulis, E. and Dyson, R.G. (1991) 'Using data envelopment analysis to assess the efficiency of the perinatal care provision in England', Warwick Business School Research Papers no. 5, Coventry: University of Warwick

Brook, R.H. *et al.* (1983) 'Does free care improve adults' health?' Results from a randomized controlled trial. *New Engl J Med*, **309**: 1426–1434

Bryce, C.L., Engberg, J.B. and Wholey, D.R. (2000) 'Comparing the agreement among alternative models in evaluating HMO efficiency', *Health Serv Res*, **35**: 509–528

Buck, D. (2000) 'The efficiency of the community dental service in England: a data envelopment analysis', *Commun Dent Oral Epidemiol,* **28**: 274–280

Burgess, J.F. and Wilson, P.W. (1993) 'Technical efficiency in Veterans Administration hospitals', in H.O. Fried, C.A.K. Lovell and S.S. Schmidt (eds) *The Measurement of Productive Efficiency*, Oxford: Oxford University Press

Burgess, J.F. and Wilson, P.W. (1995) 'Decomposing Hospital productivity changes, 1985–1988: A nonparametric Malmquist approach', *J Productiv Anal,* **6**: 343–363

Burgess, J.F. and Wilson, P.W. (1996) 'Hospital ownership and technical inefficiency', *Man Sci* **42**: 110–123

Burgess J.F. and Wilson, P.W. (1998) 'Variation in inefficiency among US hospitals', *INFOR*, **36**: 84–102

Butler, J.R.G. (1995) *Hospital Cost Functions*, Dordrecht: Kluwer Academic

Butler, T.W. and Li, L. (2005) 'The utility of returns to scale in DEA programming: an analysis of Michigan rural hospitals', *Eur J Oper Res*, **161**: 469–477

Byrnes P. and Valdmanis, V. (1989) 'Variable cost frontiers and efficiency: an investigation of labor costs in hospitals', in T. Gulledge and L. Lihl (eds) *Cost Analysis Applications of Econs*, Berlin: Springer

Byrnes, P. and Valdmanis, V. (1994) 'Analyzing technical and allocative efficiency of hospitals', in A. Charnes, W. Cooper, A. Lewin, and L. Seiford (eds) *DEA Theory, Methodology and Applications*, Boston: Kluwer

Capettini, R.A.D. and Morey, R.C. (1985) 'Reimbursement rate setting for Medicaid prescription drugs based on relative efficiencies', *J Acc Public Pol*, **4**: 83–110

Capettini, R., Dittman, D.A. and Morey, R.C. (1985) 'Variation in inefficiency among US hospitals', *J Acc Public Pol*, **4**: 83–110

Caves, D.W., Christensen, L.R. and Diewert, W.E. (1982) 'The economics theory of index numbers and the measurement of input, output and productivity', *Econometrica,* **50**: 1393–1414

Chambers, R.G., Färe, R. and Grosskopf, S. (1996) 'Productivity growth in APEC countries', *Pacific Econ Rev,* **1**: 181–190

Chang, H.H. (1998) 'Determinants of hospital efficiency: the case of central government-owned hospitals in Taiwan', *Omega Int J Man Sci*, **26**: 307–317

Chang, H., Cheng, M-A. and Das, S. (2004) 'Hospital ownership and operating efficiency: evidence from Taiwan', *Eur J Oper Res*, **159**: 513–527

Charnes, A., Cooper, W. and Rhodes, E. (1978) 'Measuring the efficiency of decision-making units', *Eur J Oper Res*, **2**: 429–444

Chattopadhyay, S. and Heffley, D. (1994) 'Are for-profit nursing homes more efficient? data envelopment analysis with a case-mix constraint', *Eastern Econ J*, **20**: 171–187

Chattopadhyay, S. and Ray, C.S. (1996) 'Technical, scale, and size efficiency in nursing home care: a non-parametric analysis of Connecticut homes', *Health Econ,* **5**: 363–373

Chen, A., Hwang, Y.C. and Shao, B. (2005) 'Measurement and sources of overall and input inefficiencies: evidence and implications in hospital services', *Eur J Oper Res*, **161**: 447–468

Chern, J.-Y. and Wan, T.T. (2000) 'The impact of the prospective payment system on the technical efficiency of hospitals', *J Med Sys*, **24**: 159–172

Chilingerian, J.A. (1995) 'Evaluating physician efficiency in hospitals: a multivariate analysis of best practices', *Eur J Oper Res*, **80**: 548–574

Chirikos, T.N. (1998) 'Identifying efficiently and economically operated hospitals: the prospects and pitfalls of applying frontier regression techniques', *J Health Polit Pol Law*, **23**: 79–904

Chirikos, T.N. (1998/99) 'Further evidence that hospital production is inefficient', *Inquiry*, **35**: 408–416

Chirikos, T.N. and Sear, A.M. (1994) 'Technical efficiency and the competitive behaviour of hospitals', *Socio-Econ Plann Sci,* **28**: 219–227

Chirikos, T.N. and Sear, A.M. (2000) 'Measuring hospital efficiency: a comparison of two approaches', *Health Serv Res*, **34**: 1389–1408

Coelli, T., Rao, D.S.P., O'Donnell, C.J. and Battesse, G. (2005) *An Introduction to Efficiency and Productivity Measurement*, New York: Springer

Cooper, W.W., Seiford, L.M. and Tone, K. (2000) *Data Envelopment Analysis: A Comprehensive Text with Models, Applications, References and DEA-solver Software*, Boston: Kluwer Academic

Cooper, W.W., Seiford, L.M. and Zhu, J. (2004) *Handbook on Data Envelopment Analysis*, Massachusetts: Kluwer Academic

Coppola, M.N., Ozcan, Y.A. and Bogacki, R. (2003) 'Evaluation of performance of dental providers on posterior restorations: Does experience matter? A data envelopment analysis (DEA) approach', *J Med Sys*, **27**: 445–456

Cornwell, C., Schmidt, P. and Sickles, R.C. (1990) 'Production frontiers with cross sectional and time-series variation in efficiency levels', *J Econometrics*, **46**: 185–200

Crivelli, L., Filippini, M. and Lunati, D. (2002) 'Regulation, ownership and efficiency in the Swiss nursing home industry', *Int J Health Care Finance Econ*, **2**: 79–97

Culyer, A.J. (1978) 'Needs, values and health status measurement', in A.J. Culyer and K.G. Wright (eds) *Economic Aspects of Health Serv*, London: Martin Robertson

Culyer, A.J. and Newhouse, J. (eds) (2000) *The Handbook of Health Econs*, Amsterdam: Elsevier

Culyer, A.J. and Wagstaff, A. (1993) 'Equity and equality in health and health care', *J Health Econ*, **93**: 321–324

Cutler, D.M. and McClellan, M. (2001) 'Is technology change in medicare worth it?', *Health Affairs*, **20**(5), 11–29.

Dalmau-Matarrodona, E. and Puig-Junoy, J. (1998) 'Market structure and hospital efficiency: Evaluating potential effects of deregulation in a national health service', *Rev Indust Org*, **13**: 447–466

DaVanzo, J. and Gertler, P. (1990) 'Household Production of Health: A Microeconomic Perspective on Health Transitions', RAND Note no. N-3014-RC, RAND Corporation

Defelice, L.C. and Bradford, W.D. (1997) 'Relative inefficiencies in production between solo and group practice physicians', *Health Econ* **6**: 455–465

Department of Health (1997) 'The New NHS. Modern. Dependable'. White Paper Cm 3807, London: HMSO

Dervaux, B. (2004) 'Comparing French and US hospital technologies: a directional input distance function approach', *Appl Econ*, **36**: 1065–1081

Dismuke, C.E. and Sena, V. (1999) 'Has DRG payment influenced the technical efficiency and productivity of diagnostic technologies in Portuguese public hospitals? An empirical analysis using parametric and non-parametric methods', *Health Care Man Sci*, **2**: 107–116

Dismuke, C. and Sena, V. (2001) 'Is there a trade-off between quality and productivity? The case of diagnostic technologies in Portugal', *Ann Oper Res* **107**: 101–116

Dittman, D.A., Capettini, R. and Morey, R.C. (1991) 'Measuring efficiency in acute care hospitals: An application of data envelopment analysis', *J Health Human Res Admin*, **14**: 89–108

Donabedian, A. (1969) *A Guide to Medical Care Administration Volume II: Medical Care Appraisal – Quality and Utilization*, Washington DC: American Public Health Association

Donaldson, L.J., Kirkup, W., Craig, N. and Parkin, D. (1994) 'Lanterns in the jungle: is the NHS driven by the wrong kind of efficiency?', *Publ Health*, **108**: 3–9

Draper, D.A., Solti, I. and Ozcan, Y.A. (2000) 'Characteristics of health maintenance organisations and their influence on efficiency', *Health Serv Man Res*, **13**: 40–56

Drummond, M., Sculpher, M., Torrance, G.W., O'Brien, B. and Stoddart, G.L. (2005) *Methods for the Economic Evaluation of Health Care Programmes*, 3rd edn, New York: Oxford University Press

Dyson, R.G. and Thanassoulis, E. (1988) 'Reducing weight flexibility in data envelopment analysis', *J Oper Res Soc*, **39**: 563–576

Erlandsen, E. and Førsund, F.R. (2002) 'Efficiency in the provision of municipal nursing and home-care Services: the Norwegian experience', in K.J. Fox (ed.) *Efficiency in the Public Sector*, Boston: Kluwer

Ersoy, K., Kavuncubasi, S., Ozcan, Y.A. and Harris, J.M. (1997) 'Technical efficiencies of Turkish hospitals: DEA approach', *J Med Syst*, **21**: 67–74

Evans, R.G. (1971) 'Behavioural cost functions for hospitals', *Canad J Econ*, **4**: 198–215

Evans, R. and Stoddart, G. (1990) 'Producing health, consuming health care', *Soc Sci Med*, **31**: 1347–1363

Färe, R., Grosskopf, S. and Knox Lovell, C.A. (1985) *The Measurement of Efficiency of Production*, Boston: Kluwer-Nijhoff

Färe, R., Grosskopf, S., Lindgren, B. and Roos, P. (1992) 'Productivity changes in Swedish pharmacies 1980–1989: a non-parametric Malmquist approach', *J Productiv Anal*, **3**: 85–101

Färe, R., Grosskopf, S., Lindgren, B. and Roos, P. (1994a) 'Productivity developments in Swedish hospitals: A Malmquist output index approach', in A. Charnes, W. Cooper, A. Lewin and L. Seiford (eds) *Data Envelopment Analysis: Theory, Methodology and Applications*, Boston: Kluwer

Färe, R., Grosskopf, S. and Lovell, C. (1994b) *Production Frontiers,* Cambridge: Cambridge University Press

Färe, R., Grosskopf, S. and Roos, P. (1995) 'Productivity and quality changes in Swedish pharmacies', *Int J Prod Econ*, **39**: 137–147

Färe, R., Grosskopf, S., Lindgren, B. and Poullier, J.P. (1997) 'Productivity growth in health care delivery', *Med Care* **35**: 354–366

Färe, R., Grosskopf, S. and Roos, P. (2002) 'Integrating consumer satisfaction into productivity indexes', in K.J. Fox (ed.) *Efficiency in the Public Sector*, Boston: Kluwer

Farrell, M.J. (1957) 'The measurement of productive efficiency', *J Roy Stat Soc*, Series A (III), 253–290

Farsi, M. and Filippini, M. (2004) 'An empirical analysis of cost efficiency in non-profit and public nursing homes', *Ann Pub Coop Econ*, **75**: 339–365

Farsi, M., Filippini, M. and Kuenzle, M. (2005) 'Unobserved heterogeneity in stochastic cost frontier models: an application to Swiss nursing homes', *Appl Econ*, **37**: 2127–2141

Feldstein, M.S. (1967) *Economic Analysis for Health Service Efficiency: Econometric Studies of the British National Health Service*, Amsterdam: North Holland

Fernandez-Castro, A. and Smith, P. (1994) 'Towards a general non-parametric model of corporate performance', *OMEGA Int J Man Sci*, **22**: 237–249

Ferrier, G.D. and Valdmanis, V. (1996) 'Rural hospital performance and its correlates', *J Productiv Anal*, **7**: 63–80

Ferrier, G.D. and Valdmanis, V.G. (2002) 'Exploring psychiatric hospital performance using data envelopment analysis and cluster analysis', *J Econ Medic*, 20(3/4): 143–153

Ferrier, G.D. and Valdmanis, V.G. (2004) 'Do mergers improve hospital productivity?', *J Oper Res Soc,* **55**: 1071–1080

Fisher, E.S., Wennberg, D.E., Stukel, T.A., Gottlieb, D.J., Lucas, F.L. and Pinder, E.L. (2003) 'The implications of regional variations in medicare spending. part 1: the content, quality, and accessibility of care', *Annals of Internal Medicine,* **138**(4), 273–286.

Fizel, J.L. and Nunnikhoven, T.S. (1993) The efficiency of nursing-home chains, *Appl Econ*, **25**: 49–55

Folland, S.T. and Hofler, R.A. (2001) 'How reliable are hospital efficiency estimates? exploiting the dual to homothetic production', *Health Econ*, **10**: 683–698

Folland, S., Goodman, A. and Stano, M. (1997) *The Economics of Health and Health Care*, 2nd edn, New Jersey: Pearson Prentice Hall

Folland, S., Goodman, A.C. and Stano, M. (2001) *The Economics of Health and Health Care*, 4th edn, New York: MacMillan

Fried, H.O., Schmidt, S.S. and Yaisawarng, S. (1998) 'Productive, scale and scope efficiencies in US hospital-based nursing homes', *INFOR*, **36**: 103–119

Fried, H.O., Lovell, C.A.K., Schmidt, S.S. and Yaisawarng, S. (2002) 'Accounting for environmental effects and statistical noise in data envelopment analysis', *J Productiv Anal*, **17**: 157–174

Ganley, J.A. and Cubbin, J.S. (1992) *Public Sector Efficiency Measurement: Applications of Data Envelopment Analysis*, Amsterdam: North Holland

Gannon, B. (2005) 'Testing for variation in technical efficiency of hospitals in Ireland', *Econ Soc Rev,* **36**: 273–294

Gaynor, M. and Pauly, M.V. (1990) 'Compensation and productive efficiency in Partnerships: evidence from medical groups practice', *J Political Econ*, **98**: 544–573

Gerard, K. and Roderick, P. (2003) 'Comparison of apparent efficiency of haemodialysis satellite units in England and Wales using data envelopment analysis', *Int J Technol Assess Health Care*, **19**: 533–539

Gerdtham, U.G., Rehnberg, C. and Tambour, M. (1999) 'The impact of internal markets on health care efficiency: evidence from health care reforms in Sweden', *Appl Econ*, **31**: 935–945

Giokas, D.I. (2001) 'Greek hospitals: how well their resources are used', *Int J Man Sci*, **29**: 73–83

Giuffrida, A. (1999) 'Productivity and efficiency changes in primary care: a Malmquist index approach', *Health Care Man Sci*, **2**: 11–26

Giuffrida, A. and Gravelle, H. (2001) 'Measuring performances in primary care: econometric analysis and DEA', *Appl Econ*, **33**: 163–175

Giuffrida, A., Gravelle, H. and Sutton, M. (2000) 'Efficiency and administrative costs in primary care, *J Health Econ*, **19**: 983–1006

Gonzalez, E. and Gascon, F. (2004) 'Sources of productivity growth in the Spanish pharmaceutical industry (1994–2000)', *Res Pol*, **33**: 735–745

Gravelle, H. and Rees, R. (1992) *Micro Economics*, Essex: Longman Group

Gravelle, H., Wildman, J. and Sutton, M. (2001) 'Income, income inequality and health: what can we learn from aggregate data?', *Soc Sci Med*, **54**: 577–589

Gravelle, H., Jacobs, R., Jones, A.M. and Street, A. (2003) 'Comparing the efficiency of national health systems: a sensitivity analysis of the WHO approach', *Appl Health Econ Health Pol*, **2**: 141–147

Greene, W.H. (1986) 'Comment on "Frontier production functions"', *Economet Rev*, **4**: 335–338

Greene, W.H. (1992) *LIMDEP Version 6.0: User's Manual and Reference Guide,* New York: Econometric Software Inc

Greene, W.H. (2004) 'Distinguishing between heterogeneity and inefficiency: stochastic frontier analysis of the World Health Organisation's panel data on national health care systems', *Health Econ*, **13**: 959–980

Grosskopf, S. and Valdmanis, V. (1987) 'Measuring hospital performance – a non-parametric approach', *J Health Econ*, **6**: 89–107

Grosskopf, S. and Valdmanis, V. (1993) 'Evaluating hospital performance with case-mix-adjusted outputs', *Med Care*, **31**: 525–532

Grosskopf, S., Margaritis, D. and Valdmanis, V. (1990) 'Nurse productivity and wages', *New Zealand Econ Papers*, **24**: 73–86

Grosskopf, S., Margaritis, D. and Valdmanis, V. (1995) 'Estimating output substitutability of hospital services: a distance function approach', *Eur J Oper Res*, **80**: 575–587

Grosskopf S., Margaritis, D. and Valdmanis, V. (2001) 'Comparing teaching and non-teaching hospitals: A frontier approach, teaching vs. non-teaching hospitals', *Health Care Man Sci*, **4**: 83–90

Grosskopf, S., Margaritis, D. and Valdmanis, V. (2004) 'Competitive effects on teaching hospitals', *Eur J Oper Res*, **154**: 515–525

Grossman, M. (1972a) 'The demand for health: a theoretical and empirical investigation', NBER Occasional Paper no. 119, New York: Columbia University Press

Grossman, M. (1972b) 'On the concepts of health capital and the demand for health', *J Politic Econ*, **80**: 223–255

Gruca, T.S. and Nath, D. (2001) 'The technical efficiency of hospitals under a single payer system: the case of Ontario community hospitals', *Health Care Man Sci*, **4**: 91–101

Grytten J. and Rongen, G. (2000) 'Efficiency in provision of public dental services in Norway', *Commun Dent Oral Epidemiol*, **28**: 170–176

Hao, S.H.S. and Pegels, C.C. (1994) 'Evaluating relative efficiencies of veterans affairs medical-centers using data envelopment, ratio, and multiple-regression analysis', *J Med Sys*, **18**: 55–67

Hadley, J. (1982) *More Medical Care, Better Health?* Washington DC: Urban Institute

Hadley, J. (1988) 'Medicare spending and mortality rates of the elderly', *Inquiry*, **25**: 485–493

Harris J., Ozgen, H. and Ozcan, Y. (2000) 'Do mergers enhance the performance of hospital efficiency?', *J Oper Res Soc*, **51**: 801–811

Harrison, J.P. and Ogniewski, R.J. (2005) 'An efficiency analysis of Veterans Health Administration hospitals', *Mil Med*, **170**: 607–611

Harrison, J.P., Coppola, M.N. and Wakefield, M. (2004) 'Efficiency of Federal hospitals in the United States', *J Med Sys*, **28**: 411–422

Helmig, B. and Lapsley, I. (2001) 'On the efficiency of public, welfare and private hospitals in Germany over time: a sectoral data envelopment analysis study', *Health Serv Man Res*, **14**: 263–274

Hofler, R. and Rungeling, B. (1994) 'US nursing homes are they cost efficient', *Econ Lett*, **44**: 301–305

Hollingsworth, B. (1997) 'A review of data envelopment analysis software', *Econ J*, **107**: 1268–1270

Hollingsworth, B. (1999) 'Data envelopment analysis and productivity analysis: a review of the options', *Econ J*, **109**: 458–462

Hollingsworth, B. (2003) 'Non-parametric and parametric applications measuring efficiency in health care', *Health Care Man Sci*, **6**: 203–218

Hollingsworth, B. and Parkin, D. (1995a) 'The efficiency of Scottish acute hospitals – an application of data envelopment analysis', *IMA J Math Appl Med Biol*, **12**: 161–173

Hollingsworth, B. and Parkin, D. (1995b) 'Efficiency measurement in health care: the use and usefulness of data envelopment analysis', paper presented at Third European Conference on Health Economics, Stockholm

Hollingsworth, B. and Parkin, D. (1998) 'Developing Efficiency Measures for use in the NHS', a report to the NHS Executive Northern & Yorkshire Region R&D Directorate, Newcastle: Health Economics Group, School of Health Sciences, University of Newcastle

Hollingsworth, B. and Parkin, D. (2001) 'The efficiency of the delivery of neonatal care in the UK', *J Publ Health Med*, **23**: 47–50

Hollingsworth, B. and Parkin, D. (2003) 'Efficiency and productivity change in the English National Health Service: can data envelopment analysis provide a robust and useful measure?', *J Health Serv Res Pol*, **8**: 230–236

Hollingsworth, B. and Smith, P. (2003) 'The use of ratios in data envelopment analysis', *Appl Econ Lett*, **10**: 733–735

Hollingsworth, B. and Street, A. (2006) 'The market for efficiency analysis of health care organisations', *Health Econ*, **15**: 1055–1059

Hollingsworth, B. and Wildman, J. (2003) 'The efficiency of health production: re-estimating the WHO panel data using parametric and nonparametric approaches to provide additional information', *Health Econ,* **12**: 493–504

Hollingsworth, B., Dawson, P. and Maniadakis, N. (1999) 'Efficiency measurement of health care: A review of non-parametric methods and applications', *Health Care Man Sci*, **2**: 161–172

Hollingsworth, B., Harris, A. and Gospodarevskaya, E. (2002) 'The efficiency of immunization of infants by local government', *Appl Econ*, **34**: 2341–2345

Huang, Y.L. and McLaughlin, C.P. (1989) 'Relative efficiency in rural primary health care: an application of data envelopment analysis', *Health Serv Res,* **24**: 143–158

Jacobs, R. (2001) 'Alternative methods to examine hospital efficiency: data envelopment analysis and stochastic frontier analysis', *Health Care Man Sci* **4**: 103–115

Johnston, K. and Gerard, K. (2001) 'Assessing efficiency in the UK breast screening programme: does size of screening unit make a difference?' *Health Pol,* **56**: 21–32

Jones, A. (2000) 'Health econometrics', in A Culyer and J Newhouse (eds) *The Handbook of Health Economics*, Amsterdam: Elsevier

Kamis-Gould, E. (1991) 'A case study in frontier production analysis, assessing the efficiency and effectiveness of New Jersey's partial-care mental health programs', *J Evaluat Prog Plann*, **14**: 385–390

Kathuria, V. and Sankar, D. (2005) 'Inter-state disparities in health outcomes in rural India: an analysis using a stochastic production frontier approach', *Dev Policy Rev*, **23**: 145–163

Kerr, C.A., Glass, J.C., McCallion, G.M. and McKillop, D.G. (1999) 'Best-practice measures of resource utilization for hospitals: a useful complement in performance assessment, *Publ Admin*, **77**: 639–650

Kirigia, J.M., Emrouznejad, A. and Sambo, L.G. (2002) 'Measurement of technical efficiency of public hospitals in Kenya: using data envelopment analysis', *J Med Sys,* **26**: 39–45

Kirigia, J.M., Emrouznejad, A., Sambo, L.G., Munguti, N. and Liambila, W. (2004) 'Using data envelopment analysis to measure the technical efficiency of public health centers in Kenya', *J Med Sys*, **28**: 155–166

Kirigia, J.M., Lambo, E. and Sambo, L.G. (2000) 'Are public hospitals in Kwazulu-Natal province of South Africa technically efficient', *Afr J Health Sci*, **7**: 25–32

Kleinsorge, I.K. and Karney, D.F. (1992) 'Management of nursing-homes using data envelopment analysis', *Socio-Econ Plann Sci*, **26**: 57–71

Kontodimopoulos, N. and Niakas, D. (2005) Efficiency measurement of hemodialysis units in Greece with data envelopment analysis, *Health Pol*, **71**: 195–204

Koop, G., Osiewalski, J. and Steel, M.F.J. (1997) 'Bayesian efficiency analysis through individual effects: Hospital cost frontiers', *J Economet*, **76**: 77–105

Kooreman, P. (1994) 'Data envelopment analysis and parametric frontier estimation – complementary tools', *J Health Econ*, **13**: 345–346

Laine, J., Linna, M., Hakkinen, U. and Noro, A. (2005a) 'Measuring the productive efficiency and clinical quality of institutional long-term care for the elderly', *Health Econ*, **14**: 245–256

Laine, J., Finne-Soveri, U.H., Bjorkgren, M., Linna, M., Noro, A. and Hakkinen, U. (2005b) 'The association between quality of care and technical efficiency in long-term care', *Int J Qual Health Care*, **17**: 259–267

Li, T. and Rosenman, R. (2001) 'Cost inefficiency in Washington hospitals: a stochastic frontier approach using panel data', *Health Care Man Sci*, **4**: 73–81

Linna, M. (1998) 'Measuring hospital cost efficiency with panel data models', *Health Econ*, **7**: 415–427

Linna, M. and Häkkinen, U. (1998) 'A comparative application of econometric frontier and DEA methods for assessing cost efficiency of Finnish hospitals', in P. Zweifel (ed.) *Health, The Medical Profession and Regulation*, Boston: Kluwer

Linna, M., Nordblad, A. and Koivu, M. (2002) 'Technical and cost efficiency of oral health care provision in Finnish health centres', *Soc Sci Med*, **56**: 343–353

Liu, X. and Mills, A. (2005) 'The effect of performance related pay for hospital doctors on hospital behaviour: a case study from Shandong, China', *Hum Resources Health,* **3**: 11 (12 pp.)

Lopez-Valcarcel, G.B. and Perez, P.B. (1996) 'Changes in the efficiency of Spanish public hospitals after the introduction of program-contracts', *Investigaciones Econ*, **20**: 377–402

Löthgren, M. and Tambour, M. (1999) 'Productivity and customer satisfaction in Swedish pharmacies: A DEA network model', *Eur J Oper Res*, **115**: 449–458

Lowey, E.H. (1980) 'Letter to the editor: cost should not be a factor in Medical Care', *New Engl J Med*, **302**: 697

Luoma, K., Järviö, M., Suuoniemi, I. and Hjerppe, R. (1996) 'Financial incentives and productive efficiency in finnish health centres', *Health Econ*, **5**: 435–445

McCallion, G.M., McKillop, D.G., Glass, J.C. and Kerr, C. (1999) 'Rationalizing Northern Ireland hospital services towards larger providers: best-practice efficiency studies and current policy', *Public Money Man*: 27–32

McCallion, G.M., Glass, J.C., Jackson, R., Kerr, C.A. and McKillop, D.G. (2000) 'Investigating productivity change and hospital size: a nonparametric frontier approach', *Appl Econ*, **32**: 161–174

McGuire, A. and Westoby, R. (1983) 'A production function analysis of acute hospitals', Health Economics Research Unit, Discussion Paper 4/83, University of Aberdeen

McGuire, A., Henderson, J. and Mooney, G. (1988) *The Economics of Health Care,* London: Routledge

McKay, N.L., Deily, M.E. and Dorner, F.H. (2002/03) 'Ownership and changes in hospital inefficiency', *Inquiry*, **39**: 388–399

McKillop, D.G., Glass, J.C., Kerr, C. and McCallion, G.M. (1999) 'Efficiency in Northern Ireland hospitals: a non-parametric analysis', *Econ Soc Rev,* **30**: 175–196

Maddala, G.S. (1988) *Introduction to Econometrics*, New York: MacMillan

Magnussen, J. (1996) 'Efficiency measurement and the operation of hospital production', *Health Serv Res*, **31**: 21–37

Magnussen, J. (2005) 'Kan vi Stole På malene for Sykehusenes produktivitet? Tidsskr Nor Laegeforen N.23', **125:** 3300–3302

Maindiratta, A. (1990) 'Largest size-efficient scale and size efficiencies of decision-making units in data envelopment analysis, *J Economet*, **46**: 57–72

Maniadakis, N. and Thanassoulis, E. (2000) 'Assessing productivity changes in UK hospitals reflecting technology and input prices', *Appl Econ*, **32**: 1575–1589

Maniadakis, N. and Thanassoulis, E. (2004) 'A cost Malmquist productivity index', *Eur J Oper Res*, **154**: 396–409

Maniadakis, N., Hollingsworth, B. and Thanassoulis, E. (1999) 'The impact of the internal market on hospital efficiency, productivity and service quality', *Health Care Man Sci*, **2**: 75–85

Malmquist, S. (1953) 'Index numbers and indifference surfaces', *Trabajos de Estatistics* **4**: 209–242

Martinussen, P.E. and Midttun, L. (2004) 'Day surgery and hospital efficiency: empirical analysis of Norwegian hospitals 1999–2001', *Health Pol*, **68**: 183–196

Mobley, L.R. (1998) 'Effects of selective contracting on hospital efficiency, costs and accessibility', *Health Econ*, **7**: 247–261

Mobley, L.R. and Magnussen, J. (1998) 'An international comparison of hospital efficiency: does institutional environment matter?' *Appl Econ*, **30**: 1089–1100

Mobley, L.R. and Magnussen, J. (2002) 'The impact of managed care penetration and hospital quality on efficiency in hospital staffing', *J Health Care Finance*, **28**: 24–42

Mooney, G., Gerard, K., Donaldson, C. and Farrar, S. (1992) 'Priority setting in purchasing: some practical guidelines', (Research Paper 6), Scotland: National Association of Health Authorities and Trusts

Morey, R.C. and Dittman, D.A. (1996) 'Cost pass-through reimbursement to hospitals and their impacts on operating efficiencies, *Anna Oper Res*, **67**: 117–139

Morey, R.C., Fine, D.J. and Loree, S.W. (1990) 'Comparing the allocative efficiencies of hospitals', *Int J Man Sci,* **18**: 71–83

Morey, R.C., Retzlaff-Roberts, D.L., Fine, D.J. and Loree, S.W. (2000) 'Assessing the operating efficiencies of teaching hospitals by an enhancement of the AHA/AAMC Method', *Acad Medi*, **75**: 28–40

Newhouse, J.P. (1994) 'Frontier estimation: how useful a tool for health economics?', *J Health Econ*, **13**: 317–322

Newhouse, J.P. and Friedlander, L.J. (1980) 'The relationship between medical resources and measures of health: some additional evidence', *J Hum Res*, **15**: 200–218

Norman, M. and Stoker, B. (1991) *Data Envelopment Analysis, The Assessment of Performance*, Chichester: John Wiley

Nunamaker, T.R. (1983) 'Measuring routine nursing service efficiency – A comparison of cost per patient day and data envelopment analysis models', *Health Serv Res*, **18**: 183–205

Nyman, J.A. and Bricker, D.L. (1989) 'Profit incentives and technical efficiency in the production of nursing home care', *Rev Econ Stat*, **71**: 586–594

Nyman, J.A., Bricker D.L. and Link, D. (1990) 'Technical efficiency in nursing homes', *Med Care*, **28**: 541–551

Okunade, A.A. (2001) 'Cost-output relation, technological progress, and clinical activity mix of US hospital pharmacies', *J Productiv Anal*, **16**: 167–193

O'Neal, P.V., Ozcan, Y.A. and Ma, Y. (2002) 'Benchmarking mechanical ventilation services in teaching hospital', *J Med Sys*, **26**: 227–240

O'Neill, L. (1998) 'Multifactor efficiency in data envelopment analysis with an application to urban hospitals', *Health Care Man Sci*, **1**: 19–27

O'Neill, L. and Dexter, F. (2004) 'Market capture of inpatient perioperative services using DEA', *Health Care Man Sci*, **7**: 263–273

Osei, D., d'Almeida, S., George, M.O., Kirigia, J.M., Mensah, A.O. and Kainyu, L.H. (2005) 'Technical efficiency of public district hospitals and health centres in Ghana: a pilot study', *Cost Effect Resource Alloc*, **3**: 9–21

Ozcan, Y.A. (1992) 'Sensitivity analysis of hospital efficiency under alternative output/input and peer groups: A review', *Int J Knowledge Trans Utilis*, **5**: 1–29

Ozcan, Y.A. (1995) 'Efficiency of hospital-service production in local markets – the balance-sheet of US medical armament', *Socio-Econ Plann Sci*, **29**: 139–150

Ozcan, Y.A. and Bannick, R.R. (1994) 'Trends in department of defense hospital efficiency', *J Med Sys*, **18**: 69–83

Ozcan, Y.A. and Cotter, J.J. (1994) 'An assessment of efficiency of area agencies on aging in Virginia through data envelopment analysis', *Gerontologist*, **34**: 363–370

Ozcan, Y.A. and Luke, R.D. (1993) 'A national study of the efficiency of hospitals in urban markets', *Health Serv Res,* **27**: 719–739

Ozcan, Y.A. and Lynch, J.R. (1992) 'Rural hospital closures: an inquiry into efficiency', *Adv Health Econ Health Serv Res*, **13**: 205–244

Ozcan, Y.A., Luke, R.D. and Haksever, C. (1992) 'Ownership and organizational performance: a comparison of technical efficiency across hospital types', *Med Care* **30**: 781–794

Ozcan, Y.A., McCue M.J. and Okasha, A.A. (1996) 'Measuring the technical efficiency of psychiatric hospitals', *J Med Sys*, **20**: 141–150

Ozcan, Y.A., Wogen, S.E. and Mau, L.W. (1998a) 'Efficiency evaluation of skilled nursing facilities', *J Med Sys*, **22**: 211–224

Ozcan, Y. A., Watts, J., Harris, J.M. and Wogen, S.E. (1998b) 'Provider experience and technical efficiency in the treatment of stroke patients: DEA approach', *J Oper Res Soc*, **49**: 573–582

Ozcan, Y.A., Begun, J.W. and McKinney, M.M. (1999) 'Benchmarking organ procurement organizations: a national study', *Health Serv Res*, **34**: 855–874

Ozcan, Y.A., Jiang, H.J. and Pai, C.-W. (2000) 'Do primary care physicians or specialists provide more efficient care?', *Health Serv Man Res*, **13**: 90–96

Ozgen, H. and Ozcan, Y.A. (2002) 'A national study of efficiency for dialysis centers: an examination of market competition and facility characteristics for production of multiple dialysis outputs', *Health Serv Res*, **37**: 711–732

Ozgen, H. and Ozcan, Y.A. (2004) 'Longitudinal analysis of efficiency in multiple output dialysis markets', *Health Care Man Sci*, **7**: 253–61

Pai, C.W., Ozcan, Y.A. and Jiang, J.H. (2000) 'Regional variation in physician practice pattern: an examination of technical and cost efficiency for treating sinusitis', *J Med Sys*, **24**: 103–117

Panzer, J. and Willig, R. (1975) 'Economics of Scale and Economics of Scope in Multi-output Production', Economic Discussion paper No. 33, USA: Bell Laborateries

Panzer, J.C. and Willig, R.U. (1981) 'Economics of Scope', *Am Econ Rev*, **71**: 268–272

Parkin, D. and Devlin, N. (2003) 'Measuring efficiency in dental care', in A. Scott, A. Maynard and R. Elliott (eds) *Advance in Health Economics*, West Sussex: Wiley

Parkin, D. and Hollingsworth, B. (1997) 'Measuring production efficiency of acute hospitals in Scotland 1991–1994: validity issues in data envelopment analysis', *Applied Econ*, **29**: 1425–1433

Parkin, D. and Hollingsworth, B. (1999) 'Comparing the efficient production of health and health care in Europe', paper presented at Second International Health Economics Association (*i*HEA) World Conference, Rotterdam

Parkin, D. and Hollingsworth, B. (2005) 'Diversification and specialisation measurement', paper presented at Health Economists' Study Group Conference, University of Newcastle, UK

Paul, C.J.M. (2002) 'Productive structure and efficiency of public hospitals', in K.J. Fox (ed.) *Efficiency in the Public Sector*, Boston: Kluwer

Pedraja-Chaparro, F., Salinas-Jiminez, J. and Smith, P. (1997) 'On the role of weight constrictions in data envelopment analysis', *J Productiv Anal*, **8**: 125–230

Pina, V. and Torres, L. (1992) 'Evaluating the efficiency of nonprofit organizations: an application of data envelopment analysis to the public health service', *Financ Accountabil Man*, **8**: 213–224

Prior, D. (1996) 'Technical efficiency and scope economies in hospitals', *Appl Econ*, **28**: 1295–1301

Prior, D. and Sola, M. (2000) 'Technical efficiency and economies of diversification in health care', *Health Care Man Sci*, **3**: 299–307

Puig-Junoy, J. (1998) 'Measuring health production performance in the OECD', *Appl Econ Lett*, **5**: 255–259

Puig-Junoy, J. and Ortún, V. (2004) 'Cost efficiency in primary care contracting: a stochastic frontier cost function approach', *Health Econ*, **13**: 1149–1165

Ramanathan, R. (2005) 'Operations assessment of hospitals in the Sultanate of Oman', *Int J Oper Prod Man*, **25**: 36–54

Ramanathan, T.V., Chandra, K.S. and Thupeng, W.M. (2003) 'A comparison of the technical efficiencies of health districts and hospitals in Botswana', *Develop South Africa*, **20**: 307–320

Register, C.A. and Bruning, E.R. (1987) 'Profit incentives and technical efficiency in the production of hospital care', *South Econ J*, **53**: 899–914

Reinhardt, U. (1998) 'Foreword' in T. Rice (ed.) *The Economics of Health Reconsidered*, 1st edn, Chicago: Health Administration Press

Renner, A., Kirigia, J.M., Zere, E.A., Barry, S.P., Kirigia, D.G., Kamara, C. and Muthusi, H. K. (2005) 'Technical efficiency of peripheral health units in Pujehun district of Sierra Leone: a DEA application', *BMC Health Serv Res*, **5**: (11 pp.)

Retzlaff-Roberts, D., Chang, C.F. and Rubin, R.M. (2004) 'Technical efficiency in the use of health care resources: a comparison of OECD countries', *Health Pol*, **69**: 55–72

Rice, T. (2002) *The Economics of Health Reconsidered*, 2nd edn, Chicago: Health Administration Press

Rollins, J., Lee, K., Xu, Y. and Ozcan, Y.A. (2001) 'Longitudinal study of health maintenance organisation efficiency', *Health Serv Man Res*, **14**: 249–262

Roos, P. (2002) 'Measuring output of hospital services', in K.J. Fox (ed.) *Efficiency in the Public Sector*, Boston: Kluwer

Rosenberg, D. (1991) 'Forget CEA. Use DEA!', *J Health Hum Res Admin*, **14**: 109–112

Rosenman, R. and Friesner, D. (2004) 'Scope and scale inefficiencies in physician practices', *Health Econ*, **13**: 1091–1116

Rosenman, R., Siddharthan, K. and Ahern, M. (1997) 'Output efficiency of health maintenance organisations in Florida', *Health Econ*, **6**: 295–302

Rosko, M. (1999) 'Impact of internal and external environmental pressures on hospital inefficiency', *Health Care Man Sci*, **2**: 63–74

Rosko, M.D. (2001a) 'Cost efficiency of US hospitals: a stochastic frontier approach', *Health Econ*, **10**: 539–551

Wagner, J.M., Shimshak, D.G. and Novak, M. (2003) 'Advances in physician profiling: the use of DEA', *Soc Econ Plan Sci*, **37**: 141–163

Wagstaff, A. (1987) 'Measuring technical efficiency in the National Health Service: a stochastic frontier analysis', Centre for Health Economics, Discussion Paper 30, University of York

Wagstaff, A. (1989) 'Estimating efficiency in the hospital sector: a comparison of three statistical cost frontier models', *Appl Econ* **21**: 659–672

Wagstaff, A. and López, G. (1996) 'Hospital costs in Catalonia: a stochastic frontier analysis', *Appl Econ Lett*, **3**: 471–474

Wang, B.B., Ozcan, Y.A., Wan, T.T.H. and Harrison, J. (1999) 'Trends in hospital efficiency among metropolitan markets', *J Med Sys*, **23**: 83–97

Wennberg, J. (1988) 'Improving the medical decision making process', *Health Affairs*, **7**: 99–106

White, K.R. and Ozcan, Y.A. (1996) 'Church ownership and hospital efficiency', *Hospit Health Serv Admin*, **41**: 297–310

World Health Report (2000) 'Health systems: improving performance', *World Health Organisation*, Geneva: WHO

Yeh, J., White K.R. and Ozcan, Y.A. (1997) 'Efficiency evaluation of community based youth services in Virginia', *Comm Mental Health J*, **33**: 487–499

Young, S.T. (1992) 'Multiple productivity measurement approaches for management', *Health Care Man Rev*, **17**: 51–58

Zavras, A.I., Tsakos, G., Economou, C. and Kyriopoulos, J. (2002) 'Using DEA to evaluate efficiency and formulate policy within a Greek national primary care network', *J Med Sys*, **26**: 285–292

Zere, E., McIntyre, D. and Addison, T. (2001) 'Technical efficiency and productivity of public sector hospitals in three South African Provinces', *South African J Econ*, **69**: 336–358

Zuckerman, S., Hadley, J. and Iezzoni, L. (1994) 'Measuring hospital efficiency with frontier cost functions', *J Health Econ*, **13**: 255–280

Index

Note: Page numbers in **bold** refer to figures and in *italics* refer to tables.